Best.

Elizabeth Hill

For Richard Hill, my loving husband, with whom I will celebrate our forty-ninth wedding anniversary on June 14, 2012; Allison and Michael Hester, our wonderful daughter and son-in-law; and Ethan and Abby Hester, our grandchildren, who give us untold joy.

The Cover
The cover is a close-up photograph of the center of a single six-pointed star stitched as the beginning of a quilt top by Mrs. Alta Elizabeth Cone Echols, the author's maternal grandmother, who lived from 1892 to 1945.

Cover Photograph
Richard Allen Hill

Cover Design
Allison Hill Hester

Co-Researcher at the National Archives
Richard Hill

Book Formatting and Design
Allison Hester

Printed in the United States of America
2012

eahill@ualr.edu

A Splendid Piece of Work

1912-2012

One Hundred Years of Arkansas's Home Demonstration and Extension Homemakers Clubs

Elizabeth Griffin Hill

I would like to see the campaign against the house fly made national, including every farm as well as every town and city.[1]

I have never been to a lecture, nor play, nor show since marriage – have been trying to save to buy a home. It has been a very monotonous road to travel. The women here in this country, where there is no help to be had, don't average a half dozen visits a year. Don't have time. I am making soap and catchup today.[2]

You will ask, 'Why not can all of your surplus vegetables and fruits?' and I will say that is one of the worst pieces of drudgery. Yes, drudgery! And with all of our care and precautions a great deal of canned stuff spoils in this hot southern climate unless put in tin, and then the doctors have talked ptomaine poisoning until people are afraid of tin cans.[3]

Endnotes

[1]Kate Adele Hill. *Home Demonstration Work in Texas.* San Antonio: The Naylor Company, ND, pages 7-13. (This is one of 2,241 replies to the October 1, 1913 letter from U.S. Department of Agriculture Secretary D. F. Houston to 55,000 wives of U.S.D.A. crop correspondents, in which he asked for suggestions to improve farm women's lives.)
[2]Ibid.
[3]Ibid.

IN MEMORIAM

**Mrs. Lugenia Bell Christmas
Local[1] Home Demonstration Agent
St. Francis County, 1917 to 1942**

Lugenia B. Christmas had lovely handwriting, with the extended crossbar of her t's slanting at the angle of a child's crayoned rooftop in a construction-paper scene. Only the obligatory chimney and its curling smoke were missing. Her early reports were in long-hand and were difficult to read despite their uniformity. Her reports were filled with individuals' accomplishments; she seldom used the personal pronoun "I." Her rhetorical stance was one of encouragement and praise. Her reports were a delight to read; her favorite adjective was "splendid," and each project or accomplishment was a "piece of work." As the years went on, her lovely slanted writing changed to a more hurried style that angled toward the lower right-hand corner of the page. Even later, she displayed a skill at the typewriter that was woefully lacking. Christmas' narrative reports, however, provided a vivid view of the lives and accomplishments of the black women with whom she worked as well as a glimpse at their communities.

In 1927, she wrote about Mrs. Mittie B. Wade, a member of the Shady Grove club in Forrest City, who won the twenty-five dollars given by the Chamber of Commerce for the best year-round garden in the county in 1927—*even though cows broke into her garden only a few days before the County Fair on September 28!* Christmas continued—with a lyrical playfulness not anticipated in a government report:

> For our Thanksgiving dinner in our home we had bleached celery, ripe tomatoes, headed lettuce, lovely green parsley [and] carrots from Mrs. Wade's garden. We could have had cabbage, cauliflower, beets and spinach from Mrs. O. B. Huddleston's garden. She is of Shiloh Community, Palestine, Rt 1. We could have had English peas from Mrs. E. L. Pettigrew's garden at Caldwell. We could have had collards, cabbage, turnips, spinach, pimentos, lettuce from Mrs. Mattie B. Hare's garden, Caldwell.[2]

Christmas emphasized home and garden beautification. She noted that Mrs. Etta Hughes' vegetable garden was beautifully bordered with flowers in bloom. In 1933, a local newspaper included a letter from Better Homes in America, 42 Broadway, New York City, granting a Special Merit Award to the Better Homes program for the colored citizens of St. Francis County for 1933. The award read, in part, as follows: "This award was made primarily for the instructive educational tours conducted by your committee and for the extensive work in home improvement and the widespread participation in contests. St. Francis County, under your direction, has developed a significant community campaign for home improvement. . . ."[3]

Christmas also dealt with the mundane but necessary aspects of the program. Under the heading "Rural Engineering," she noted an improvement of the tenant houses after the Great Flood—more light, more rooms and many with outhouses.[4] For rodents, she told of success with arsenate of lead and slacked lime, sprayed or dusted.[5] She reported that Mrs. O. B. Huddleston— whose cabbage, cauliflower, beets, and spinach were mentioned above—improved her fifty-six barred rock hens' output from twenty-five to forty eggs daily by culling the flock and feeding the remaining hens more balanced rations. Mrs. Lottie Bond, of Madison, was able to pay fifteen dollars board monthly for her son at Fargo Industrial School at Brinkley[6] by selling weekly, among other products, eight pounds of butter at twenty-five cents per pound.[7]

Christmas provided a concise picture of improved health and sanitation conditions among black families and schools. At Wheatley, for example, Miss Morse, the county nurse, examined and inoculated 200 children against typhoid, diphtheria, and small pox, with the assistance of Mrs. V. E. Gates, home demonstration health and sanitation volunteer leader for the county. Sanitary closets were built at fifty-eight homes during the year. The Colt school had two sanitary closets built under the recommendation of Mrs. Mattie B. Hare, leader and county council president. Material was furnished by the school board, the work was done by patrons, and lunch was served to workers by 4-H[8] club girls. Fifty-one homes were screened for the first time. Mrs. Etta Hughes, of Bolden, made her own screens with poultry products money.[9]

Endnotes

[1] The early annual reports found in Record Group 33 at the National Archives Southwestern Branch, Fort Worth, Texas, revealed that the term "local home demonstration agent" was the title given to African American agents. However, their supervisor's title was "Negro District home demonstration agent."

[2] 1927 Annual Narrative Report, St. Francis County Local Home Demonstration Agent (HDA), Record Group (RG) 33, National Archives and Records Administration Southwestern Branch (NARA), Fort Worth, Texas.

[3] 1933 Annual Narrative Report, St. Francis County Local HDA, RG 33, NARA/Fort Worth, Texas.

[4] 1927 Annual Narrative Report, St. Francis County Local HDA, RG 33, NARA/Fort Worth, Texas.

[5] 1933 Annual Narrative Report, St. Francis County Local HDA, RG 33, NARA/Fort Worth, Texas.

[6] "Floyd Brown-Fargo Agricultural School Museum," accessed January 4, 2012. http://www.arkansas.com/attractions/detail.aspx?r=Delta&id=92495&lr=. Floyd Brown started the Fargo Agricultural School in 1919 for a reported $2.85. The school provided a high school education for thousands of black students for thirty years.

[7] 1933 Annual Narrative Report, St. Francis County Local HDA, RG 30, NARA/Fort Worth, Texas.

[8] The 4-H work was—and is—the youth program of the Cooperative Extension Service. The 4-H youth development program provides opportunities for youth to acquire knowledge, develop skills, form attitudes, and practice behavior that will enable them to become self-directing, productive, and contributing members of society. The name represents four personal development areas of focus for the organization: head, heart, hands, and health. See University of Arkansas, Division of Agriculture, Research and Extension, University of Arkansas System, Cooperative Extension Service, 4-H Youth Development website (http://www.kidsarus.org/).

[9] 1933 Annual Narrative Report, St. Francis County Local HDA, RG 30. NARA/Fort Worth, Texas.

Contents

The Situation

In Memoriam

About the Picture Gallery

Introduction   1

The Beginning of Demonstration Work in the
     South   3

Early Home Demonstration Work in Arkansas   10

The 1920s:

     Time of Agricultural Depression   32

     1927: Year of Destruction   59

     The Early School Lunch Work   84

The 1930s:

     Keeping the Work Going: Hiring, Retaining,
         Continuing the Funding   96

     The Work Goes On   106

     A Time for Evaluation and Change   132

     All Work and No Play: Having Fun, Getting
         Together, and Reaching Out   142

         "Learn and Live" by Claudia Cranston   154

The 1940s:

     The War Years   169

     After the War   197

The Picture Gallery   219

The 1950s: Time of Change for Women   238

The 1960s: Time of Social Change   253

Long-Term Commitments to Children and
     Youth   265

The Rest of the Story   277

Bibliography   331

Contributors to the History   347

About the Picture Gallery

All of the photographs in The Picture Gallery were found throughout Record Group 33 at the National Archives and Records Administration Southwestern Branch, Fort Worth, Texas. The pictures have not been identified and were chosen from hundreds of photographs copied at the archives to represent home demonstration agents, club members, youths, and children throughout the entire state of Arkansas. It was difficult to leave any of the photographs at the archives without bringing a copy back to Arkansas. The author considers the photographs—as well as the agents' narrative reports found in the archives—to be a precious gift to us from the past.

A Splendid
Piece of Work

Introduction

As the phrase "home demonstration clubs" was mentioned to acquaintances and current Extension Homemakers Club members, often the response was one of memories of grandmothers painstakingly preparing tea and cookies for other ladies who gathered in the parlor for quilting. In scrapbooks and archival newspapers, society-page blurbs described club meetings in glowing society-page terms: the hostess, the refreshments, the program title. Pictures were of smiling club members showing off a recent project.

These remnants of memories are surely an insult to the bright, energetic, shrewd, sometimes heroic agents who helped Arkansas's farm wives improve their lives during the early twentieth century. The Smith-Lever Act of 1914, which funded home demonstration as well as agricultural demonstration work, was enacted during a time of peace and prosperity for the nation's farmers and farm families. Nevertheless, these agents taught Arkansas's women thrift and self-sufficiency during times of war, drought, floods, and economic depression.

These memories also do not do justice to the rural women themselves. Women developed leadership skills and were empowered as they became the trainers who provided demonstrations when one agent was unable to reach an entire county. As club members focused on the safe and efficient canning of meats, vegetables, and fruits—and as they came to understand more about

1

nutrition—they began to make sure that undernourished children in rural schools had adequate hot lunches during the winter months.

And that was just the beginning. In the 1930s, the women cooperated with public relief agencies to use up surplus cotton by helping thousands of Arkansans make cotton mattresses—often the first time families had a mattress made from something other than straw. They also began a tradition of providing untold numbers of cans and jars of nutritious food for the struggling Arkansas Children's Home and Hospital.

Throughout the one hundred-year history, Arkansas's Cooperative Extension Service managers struggled with the needs of rural families and adjusted the work to fit those needs. During the mid-1930s, rural sociologists and economists helped the organization determine that the men's and women's work must cooperate to focus on the family as a unit. After World War II, management struggled with the changes wrought by the war. In the 1950s, home demonstration work expanded to urban areas and focused on meeting the needs of women in the workforce. In the 1960s, the segregated work halted as black and white clubs were combined under the newly reorganized Extension Homemakers Council.

During the state meeting at Hot Springs in June 2011, thirty-six members and agents from throughout the state provided thoughtful insight into the work and where it is heading. In interviews of three or four, they voiced concerns for the organization, but they also provided exciting possibilities as members embrace the future.

1

The Beginning of Demonstration Work in the South

During the latter nineteenth century and early twentieth century, several factors seemed to come together in something of a perfect storm that led to the creation of the Cooperative Extension Service of the U. S. Department of Agriculture. During the mid-nineteenth century, the U. S. Congress determined that for the nation to grow and prosper, its farmers must have improved methods, which would encourage farm families to stay and work the land. In 1862, the Morrill Land-Grant College Act was passed, giving federal land scrip to states to establish agricultural and mechanical colleges. Most states—including Arkansas—sold the land and used the proceeds to establish the schools.[1]

Throughout their first twenty-five years, land-grant colleges struggled to convince young rural men—to whom land was readily available—to enter college to improve their agricultural methods. Many preferred learning by doing rather than by studying. Simply put, agricultural education was not economically feasible because fertile land was abundant, and working that land required no college certificate. One of the major deficiencies was the schools' lack of scientific research to share with their students. As a result, in 1887 the Hatch Experiment Station Act was passed, providing that a research station was to be built in conjunction with each land-grant college.[2]

The Demonstration Work

Over the following twenty-five years, land-grant colleges continued to struggle to attract students. High schools were scarce in rural areas, and most rural young people did not attend school beyond the elementary grades. Farmers saw no need to enroll in college in order to learn so-called "book farming." Because of farmers' reluctance to come to them, the schools found ways to take research findings to the farmers. The colleges established farmers' institutes, also known as movable schools, as well as farm trains, which provided demonstrations to farmers along the routes. They also offered short courses at the universities.[3]

With each of these methods, the notion of *demonstration* became the accepted way to teach farmers. As the term implies, professors would *demonstrate* new methods based upon scientific research. By 1914, the institutes had outlived their usefulness; farmers needed answers to specific questions. For example, an institute speaker could not answer questions about a sick cow without seeing the animal. Institutes were essentially a transitional stage in educating farmers: they provided contact between professors and farmers and opened farmers' eyes to the opportunities that science offered. However, they simply did not provide the guidance individual farmers needed.[4]

Seaman Knapp

In 1902, Seaman Knapp, something of a Renaissance man—an Eastern-college-educated, "bucolic [Benjamin] Franklin,"[5] with frock coat, old-fashioned derby, and a special rapport with farmers—was selected by the Department of Agriculture as special agent for the promotion of agriculture in the South. In 1903, Knapp successfully showed Texas farmers how an independent, privately owned farm could improve as its owner followed the government's scientifically proven methods. Knapp's success was recognized just in time as a wave of fear swept across Texas because of a massive cotton crop boll weevil infestation.[6]

Knapp's program, which was funded by a $250,000 congressional appropriation, enrolled banks and merchants to convince skeptical farmers to raise a guaranty fund and then select one or more local farmers to use ten acres of their land to follow governmental recommendations for weevil eradication. Participating farmers were to burn all stalks and other hibernation places, plow cotton land in the fall, and plant early the following spring. The instructions were based on scientific studies of the weevil's life cycle. Success of the program allowed Knapp to crusade for basic farm demonstrations throughout the South.[7]

Thus, the beginning of demonstration work among Southern farmers.

In spite of these accomplishments, Knapp realized the farmers' demonstration work was not sufficient to improve rural Southern life. Knapp found the South's problems to include dilapidated farm homes, malnutrition, and "poverty of spirit";[8] thus, his goal became to reach farm women and their children. Although he was interested in educating children for their own sakes, Knapp also believed he could reach skeptical parents if their children were successful using the methods he touted.

Following the example of Northern leaders working to help boys learn better corn-production methods, one of Knapp's agents recruited boys to join a so-called "corn club." As members, the boys would grow corn using governmental methods and show it at the local fair the following fall. Using seed provided by the Rock Island Railroad, one hundred thirty-seven boys displayed their corn. At about the same time, several corn clubs were established in Louisiana. Corn clubs were followed closely by pig, potato, and baby beef clubs. In addition to learning good production methods, the children were learning to read, think, and reason.[9]

In 1910, Knapp spoke to a group of South Carolina teachers and challenged them to take up club work with girls. One of the teachers accepted the challenge and chose tomato clubs because of the tomato's popularity, its versatility, its length of growing season, and the ease with which it could be grown.[10]

But more about tomato clubs later.

The Progressive Movement

While Seaman Knapp was working with Southern farmers, a national movement was focused in part toward improving the lot of those same farmers and their families. The Progressive Movement, with Theodore

Roosevelt as its political leader and spokesman, defined the entire era with its emphasis on eliminating deficiencies within the nation and solving social ills. The Progressives were not a single group that focused on the improvement of one aspect of American life. Instead, concerns ran the gamut from the urban poor to governmental corruption to women's right to vote. Roosevelt appointed a Country Life Commission in 1908 to determine deficiencies in rural life as well as the best methods to correct them. At about the same time, philanthropist John D. Rockefeller established the General Education Board, which supported youth work in the South.[11]

African American Reform Movement

With their own goals and efforts parallel but separate from those of white rural reformers, African American activists—including particularly Booker T. Washington and George Washington Carver—viewed black farm women as vital to their families. They encouraged black women to help their families achieve economic independence from the sharecropping and tenancy systems of the time through farm ownership.[12]

At black farmers' annual conferences at Tuskegee Institute in Alabama and Hampton Institute in Virginia, black women were assured that "[t]he physical health and moral welfare of the race rested upon their shoulders; mothers could stem a high death rate among children by feeding and clothing them properly and maintaining clean and well-ventilated homes."[13]

Early Home Demonstration Work in the South

Just as Seaman Knapp had planned, girls' tomato clubs followed on the heels of boys' corn clubs in the South. Tomatoes were relatively easy to grow and can and were already a staple of Southern dinner tables. The program for girls in growing and preserving tomatoes, which began in some Southern states in 1910, led to the beginning of projects with rural women as farm wives took an interest in their daughters' activities, as Knapp had anticipated.[14]

By 1915, home demonstration work, as conducted in fifteen Southern states, included about sixty thousand girls and thirty thousand women, who had "undertaken definite work for the improvement and rebuilding of country life."[15] State and county home demonstration agents planned and coordinated the projects, with the aid of specialists who contributed information on such topics as horticulture, poultry work, and dairying.[16]

Early on, a state leader was appointed to oversee the girls' canning work. To help in each county, a woman was employed for about two months to give canning demonstrations during the summer. Any assistance she gave in the spring or fall was without pay. The girls' canning projects were based on a tenth-acre garden plot, and each girl became a demonstrator as she followed the agent's instruction and used only approved methods.[17]

Although 1915 was the first year in which formal home demonstration work was undertaken among women, initial reports to the Department of Agriculture indicated women were quickly embracing more than just the canning of tomatoes. Nationally, women reported making or purchasing fireless cookers, iceless refrigerators, kerosene stoves, home water works systems, inexpensive shower baths, and improved sewage disposals as a result of agents' demonstrations.[18]

Endnotes

[1]Wayne D. Rasmussen. *Taking the University to the People: Seventy-five Years of Cooperative Extension* (Ames: Iowa State University Press, 1989), 22-25.

[2]Ibid., 25-26.
Roy V. Scott. *The Reluctant Farmer: The Rise of Agricultural Extension to 1914* (Urbana: University of Illinois Press, 1970), 28.

[3]Rasmussen, 28-35.

[4]Scott, 210.
Rasmussen, 28-35.

[5]Scott, 210.

[6]Scott, 208-214.

[7]Ibid.

[8]Ibid., 237.

[9]Ibid., 237-247

[10]Ibid., 247-249

[11]Rasmussen, 41.
Joan Jensen, *With These Hands: Women Working on the Land* (Old Westbury, New York: The Feminist Press, 1981), 148-149. (Country Life Movement reformers were drawn mostly from agricultural colleges and federal and state governments. Their solution to many rural problems was the application of good business principles to farm management.)
Scott, 222-223. (The General Education Board found numerous problems with Southern school systems: too little money devoted to education, extremely low teachers' salaries, and inadequate school terms. The root of these problems was the Southern economy with its rural poor.)

[12]Lu Ann Jones, *Mama Learned Us to Work: Farm Women in the New South* (Chapel Hill: The University of North Carolina Press, 2002), 16.

[13]Ibid.

[14]Jane S. McKimmon, "Home Demonstration Work–Its Beginning" (part of a talk at the Association of Southern Agricultural Workers Thirtieth Annual Convention, Houston, February 1928) in *The Spirit and Philosophy of Extension Work As Recorded in Significant Extension Papers*, edited by R. K. Bliss, T. B. Symons, and M. L. Wilson. (Washington D.C.: Graduate School, United States Department of Agriculture and Epsilon Sigma Phi/National Honorary Extension Fraternity, 1952), 66-69.

[15]Mary E. Creswell, "The Home Demonstration Work," *Annals of the American Academy of Political and Social Science*, Vol. 67, New Possibilities in Education (Sep., 1916), 241.

[16]Ibid., 243.

[17]Ibid., 242-243.

[18]Ibid., 247-248.

2

Early Home Demonstration Work in Arkansas

Miss Leila Goodwin, Drew County agent, taught bread making by spending the night at the home of one girl – having written to the nearest club member and invited her to come also. The bread was set at night and baked the next day. Miss Goodwin visited local gardens and returned for the next process when the bread was ready.[1]

Canning Clubs for Girls

In 1911, the General Education Board appropriated $300 to each of four Southern states to finance the two-month employment of rural school teachers to conduct canning club work. The women were paid one dollar yearly by the federal government so that they could have unlimited franking privileges and government bulletins to distribute. Although Arkansas was not one of the four initial states, canning club work began within the state in 1912 when agents—mostly rural school teachers— were placed in two-month positions in ten counties, chosen mostly because of railroad accessibility. The $1,500 funding came from the General Education Board through the Secretary of Agriculture.[2]

The agents and their counties are listed below:

Miss Anna Camp, Bradley County
Miss Jeanette V. Bietz, Conway County
Miss Bertha Wilson, Faulkner County
Miss Anna Gill, Garland County
Mrs. Minnie J. Clark, Miller County
Miss Dauphine Kapp, Ouachita County
Miss Emma Archer, Pulaski County
Miss Elizabeth Jackson, Randolph County
Mrs. Ella Lambert, White County
Miss Zelma Sands, Sebastian County[3]

We are deeply indebted to Miss Mena Hogan for providing information about the earliest work in her circa 1942 master's thesis from the University of Wisconsin. A copy of the thesis is on file in the Butler Center of the Central Arkansas Library System. Much of Hogan's information came from Miss Emma Archer's "History of Home Demonstration Work for 1912."[4]

In January 1912, Emma Archer organized the first canning club work in the state even though she was teaching in the Mabelvale School. It was reported that George Pye, county agricultural agent, actually enrolled most of the girls because Archer continued to teach until March 1, when she was officially appointed as an agent by the Department of Education. However, Archer performed office work for Pye on Saturdays while he did field work for her on weekdays.[5]

One of the requirements of club work was that girls be from ten through eighteen years of age. Pye did not strictly observe the age limit; several members were older than eighteen. The young women were enrolled with the understanding that they could participate but could not receive prizes. The older girls actually acted as leaders to the younger ones. Two of the Mabelvale girls became county agents. Charter members of the Mabelvale club are included below, just as Hogan listed them:[6]

Viola Lewis	Ora Red
Cora Lewis	Pearl Cochrane
Lillian Martin	Emma Jaynes
Lillian Sherrill	Abbie Jaynes
Nettie Morehart	Cora White
Lillie Van Dyke	Lillian Scott
Sue Vandyke	Flora Hart
Etta Red	Bess Fowler[7]

During the first year, 400 canning club girls were enrolled within the ten counties. Archer and the other agents realized the tremendous possibilities of the program. Archer provided amazing insight into the earliest work, as reported in Hogan's thesis, as follows:

Not a great deal was accomplished the first year except the laying of a deep broad foundation for future operations. The whole was in a primitive stage. Its recognized value lay in the fact that it gave vocational training, broke away from prescribed lines and methods, and reached all classes. At the end of the year it was found that only those agents who gave freely of their time and talent without reference to the money they received were successful. It was those who loved their work because of the good accomplished and put in many long hours of toil outside of contract lines who paved the way for the future success achieved. The work depends wholly upon individual effort. Each agent must visit the girls as often as possible or they become discouraged and quit. The little girl living far back in the country never in touch with commercial activities, located where opportunity seldom knocks, can hardly understand why a stranger should show an interest in her welfare and that without money or price. Parents as well as children are slow to believe. Tact and patience must be exercised and many explanations made. In my experience I found one little girl who, as well as her parents, would not believe that I would not charge them for the help I gave. If I did not ask a fee for my visit, the girl felt sure she would have to pay for the tin cans I used to teach her. She would not put up a can at my canning school for fear she would have to pay for it. It was only after the year's work was done and I had helped her finish her record book that I at last gained her full confidence.

It is in this broad field that the home demonstration agent labors. Her schoolroom is bound by the confines of her county; her pupils are all the girls and women she enrolls. Following the example of the great teacher, she, by percept and example, aids the poor, encourages the weak, teaches industry and thrift, educates the mind, instills beauty, purity, and love in the heart, trains the hands to labor efficiently and intelligently, and crowns the whole with the strength and health that comes

to a body well-nourished and exercised. It is
a great missionary wait that combines mental,
physical, and spiritual uplift and makes for a
strong self-reliant, God-fearing womankind.[8]

During 1916, girls' canning clubs incorporated bread
making into their agendas. During the year, the girls
made 3,954 loaves of light bread, with Drew County
leading the state with 2,000 loaves. As an example of the
work, Miss Marcella Arthur and Miss Isabella Thursby,
cooking specialists, held seventy-six two-day cooking
schools and two three-day schools in forty-five counties.
Twenty of the counties had home demonstration agents.
In some counties, the cooking schools helped to create
interest in the home demonstration work. In some
small schools, which were financially unable to have
home economics departments, regular teachers or local
club women taught the cooking lessons based on the
specialists' plans.[9]

The Work with Women

In Arkansas, organized home demonstration activities
for women under the Smith-Lever Act of 1914 began
in 1915 with seven counties taking up the work. Early
report forms incorporated statistics for both women
and girls. County agents reported the women were
eager to learn the same canning methods as girls
who participated in canning clubs. Agents held 286
canning schools for women with an average of twenty in
attendance for a total of 5,720 who received instructions
that first year.[10]

Although specific information about home
demonstration work with Arkansas women before 1918

14

is incomplete, six county agents' 1917 reports found in the National Archives at Fort Worth provided a snapshot of how the early work was progressing. Because the statistics were taken from preprinted forms, the grid portrayed activities considered important by the U. S. Department of Agriculture.

In the six counties, only twenty-one clubs had been established, with 517 women actively participating in the clubs. Most important demonstrations given by the agent included bread making, canning, cooking, drying, and fireless cookers. One hundred eleven women made bread; substitutions most often combined with wheat were rice, corn, sweet potatoes, and peanuts. (The substitutions for wheat in bread making were in deference to the shortage of wheat and the widespread starvation in Europe during the World War.) Labor-saving devices installed in homes included fireless cookers, iceless refrigerators, fly traps, fly screens, ironing boards, kitchen cabinets, and water systems. Other categories on the preprinted form were restrooms established for farm women, butter making, food preservation, poultry and poultry sales, and number of women making a winter garden demonstration. The butter-making category showed no activity in the six counties.[11]

The preprinted federal report form for 1917 indicated how quickly the women's work evolved from simply canning tomatoes, even though the number of women and clubs was small. In some counties, the number of individual women actually demonstrating exceeded the number of women in organized clubs. This continued to be the case for several years. The concept of clubs was a natural outgrowth of the realities of a program in which one agent was responsible to reach rural women throughout an entire county in spite of somewhat primitive transportation and communication systems.

Definitions of the terms "method demonstration," "results demonstration," and "demonstrator" are vital to an understanding of home demonstration work and are printed directly from a "Definition of Terms" page of the 1930 annual report form, as follows:

> A method demonstration is a demonstration given by an extension worker or other trained leader for the purpose of showing how to carry out a practice. Examples: Demonstrations of how to can fruits and vegetables, mix spray materials, and cull poultry.

> A result demonstration is a demonstration conducted by a farmer, home maker, boy, or girl under the direct supervision of the extension worker, to show locally the value of a recommended practice. Such a demonstration involves a substantial period of time and records of results and comparisons, and is designed to teach others in addition to the person conducting the demonstration. Examples: Demonstrating that the application of fertilizer to cotton will result in more profitable yields, that underweight of certain children can be corrected through proper diet, or that the use of certified seed in growing potatoes is a good investment.

The adoption of a farm or home practice resulting from a demonstration or other teaching activity employed by the extension worker as a means of teaching is not in itself a demonstration.

A result demonstrator is an adult, boy, or girl who conducts a result demonstration as defined above.[12]

The variety of demonstrations reflected the democratic practice of allowing a county's women to voice their interests and plan their agendas. Bread making, canning, drying, and the use of fireless cookers were considered important demonstrations in the greatest number of counties. The interest in labor-saving devices in the six Arkansas counties was typical of the national reports mentioned previously. Inclusion of a question as to the number of restrooms established for farm women, however, seemed to indicate a concern for women's welfare beyond what might be expected.

World and National Influences on the Work

In looking back, we realize that the item on bread making and substitutes for wheat in an earlier paragraph was simply a precursor of things to come. It was symbolic of what home demonstration work was all about. The work with rural women was not a social club that could be separated from events in the world. The meetings and the work provided longed-for socialization for the isolated rural women. However, the meetings were not places of refuge where outside cares and pressures could be left at the front door along with wet boots. Club members were affected by world and national events, and their work was tailored to their families' needs in response to those outside forces. Their families' livelihoods rose and fell because of what was happening outside their own walls. By the same token, this study of home demonstration work cannot be separated from outside influences and pressures.

The World War and Famine in Europe

For example, toward the end of the century's second decade, cottage cheese was a topic of discussion in every report. There were statistics on the number of women and girls making cottage cheese and the number of pounds of cottage cheese sold through curb markets. There were no explanations given since the reader would know of the shortage of meat and widespread starvation in Europe because of the ravages of the World War. One poster prepared by the United States Food Administration read:

Hunger

For three years America has fought starvation in Belgium.
Will you eat less – wheat, meat, fats and sugar – that we may still send food in ship loads?[13]

Of course Arkansas's home demonstration women would eat less meat. And they would make cottage cheese as a substitute. Statewide, 489 demonstrators were enrolled in cottage cheese making. Washington County members made 7,024 pounds in two months; Randolph County reported 1,200 pounds during the year, and Mississippi County – 1,796. During the summer of 1918, a cottage cheese specialist was added to the state staff, along with a canning specialist and child nutrition specialist.

And there were other ways in which they could help. In Crawford County, women pledged to grow fall chickens in order to save meat. Seven hundred women raised an average of one hundred fall chickens each, thus releasing a carload of smoked meat for other uses.[14]

The following recipe, found on the Cornell University home economics archives website, was distributed to assist in the meatless cooking endeavor:

Cottage Cheese Sausage

1 cup cottage cheese
1/2 tsp thyme
1 cup dry bread crumbs (or 1/2 cup cold cooked rice and 1/2 cup bread crumbs)
1 TB milk
1 tsp salt
1 TB peanut butter (or 1 TB of fat)
1/4 tsp pepper
1/4 cup peanut meats
1/3 tsp soda
1/2 tsp sage
1 TB finely chopped onion

Cook onion in the fat until tender but not brown, or mix onion with peanut butter if that is used. Dissolve soda in milk and work it into the cheese. Mix all other dry ingredients with bread crumbs. Then combine mixtures. Form into cakes, dust with bread crumbs or cornmeal and fry a delicate brown, using very little fat for frying.

Flavorful, light but protein-rich finger food [15]

Annual reports during the war years included a page entitled "Emergency Work in Food Production and Conservation." The numbers were to include work in rural areas as well as in towns and villages—whether by the agent or her demonstrators. Home demonstration agents and women participated and often seemed to take the lead in war efforts, as follows:

> In Southwest Arkansas, sixteen demonstration kitchens and twelve school laboratories were established and used by women and girls for demonstrations in war cookery and food conservation.[16]

> At Murfreesboro, Pike County, Miss Ruth Dean's girls and women sold war bread sandwiches and gave a program at the picture show to secure funds for a large portion of their equipment for the kitchen.[17]

> Mrs. Howard also sold $3,000 of Liberty Bonds, $6,000 of War Savings stamps and collected for the United War Fund drive $2,796.00.[18]

> Several of the agents were made County Chairman of the War Savings Stamp drive and also of the Junior Red Cross Association. I did not approve of this, but as they were able to come in contact with a great many more people because of it, they continued to hold the office for a while.[19]

> Mrs. Sarah J. Trussell of Hot Springs, Garland County, began work when salaries were only

about $400 per year. She wanted to hold on to her job so kept a secret that she was helping the mess sergeant at the Army and Navy Hospital to can beans, peas, and corn in 10-pound cans with hot water canner. She told him it would be an experiment but was willing to try. A canner with the exact capacity of twelve ten-pound cans was made to fit the gas stove. Total: 951 10-pound cans. 8 spoiled. The mess sergeant said the only disagreeable feature about the whole thing was that Mrs. Trussell didn't have a telephone under her pillow and let him call her in the middle of the night if there was trouble.[20]

The Great Influenza Epidemic of 1918

Compounding the difficulties for rural families during 1918 and 1919 were the great influenza epidemic and the intense drought throughout Arkansas. The influenza epidemic was unimaginably devastating. In fact, it killed more people in one year than the Black Death did in an entire century. In Arkansas, about 7,000 people died from the disease. Many rural deaths went unreported. Sometimes families were wiped out because no one had the strength to draw water or prepare food. Although rural people were known for helping each other, they generally could not or would not help their neighbors.[21]

During the epidemic and subsequent quarantines, most of the sixty-eight home demonstration kitchens throughout Arkansas were converted into diet kitchens. Soups and other foods were prepared and sent out to those with the disease. Over 2,000 people were provided sustenance in Little Rock alone.[22]

Glimpses at Other Pre-1920s Work

Despite the ravages of the influenza epidemic, North Central counties seemed surprisingly engaged in the work. Perhaps these activities took place before the epidemic spread to that area. Mrs. Elizabeth Temple, Emergency District agent, provided wonderful details of life in the isolated, mountainous counties:

> Bessie Morris of Cassville sold enough tomatoes to buy a registered Holstein calf. Mrs. Banks reported $13,000 in Liberty Loan subscriptions, besides helping in other war work. Miss Ora Carlile enthused a country school to the point that patrons donated the lumber for a domestic science room, which the boys are now building under guidance of a neighboring carpenter farmer. They are already collecting funds to equip the kitchen when completed. This little school is completely isolated in its rough mountain county.[23]

> Mrs. Spradlin helped to manage a fair in Newton County, the first ever held there. The schools cooperated with the two agents. 1200 people came to the fair, a thing almost unbelievable in so rough a district. Club girls exhibited pure bred poultry of a very high standard, the first owned in the county. The women's canning and jellies were exceptionally fine. Carroll county merchants reported selling 60 home canners this year.[24]

> Mrs. A. L. Watkins has a Turkey Club in Searcy County with three members. One little girl set

four turkey eggs under a bantam hen and raised all four turkeys. The women of this club raised 35 turkeys and sold them at 20 cents a pound, while the third member, a girl, raised and sold 65 turkeys. We are especially proud of Mrs. Watkins' work in organizing three community clubs, each of which purchased a $60 steam pressure canner. One club of 7 members canned 600 quarts of late corn and beans, not losing a single can. Mrs. Watkins wrote: "Here in the Heart of the Ozarks the roads are often impassable . . . but we intend to lead the state in steam pressure canning."[25]

The following vignettes from the pre-1920 years provide a glimpse into the richness of early home demonstration work in other parts of the state. Since agents worked with children as well as with women, it is appropriate to share some of the work with boys and girls as well as with women, as follows:

[In the Northeast district,] a short course for boys and girls was held. $64 of bananas was consumed in one afternoon.[26]

Miss Margaret Callahan of Lake Village worked beautifully with Italians in her county – in the care and feeding of children, bread making, canning – interpreted by the Italian women and the Catholic priest. It was necessary for her to get in a boat and row down the lake on several occasions alone to keep her engagements with these people. Every child 10 years of age became a member of the Red Cross and did knitting.

Miss Roxy Hobbs of Warren, Bradley County, taught bread work. When the wheat shortage came she taught these same women to use the substitutes.[27]

[In Northwest Arkansas, two counties had agents on emergency funds.] The agents assisted in putting on a district short course [in agriculture and home economics] at Russellville Agricultural School in August for club members – 369 girls and boys. Two girls had never seen a railroad train before. Three boys walked 35 miles together to reach the train to attend the course. One man brought his children 42 miles in a wagon in order to get them there.[28]

Growing Appreciation for the Work

In his narrative report for the fiscal year that ended June 30, 1919, the state Extension agent in Arkansas, whose analytical essays provided the overall picture of Extension work, gave the following summary:

Effort was made to show the relationship of the work of the county agents to the general governmental campaign for thrift. The fact that demonstration work is founded upon the principles of thrift was not realized by a great many people until the Thrift Campaign was fully in [unreadable]. . . .

A greater appreciation of the home demonstration work to the people at large is manifested not only in the quorum courts but on the part of men and women throughout the length and breadth of the state. A greater realization of the value of the fundamental basis on which the home demonstration work is placed is evident. More and more people are realizing the fact that home demonstration work is founded on the fundamental principles of thrift as applied to every day life including not only the problem of saving but the problems of increased production in connection with every day life.[29]

Organization, Public Relations, and Increased Local Support

The following letter from Mrs. Whatley to the county and quorum courts, which was found with Prairie County agents' 1917 narrative reports, provides additional insight into the earliest work. As can be seen in the letter, the work was demanding and involved building a county-wide program from the ground up.

To the Honorable County and Quorum Courts:

I beg to submit to you a summary of the work I have done in the Canning Club and Home Demonstration work this year, up to date. I have enlisted 307 members in the different clubs. I have made 1500 visits to the club members and homes; have had 700 consultations with women and girls. I have sent out at least 12,000 bulletins and circulars on canning, gardening and cooking.

I have traveled by rail 2100 miles; by auto about 440 miles; by team 1000 miles.

All of my club members have canned plenty of fruit and vegetables for home use, and a few have done extensive canning for market. I have superintended this market canning closely, and our product is much superior to the factory product. We have canned for home use everything in the fruit line, and everything in the vegetable line – viz., beans, peas, okra, carrots, beets, corn, tomatoes, soup mixtures, even to balanced meals in a single container; also field peas, potatoes, pumpkin, hominy, kraut, and pickles of every kind.

Most of the members in my clubs have done their gardening according to instructions. We have three regular cooking schools in the county, which meet twice a month. I have held 125 public demonstrations in canning, and have canned in every home where I have been called.

The girls are now learning government methods in making their canning club caps and aprons, and plans are now on foot for more extensive next year. Only a few club members were eligible for market canning this year, but all this year members will come in for market canning next year, since they must understand the work, as we will have nothing but a perfect product.

I have been in 85 community meetings with an attendance of 4750 people.

Signature: Mrs. Whatley[30]

The purpose of the letter was to report accomplishments to the local entities responsible for funding part of Mrs. Whatley's work. Agents' salaries were provided equally by federal, state, and county governments. The county's contribution, however, was vital to the program; it set the salary amount as the state and federal governments provided matching contributions.[31]

From the beginning, some counties were unable or unwilling to fund home demonstration agents. During the late 1920s, Connie Bonslagel, state home demonstration agent, annually juggled the work and agents among various counties because there never seemed to be enough funding to meet all the needs. She commented that in election years, the "'spoils system' trend offered difficulty with the women agents suffering for their own failure to conform [and thus] [lose out to their (difficult to read)] co-worker frequently."[32] Bonslagel's remark indicated that the women agents lost out to the male agricultural agents when newly elected county officials decided to cut expenditures within the county.

Agents surreptitiously courted the favor of businessmen, men's civic organizations, and often the County Federation of Women's Clubs. One agent admitted in her report, "Whenever the opportunity presented itself, the home demonstration agent made the acquaintance of Justices of the Peace but she did not make it noticeable."[33]

This agent also disclosed that her policy was "to meet and know the officers and most wide-awake member of the County Federation of Women's Clubs."[34] Bonslagel

27

also wooed the women's clubs. As early as 1920, she served as home economics chairman for the statewide federation.[35]

Women's Federation members wrote letters of recommendation to the quorum courts for funding of the home demonstration agents' work. In addition, the federations sometimes accepted the white rural women's clubs into their membership. In Saline County, for example, all the rural clubs were federated—along with several parent-teacher associations and school improvement organizations. In 1927, the agent reported that nearly all club officers were rural women. There often seemed to be a hint of pride in the rural agents' reports that the town clubs had accepted the rural women into their ranks.[36]

Early on, most counties formed umbrella organizations to oversee the work of the men's and women's work. One particularly honest agent expressed profound pleasure that her newly formed county organization would be responsible to contact the quorum court members for funding. The agent reported that many of the "embarrassing factors relative to seeking aid"[38] had thus been taken away from her.

As it turned out, one of the most effective means of impressing the county officials, civic clubs, and farmers of the importance of the work was the community tour held each year in numerous areas. One example follows:

> An added feature to our plan of work was the county auto tour for inspection of demonstration plots and club activities. These tours were made

during the season of the year when the yards, gardens, sweet corn plots, etc., were all in bloom. The idea of making such a tour was surely worth while. Many farmers and business men made these tours and saw many club projects, poultry houses, homes that had been white washed or painted, screened or otherwise made attractive and inviting by beautiful flowers, shrubs, etc. Many of the farmers were frank in their expressions as to what the trip had meant to them, declaring that it was a revelation to them, and that for the first time, they had been able to see what is meant by demonstration work.[39]

The cooperation and encouragement of local civic clubs and county officials certainly seemed to give a thumbs-up to the work. Since home demonstration membership was voluntary, the women's participation was, again, a vote of approval and an indication that at least some needs were being met.

Endnotes

[1] 1916 Annual Narrative Report of State Home Demonstration Agent (HDA). (Cover page was missing, but the text indicated the source.) Record Group 33, Arkansas Cooperative Extension Service, National Archives and Records Administration Southwestern Region, Fort Worth, Texas (will be cited throughout the remainder of the history as "RG 33, NARA/Fort Worth, Texas").

[2] Mena Hogan, "A History of the Agricultural Extension Service in Arkansas," (Master's thesis, University of Wisconsin, circa 1942. The thesis is undated; however, the bibliography indicated the use of unpublished Extension Service annual reports from 1912 through 1941), 39-49.

[3] Ibid., 45.

[4] Ibid., 39-49.

[5] Ibid.

[6] Ibid.

[7] Ibid., 46-47.

[8] Emma Archer, "History of Home Demonstration Work for 1912," 2, as quoted in Hogan, 48-49. (Hogan's bibliography did not list Archer's work. This may indicate that it was a narrative found among unpublished annual reports available to Hogan at the Arkansas Agricultural Extension Service, Little Rock, Arkansas.)

[9] 1916 Annual Narrative Report, State HDA, RG 33, NARA/Fort Worth, Texas. (Cover page was missing, but the text indicated the source.)

[10] 1915 State Canning Report, RG 33, NARA/Fort Worth, Texas.

[11] 1917 Annual Narrative Reports for Independence, Ouachita, Phillips (or Prairie), Saline, Sevier, and Union County HDAs, RG 33, NARA/Fort Worth, Texas.

[12] 1930 Annual Report, Saline County HDA, RG 33, NARA/Fort Worth, Texas. (Note: The Annual Report was a statistical report and was separate from the Annual Narrative Report used most frequently throughout this history.)

[13] National Archives Wiki for Researchers. http://www.ourarchives.wikispaces.net/World+War++1+{posters (ARC identifier 512582/Local Identifier 4-P-143). Retrieved 06/30/11.

[14] 1918 Annual Narrative Reports for State, Northwest District, and Northeast District HDAs, RG 33, NARA/Fort Worth, Texas. 1919 Annual Narrative Report, State HDA, RG 33, NARA/Fort Worth, Texas.

[15] From: University of California Dept. of Home Economics. Volunteer Student Service. "Save Meat." War Emergency Series No. 8. November 1918. Found in: The American Association of Family and Consumer Sciences Records, #6578, Division of Rare and Manuscript Collections, Cornell University Library. http://exhibits.mannlib.cornell.edu/meatlesswheatless/meatless-wheatless.php?content=ten. Retrieved 06/30/11.

[16] 1918 Annual Narrative Report, Southwest District HDA, RG 33, NARA/Fort Worth, Texas.

[17] Ibid.

[18] 1918 Annual Narrative Report, Northeast District HDA, RG 33, NARA/Fort Worth, Texas.

[19] 1918 Annual Narrative Report, Southeast District HDA, RG 33, NARA/Fort Worth, Texas.

[20]1918 Annual Narrative Report, Southwest District HDA, RG 33, NARA/Fort Worth, Texas.
[21]"Flu Epidemic of 1918," The Encyclopedia of Arkansas History & Culture. http://encyclopediaofArkansas.net/encyclopedia/ entry-detail.aspx?entryID=2229. Retrieved 03/03/12.
[22]1918 Annual Narrative Report, State HDA, RG 33, NARA/Fort Worth, Texas.
[23]1918 Annual Narrative Report, Emergency District HDA, RG 33, NARA/Fort Worth, Texas.
[24]Ibid.
[25]Ibid.
[26]1918 Annual Narrative Report, Northeast District HDA, RG 33, NARA/Fort Worth, Texas.
[27]1918 Annual Narrative Report, Southeast District HDA, RG 33, NARA/Fort Worth, Texas.
[28]1918 Annual Narrative Report, Northwest District HDA, RG 33, NARA/Fort Worth, Texas.
[29]1919 Annual Narrative Report, State Extension Agent, RG 33, NARA/Fort Worth, Texas.
[30]1917 Annual Narrative Report, Prairie County HDA, RG 33, NARA/Fort Worth, Texas. Several sentences have been incorporated into paragraphs for printing purposes.
[31]Gary Zellar. "H. C. Ray and Racial Politics in the African American Extension Service Program in Arkansas, 1915-1929, in Agricultural History, Vol. 72, No. 2, African Americans in Southern Agriculture:1877-1945 (Spring, 1998), 434. URL: http://www.jstor.org/stable/3744391. Accessed October 12, 2011.
[32]1928 Annual Narrative Report, State HDA, RG 33, NARA/Fort Worth, Texas. (Some words of the quotation were partially covered by the camera's date stamp.)
[33]1927 Annual Report, Saline County HDA, RG 33, NARA/Fort Worth, Texas.
[34]Ibid.
[35]1920 Annual Narrative Report, State HDA, RG 33, NARA/Fort Worth, Texas.
[36]1927 Annual Narrative Report, Saline County HDA, RG 33, NARA/Fort Worth, Texas.
[37]1933 Annual Narrative Report, St. Francis County HDA, RG 33, NARA/Fort Worth, Texas.
[38]Ibid.
[39]1921 Annual Narrative Report, Negro District HDA, RG 33, NARA/Fort Worth, Texas.

3

The 1920s: Time of Agricultural Depression

In her 1920 report, the Northwest District agent, whose counties included Benton, Washington, Madison, Crawford, Sebastian, Scott, Franklin, Johnson, Logan, Pope, Yell, Conway, Perry, Faulkner, and Pulaski, summed up one of the women's major needs. Among other things, the agent averred, women were interested in "making home drudgery into a systematized plan instead of an everlasting burden." During 1921, 1,392 women participated in 239 organized clubs in thirty-five counties. Women demonstrators who were not in clubs totaled 1,518. There were 4,554 girls in 509 organized clubs, and 856 girl demonstrators worked outside the club organization. Demonstrations were given in seventeen counties in which there were no agents.[1]

Agents' and club members' efforts in the war effort and influenza epidemic no doubt had a positive effect on the general populace as well as on the county quorum courts responsible for funding the work. The male agricultural agents had cooperated as well with overall governmental efforts to increase food supplies. With the end of the war, however, there was suddenly a surplus of food that combined with other mitigating factors to create a devastating depression for farm families at least nine years before the stock market crashed on October 25, 1929.

Re-evaluation of Extension Programs

By 1921, "[d]istressed rural conditions, brought about by the general business depression and low market value of farm products"[2] forced the state Extension staff to reevaluate and revamp the entire program. District and county agricultural and home demonstration agents were called in to meet with specialists and the state agents to formulate a state plan that would meet the needs of the farmstead during this critical period. Overall activities were adopted in the following order of priority: (1) community organization (for men, women, boys, and girls); (2) boys' and girls' club work; (3) field crop demonstrations; (4) horticultural demonstrations; (5) soil improvement demonstrations; (6) cooperative marketing; (7) livestock demonstrations; (8) food production (garden, family cow, poultry, bees); (9) food conservation (canning, drying, meat curing); (10) food preparation and utilization; and (11) textiles and clothing.[3]

As a result of the reassessment and planning described above, the seven newly prioritized home demonstration programs were (1) poultry raising, (2) gardening, (3) home dairy work, (4) canning, (5) nutrition and cookery, (6) textiles and clothing, and (7) improvement of house and yard. Noting that "poultry raising" had become the number one priority for home demonstration work, it should come as no surprise that—out in the counties—1921 was not a good year for old, unproductive chickens! Some examples follow:[4]

In Polk County, the home demonstration agent put on a "Swat the Scrub Rooster" campaign. 200 mongrel roosters were disposed of and those of standard breed were purchased instead. The banks cooperated in this piece of work.[5]

In Clay County, a special drive was made in culling flocks to get rid of hens that were poor layers.[6]

In Fulton County, teaching the farm women to cull their flocks was a line of work emphasized by Miss Wilmetta Scott. The poultry flocks in this county average from 15 to 100 in number. In the course of her year, Miss Scott culled out 1362 non-layers. These were sent to market at an average price of 27 1/3 cents. The feed saved on these hens would have cost at least one dollar a year - $1362. The laying hens retained showed a much higher rate of profit than formerly.[7]

The all day get together meeting held at Newport in Jackson County was a real success, bringing together the women from all over the county. The Chamber of Commerce furnished materials for lunch for the 75 guests. Work of the morning centered around preparation of dinner: old roosters made quite tender in the steam pressure cooker and a pot roast in the fireless cooker. Meat and lettuce sandwiches, chicken salad, deviled eggs, oatmeal and honey cookies with lemonade.[8]

The Gardening, Canning, and Nutrition Work

Because gardening and canning were at the very heart of the beginning of home demonstration work, it seems quite natural to trace the topic throughout the decade of the 1920s before turning to other programs such as clothing and home improvement work. Included under this heading will be the canning of meats as well as vegetables and fruits, gardening, and the ever-growing understanding of nutrition. One other factor must be included and explored, however: a discussion of food production, canning, and nutrition work would simply not be complete without consideration of the rural women's almost immediate concern for hungry, often malnourished children in their communities. But this splendid "piece of work," as the agents might say, will be addressed toward the end of the 1920s.

Bread Making

Other than growing and canning tomatoes, bread making was the most prolific topic under the heading "nutrition" in the very earliest reports. Mary L. Ray, who supervised African American agents throughout the state from 1917 until her untimely death in 1934, provided an amazing description of the early work. Ray commented, "A very easily discouraged person could not have pushed the work, when we realize the unfavorable conditions under which the initial demonstrations were given."[9] She continued with a detailed account of the labor entailed in providing a bread making demonstration at a rural schoolhouse. The description is included in the following:

> On bread making day one would usually see
> a farm wagon coming to the schoolhouse

containing a range and cooking utensils that had been borrowed from some member of the club. Often times a hard fight would have to be made before the stove pipe was subdued and remained intact; suitable wood and water were made plentiful and the many other little things so necessary to insure the success of the demonstration. But no one would shrink from their duty when the many anxious, happy, and appealing faces were there, because they wanted to learn.

Pattern recipes were given to the club members, according to the class in which they were enrolled. Quite often, the demonstration would be repeated the same day by the club members. The mistakes would be pointed out by the agent and they would be ready to practice the lesson until the agent came for the next public demonstration. . . .

The principal aim of these lessons was to teach skill in the manipulative process and also to teach a part of that larger problem of preparing the meals in the home, and the necessity of doing the work in as short a time as possible. We are convinced that it is important that we develop speed and skill in all of our work; and we must plan for sufficient repetition to enable club members to do things rapidly.

Nine counties held bread exhibitions and parades. For this phase of the work a display of banners and posters were used which showed

the value of better bread in the home. To
me, this has been an extremely interesting
and profitable piece of work. It has laid the
foundation for better and more effective bread
club work in the future.[10]

Health and Nutrition Concerns

One hundred years ago, the average woman's life
expectancy was a little more than forty-eight years.
People died of such diseases as dysentery, tuberculosis,
smallpox, or influenza before they grew old enough to
be concerned about the infirmities of today's elderly
population. As late as 1918, there were 250,000 infant
deaths annually in the United States, the eleventh
highest rate in the world. Mothers worried about getting
their toddlers through the second summer during a time
when clean milk was not universally available. Most
children experienced the loss of a brother or sister.[11]

In parts of Arkansas, rural families' diets during
this time often contributed to major health concerns.
So-called "close-to-subsistence" farmers ate monotonous
diets based on a few staples that were abundant in their
region. Often the staples of choice were corn, which was
fairly easy to grow, and pork, which did not require a
great deal of attention and was fairly simple to preserve
by salting and smoking. Archaeological examinations
of tenant farmers buried in an Arkansas cemetery
around 1900 revealed a variety of bone abnormalities
that indicated diets deficient in vitamins B, C, and D,
iron, and protein. The individuals most likely consumed
corn—as hominy and corn bread, along with pork—
usually as fat bacon or salt pork.[12]

Diseases caused by inadequate diets included weaning diarrhea, which was often fatal and resulted from protein malnutrition in children taken off breast milk and placed on amino acid-deficient foods. Another deficiency disease was pellagra, a debilitating condition caused by a lack of vitamin B3 (niacin). Pellagra is still common in parts of the world where individuals' diets are predominantly corn-based. Symptoms include diarrhea, inflamed mucus membranes, delusions, mental confusion, and scaly skin sores.[13]

During the Great Flood of 1927, the extent of pellagra cases in the state came to light as tenant families were removed from their homes and housed in Red Cross camps in which home demonstration agents often served as nutritionists or food service supervisors. Arkansas's governor even called a state-wide conference to work toward the eradication of the disease during the floods. Combined with poor sanitary conditions, malnutrition provided a perfect setting for tuberculosis, pneumonia, and other respiratory illnesses.[14]

Certainly all of Arkansas's rural families did not fall into the category of "close-to-subsistence farmers"; however, an overall study of Arkansas home demonstration work leaves no doubt that lives were saved and debilitating conditions were alleviated through its garden, canning, and nutrition programs. Reports as early as 1918 mentioned severe droughts in parts of Arkansas. Droughts continued throughout the following decade and were then overshadowed by the devastating floods of 1927. Home demonstration women and agents weathered these conditions, and the work was tailored to the families' most pressing needs.

An Abundance of Need

Although the 1920s were prosperous for many sectors of the economy, agriculture suffered because of overproduction and competition from other parts of the world. In the South, the failure to diversify—particularly because of dependence on cotton—as well as continued farming on exhausted land made the situation even more difficult. Historian Martha Swain reported that during the period 1929 to 1933, which she called the years of the locust, the extreme drought "wrought unbelievable hardship."[15] In Arkansas, one widow wrote to the American Red Cross, "I wish if you will please send me some clothes. Just enough to wear to the cotton patch."[16] Desperate Southern women even wrote to Lou Henry Hoover, the president's wife, asking for help.[17]

One perceptive agent, who seemed overwhelmed by the poverty and abundance of need she found in her county, summed up the goals of the foods and nutrition program in her 1927 report, which is shared below:

> Greatest needs were the needs of the children. Many showed evidence of malnutrition. If mothers had good gardens the year round, a good orchard to supply different fruits, poultry and dairy products and better home conditions, it is not unreasonable to believe that she would can and preserve fruits, vegetables, and meats to take care of her family's needs. If she did not know canning principles she would be eager to learn. She would also have her mind free to think of the preparation of food and the clothing for the family.[18]

The Growth of Nutrition Work

Lu Ann Jones interviewed 200 rural Southerners for her project for the Smithsonian Institute entitled "An Oral History of Southern Agriculture." Most of the interviewees were born during the first two decades of the twentieth century and came of age during the Great Depression. Through these interviews, Jones learned that even as Southerners continued to depend on cash crops such as cotton, women's work helped families to remain as "self-provisioning"[19] as possible by using a "live-at-home"[20] philosophy. In other words, women grew and produced much of what their families needed. Over and over, Jones heard the statement, "We didn't go hungry."[21] Arkansas's home demonstration program stressed the "live-at-home" philosophy throughout the decades. And in many instances, the women succeeded in providing sustenance for their families.

A review of Arkansas's early home demonstration work reveals a gradual growth in the understanding of nutrition and how foods affect health. Reports before 1920 usually discussed white bread making under the "nutrition" category. Eventually, discussions included the benefits of whole wheat and bran breads. Vegetables and salads became topics of demonstrations. Women became aware of some of the ways in which appropriate foods could improve their families' health.

The following excerpts provide a glimpse into the early gardening, nutrition, and foods work:

> The carrot has about come into its own.
> Spinach, rhubarb, celery, head lettuce, parsley,
> kohl rabbi are some of our new vegetables.[22]

The foods and nutrition specialist demonstrated leafy vegetables in the diet in Nevada County. As a result two women grew endive for the first time; four, celery; three, parsnips; six, asparagus; ten, spinach; twelve, carrots; ten, pimientos; six, parsley; three, eggplant; one, bush beans; one, Chinese cabbage; three, rhubarb; one, beans. In Ouachita County 155 women grew fall gardens.[23]

Mrs. Trussell of Garland County has for years followed the practice of training her club girls to furnish certain of the club women in Hot Springs with soup mixture, relishes, and other 4-H club products, the like of which are not to be found on the market. She further has club girls to do much of the canning for the Army and Navy Hospital whose steward insists that the beets, peaches, and other products which these 4-H girls put up for him are of better quality than he can procure other wheres [sic.]. This year Mrs. Trussell has taught or had some of her demonstrators to teach the matron of the county home for the aged and indigent how to can fruits and vegetables.[24]

The average club member feels that the canning of fruit is the one subject that she knows the most about. But the idea of canning vegetables and meats has been of untold value to them. The steam pressure canner has been introduced into the club work and is being used quite generally by the organized clubs in carrying on this line of canning.[25]

Miss Gertrude Conant, state foods and nutrition specialist has given two series of lessons in each county with splendid interest shown and substantial results. Three years ago, the words salads and cream soups were hardly known on the farms of my district and now these articles are on the tables everywhere.[26]

Nearly every family is interested in canning of meats at home. In 5 different counties I have given demonstrations in canning a whole beef, canning roasts, stew, steak, kidney, ox tail soup, heart, tongue, soup stock and using the bones for chicken feed so that no part of the animal is wasted. In Crawford County 13 whole beeves have been canned and 5 in Cleveland County. In addition to beef canning we have canned chicken, mutton, pork, goat meat, rabbit, squirrel—in fact about every kind of meat that is edible.[27]

6,782 pounds of cured meat, sausage, and lard were saved, with a total value of $6,300. The women used all of the fat which otherwise would have gone to waste, in making soap. 4,558 pounds of soap were made, at a savings of at least $227.90 to the homes.[28]

The outstanding progress made in food preservation work this year has been more or less apart from the amount of food canned. First, the developing of leadership and the consequent strengthening of the county program through the training of local canning leaders

in seven counties; second, the development
of community organization and of the
demonstration spirit in one community in each
of our counties; and third, the standardization
of products through demonstration [unreadable]
at fairs, are outstanding achievements in this
field.[29]

The Clothing Work

The history of clothing work in the United States is
a vital part of the history of women and their labors.
In colonial times and during the nation's early years,
women made the cloth they used for their families'
needs. Even into the early 1800s, Secretary of the
Treasury Albert Gallatin estimated that two-thirds of
household linens and clothing used by non-urban
households were produced within the home.[30]

By the second half of the nineteenth century,
seamstresses operated as independent craftswomen
for families who could afford their services. Even
the wealthy conserved cloth; women of means did
some needlework. *The Young Lady's Friend,* a popular
etiquette book, devoted two pages to instructions on
darning. The author admonished readers, "A woman
who does not know how to sew is as deficient in her
education as a man who cannot write."[31]

Elias Howe's patent for a sewing machine in 1846
became the prototype for many later models. However,
sewing machines simply cost too much for individual
families or seamstresses to purchase alone. Even the
cast-iron stove cost very little compared to a sewing
machine, with its precise moving parts. *Godey's Lady's*

Book suggested that in each country village, ten families should go together to purchase one machine. Isaac Singer's partner, Edward Clark, however, came up with a solution that would sell ten machines to ten families instead: the installment plan, with its five dollars down and high interest rates. Women often managed to buy the machines to provide income as well as clothing for their families.[32]

Some historians found that the sewing machine actually contributed to sending garment making out of the home. Between 1884 and 1920, the Sears Roebuck catalog's display of women's ready-to-wear clothing increased from none at all to ninety illustrated pages. For a time, hand-sewing was considered a confession that one could not afford a sewing machine or "boughten" clothes.[33] The head of the fabric department in a large retail store noted that in the mid-1920s the department sold only a fraction of the amount sold in 1890.[34]

Did these changes, however, reflect what rural Arkansas women were doing to clothe their families?

Clothing Specialist Employed

In her 1918 report, state agent Connie Bonslagel found that throughout Arkansas, approximately one thousand home demonstration women were engaged in the conservation of clothing, such as remodeling and making children's garments from old suits. Clothing work also consisted of teaching good workmanship as well as the details of correct cutting and fitting in order for women and girls to make their own clothes.[35]

As was noted previously, during 1921—following a drastic downturn in the rural economy—Bonslagel met with other Extension managers to assess the work and to set specific goals in order for the Extension programs to survive. Of the seven prioritized programs of work, clothing and textiles came in as number six. In spite of its sixth-place status, however, a textiles and clothing specialist was added during the second half of 1921.[36]

The following excerpt from the newly hired clothing specialist's 1922 report reveals her early concerns:

> The chief problems confronting the clothing work were poor taste in the selection and buying of materials in appropriate dress for various occasions, waste of both new and old material, and a lack of knowledge of color and design as adapted to the different types of individuals. To teach proper selection of clothing both as to color and occasion has demanded much time especially among the school girls.[37]

As she continued, the specialist addressed more practical issues, stating that the clothing work goal was for Arkansas's rural women to be dressed suitably and economically and to know enough about textiles to receive appropriate value for their purchases. She hoped for every garment or piece of material to be utilized over and over until there was nothing left to use. Finally, she looked forward to "the time when our girls and women will wear sensible shoes, those that conform to the lines of the feet and tend to make better [unreadable] and less pain and fretfulness."[38]

The clothing specialist—whose name was not included on the typed report—also discussed clothing clinics, in which she demonstrated cleaning, pressing, and making over a garment. Participants would actually make over a garment at the meeting and then do the same demonstration for the women in their own clubs, spreading the knowledge throughout the county. A savings of $2,506 was reported in seventeen counties.[39]

One other early demonstration was the making of children's garments. In one example, the county agent brought to a central location two leaders from each of five communities. The specialist provided samples of suitable children's clothing based on color, design, material, and cost. She also provided stencils and patterns for the women, who each made a garment. Each one then took the stencil and pattern back and shared the process with fellow club members.[40]

Remodeling of Worn Clothing

By the mid-1920s, the clothing program had become an important part of home demonstration work. In archival photographs of club members, the women appeared neatly dressed and well groomed. In some instances, their appearance would seem incongruous to their economic and social status. However, further research revealed the women had successfully constructed attractive clothing—sometimes by taking an old garment apart, eliminating the worn spots, and making a new piece. Over and over again, the agents reported club members learned to remodel worn clothing to make new garments for their families.[41]

Some women, including one St. Francis County member, were able to increase their families' incomes by remodeling clothing, as follows:

> Mrs. Mattie B. Wade, Rt 2 Forrest City, has remodeled 22 wool and silk dresses for women, some of which had been in service 7 years. She changed them into dresses that looked like new. She has also remodeled 34 children's dresses and coats made from clothing of adults. She has remodeled 10 dresses and over coats for men one of whom was her husband E.F. Wade and one for Dr. S.B. Banks, practicing physician of Forrest City. Dr. Banks feels that her remodeling and renovating for himself and wife, children saved him more than $200.00 this year.[42]

Cotton Bags into Clothing

Beginning in the latter nineteenth century, cotton bags replaced wooden barrels as containers for staples such as flour. There is some evidence women recycled flour bags into clothing before the turn of the century. Lu Ann Jones, who provided an account of the use of cotton bags for clothing, commented that during the 1920s and 1930s clothing made from cotton bags became "an emblem of poverty, a testament to ingenuity, and a badge of pride. Depression era photographs show the poorest of the poor clad in sack garments."[43]

Women dyed the bags with natural products such as black walnuts and sumac berries and found a way to remove inked wording from the sacks. By the 1940s—which seems an extraordinarily long time to figure out a solution—manufacturers were making paper-band labels and turning out sacks in prints and flowers. By 1947, farm women collaborated with fabric designers to define fashion for the Bemis Bag Company![44]

In the meantime, district agent Mary Ray reported that as tenant 4-H girls made their gardens, "[n]ot an empty sack was allowed to be thrown away but was used to make sewing bags, caps and aprons, uniform dresses."[45] One agent reported that the women considered it a pleasure to make garments from sugar, meal, salt, and flour sacks. First, a demonstration was made in bleaching and cleaning the sacks. Items made from the sacks included scarfs, pillowcases, towels, curtains, aprons, and children's underwear.[46]

Just a few additional comments follow to add insight into the clothing work:

> The tendency in sewing for so many years has leaned toward the fancy work until a housedress contest is unique. The farm women are rather attracted to the idea of simplicity in design for house and school dresses.[47]

> Clubs have had a fashion of bringing the sewing along, and discussing their work together. It has been a very pleasant feature of the club meetings, and many have been the new stitches learned and ideas exchanged.[48]

> The use of dye and tie-and-dye [dashes added for clarity] has improved the looks of old materials. Does not look as cheap when dyed in

colors as it does in white or cream. Girls and young women like the possibilities for clothing and home furnishings in tieing and dying.[49]

Women were more interested in clothing and textiles than in previous years: demonstrations in testing of materials, color combinations, choice and selection of materials, remodeling and millinery in addition to sewing required in girls' clubs. The girls entering the clothing contests were required to choose the materials and patterns used and were graded on the suitability to the wearer of the color and design of the garments made.[50]

The making of hats was discouraged but five or six were remodeled.[51]

In her 1927 report, Connie Bonslagel indicated notable progress in the clothing and textiles work that year. The specialist had devoted untold hours to the program. She had assisted local agents in training local leaders, who could assist with newly enrolled women demonstrators as well as with the elementary-level sewing prescribed for first and second-year club girls. Bonslagel continued:

The cotton house dress contest for farm women has been discussed in part in connection with our annual Farmers' Week [held annually for farmers and wives at the University of Arkansas at Fayetteville]. This contest has been developed into an excellent means of teaching and putting into practice the principles of dress design, garment construction, pattern alteration, . . .

and selection of materials. . . . The contest [has become] an exciting event of the club year in many communities, the entire membership of many home demonstration clubs entering the contest frequently. In Carroll County 150 farm women entered the county contest. A total of 1418, representing an increase of 1000 over last year's entries, took active part in this contest this year. Of this number, 64 attended Farmers' Week and were entered in the finals there. In many counties the winning woman is awarded a free trip to Farmers' Week.[52]

Although numerous house dress and Sunday dress contests were reported, most narratives did not specifically mention bags or sacks. However, in 1933, Lugenia Christmas reported a county contest for women and girls—school dress for girls, house dress and Sunday dress for women—all made from bags.[53]

An Intangible Benefit

Historians have noted that by the 1920s rural life was regarded as inferior to town living. Throughout the agents' reports, there were hints of this sense of inferiority, as was mentioned previously. Although not overtly stated, there was a need for acceptance that was somewhat satisfied when the farm women's organizations were invited to join the County Federation of Women's Clubs.

In some ways the clothing program may have been just what the rural women needed. Although it could not fix everything—or even very many things—it could provide the women with a sense of pride and wellbeing by allowing them to feel they looked as good as the town women. In 1927, Flora Ferrill of Lee County said exactly that: The rural women of the county were "as tastefully and stylishly dressed as the town women, with of course a few exceptions"[!][54] Ferrill's likely unintended humor brings a muffled chuckle these eighty-five years later.

The Home Improvement Work

In December of 1920, Sallie Chamberlin, Southeast District agent, compiled the "Improvements on House and Yard Based on Agent's Advice or Suggestions" portion of the annual report. The data was based on agents' submissions for Ashley, Chicot, Cleveland, Desha, Drew, Jefferson, Lincoln, Lonoke, and Union counties. The results capture this aspect of the work in one of five districts at the beginning of the 1920s:

> *Demonstrators following a definite plan for improvement of the home: 98*
>> New houses built: 8
>> Houses remodeled: 19
>> Houses repaired: 28
>> Lighting systems installed: 35
>> Heating systems: 4
>> Water systems: 9
>> Kitchens improved by screening: 101
>> Rearrangement of equipment: 30
>> Improvement of floors: 24
> *Labor Saving Devices [obtained]:*
>> Kitchen cabinets: 6
>> Wood boxes: 12
>> Fireless cookers: 27
>> Bread mixers: 1
>> Food choppers: 17

Clothes hampers or laundry bags: 48
Ironing boards: 19
Sleeping porches: 6
Flower boxes: 30

Improvements in Other Parts of the House through:
Improvement of floors: 21
Improvement of walls: 19

Furnishings bought or made:
Luncheon sets: 49
Sewing screens: 4
Wall pockets: 8

Improvements in yard:
Fences repaired: 51
Trees planted: 54
Shrubs planted: 28
Unsightly buildings repaired or removed: 17
Lawns or grass planted: 10
Bread raisers: 4

Laundry Equipment:
Washing machines: 8
Plantings of flowers, vines, other plants: 132[54a]

The following reports on home improvement provide additional insight into the work:

Home conveniences are badly needed, especially since the women and children help do the field work, therefore, having less time in the home. Springs and water at a shallow depth would make water-works in the homes more easily obtained. With a little money added to the income home conveniences could be purchased.[55]

Misses Clara and Ida Helmich, assisted by their father and brothers, are following an extensive plan of home beautification. . . .They have remodeled the house so as to have the largest room in the house on the front and use it for a living room. They changed a window to a door, added a window and remodeled a side porch to be the front of the home.[56]

The $10 prize for best kitchen improvement . . . was won by Mrs. Sara Hooks of Caldwell—only two rooms to her and husband's house on a little 40 acre farm of their own. She says she arises at 3:30 a.m. daily in order to attend her home duties – garden and other domestic duties and assist her husband on the farm. They have stock, cattle, hogs, turkeys, geese, ducks, chickens and guineas and one of the best gardens in the county.[57]

[The work] is centered around improved dwellings and poultry houses. Seven women installed lighting systems, five water systems, three pump and tank systems installed (a pump at the well which pumps the water to a tank or barrel just outside the kitchen and above the sink). A sink, faucet, and a few yards of piping finished the system. One bath room was added, one sewage disposal system, two screened sleeping porches, several natural gas connections for cooking and heating. . . . Seven water systems, seven sinks, twelve gasoline or electric irons, six washing machines add to the health and leisure time of the women.[58]

The Home and Community Beautification Work

The women of Jasper, in the North Central district, surely won the prize, hands down, for beautification work in 1920. The story follows. Hold on to your hat!

In Newton County, a conspicuously good piece of work was done by the Booster's Club, organized at Jasper with the help of the two agents, and having both a men's and a women's section. Early in the year they agreed to entertain 150 club boys and girls at a club short course during August. Then they wanted a clean town as an example to the visitors from the county. A clean up day was appointed and fifty wagon loads of trash were removed from the streets free of charge. Then, seeing that the stock running at large would soon spoil the work already done, they asked for and secured a stock law shutting hogs, cattle and horses off their clean streets. The public square was cleaned, the court house fence repaired and the trees trimmed and the lawn sown to blue grass. Again the cemetery was cleaned, the fences fixed up and the road leading to it improved, the women promising to serve dinner to all who worked.[59]

Another version of this story gave all the credit to the women of the community, especially Mrs. Spradlin, who had not been able to get a woman's club in Jasper until she and her husband started the Booster Club. The women's section of the club eventually became a home demonstration club.

Other reports of home and community beautification follow:

> Rural women improved home grounds by planting flowers around the base of houses and in porch boxes, and by using potted plants. [Women were encouraged to use] rocks: water worn rock, slate appearing rock found in streams and ditches, grey rock, and glass rock in colors and white with the appearance of glass.[60]

> [Home Beautification report:] 600 club members working along this important line. This phase of work deserves more attention than is ordinarily given to it. As the farmers become more prosperous, it will be possible to improve the surroundings of the farm home by doing the things which must be left off under the present conditions which prevail on a majority of the farms.[61]

> [In Ashley County,] [o]ne of the most interesting features of the fair was the flower show. Twenty entries were made. . . . The effectiveness of the display caused many flower lovers to renew their interest and set higher standards for next year. . . . The annual flower show was held in November under the auspices of the civic league. . . . There were 28 entries including chrysanthemums, roses, marigolds, zinnias, cannas, violets, dahlias, and other late blooming flowers.[62]

Endnotes

[1]1920 Annual Narrative Report, Northwest Arkansas District HDA, RG 33, NARA/Fort Worth, Texas.

1921 Annual Narrative Report, State HDA, RG 33, NARA/Fort Worth, Texas.

[2]1921 Annual Narrative Report, State Extension Agent, RG 33, NARA/Fort Worth, Texas.

[3]Ibid.

[4]1921 Annual Narrative Report, State HDA, RG 33, NARA/Fort Worth, Texas.

[5]Ibid.

[6]Ibid.

[7]1921 Annual Narrative Report, North Central District HDA, RG 33, NARA/Fort Worth, Texas.

[8]Ibid.

[9]1922 Annual Narrative Report, Negro District HDA, RG 33, NARA/Fort Worth, Texas.

[10]Ibid.

[11]Dorothy Schneider and Carl J. Schneider, *American Women in the Progressive Era, 1900-1920* (New York: Facts on File, 1993), 2-8.

[12]Susan Strasser, *Never Done: A History of American Housework* (New York: Pantheon Books, 1982), 14.

Carl H. Moneyhon, *Arkansas and the New South* (Fayetteville: The University of Arkansas Press, 1997), 71.

[13]Moneyhon, *Arkansas and the New South*, 71.

[14]1927 Annual Narrative Report, State Nutrition Specialist, RG 33, NARA/Fort Worth, Texas.

Moneyhon, *Arkansas and the New South*, 71.

[15]Martha A. Swain, "A New Deal for Southern Women: Gender and Race in Women's Relief Work," in *Women of the American South: A Multicultural Reader*, ed. Christie Anne Farnham (New York: New York University Press, 1997), 243.

[16]Ibid.

[17]Ibid.

[18]1927 Annual Narrative Report, Saline County HDA, RG 33, NARA/Fort Worth, Texas.

[19]Lu Ann Jones, *Mama Learned Us to Work: Farm Women in the New South* (Chapel Hill: The University of North Carolina Press, 2002), 4-5.

[20]Ibid., 5.

[21]Ibid.

[22]1927 Annual Narrative Report, Union County HDA, RG 33, NARA/Fort Worth, Texas.

[23]1927 Annual Narrative Report, State HDA, RG 33, NARA/Fort Worth, Texas.

[24] Ibid.

[25]1922 Annual Narrative Report, Negro District HDA, RG 33, NARA/Fort Worth, Texas.

[26]1920 Annual Narrative Report, North Central District HDA, RG 33, NARA/Fort Worth, Texas.

[27]1920 Annual Narrative Report, State HDA, RG 33, NARA/Fort Worth, Texas.

[28] 1922 Annual Narrative Report, Negro District HDA, RG 33, NARA/Fort Worth, Texas.

[29] 1927 Annual Narrative Report, State HDA, RG 33, NARA/Fort Worth, Texas.

[30] Strasser, 125-130.

[31] Ibid., 131-132 (quotation from page 132).

[32] Ibid., 138-139.

[33] Schneider, 29.

[34] Strasser, 143-145.

[35] 1918 Annual Narrative Report, State HDA, RG 33, NARA/Fort Worth, Texas.

[36] 1921 Annual Narrative Report, State HDA, RG 33, NARA/Fort Worth, Texas.

[37] 1922 Annual Narrative Report, State Clothing Specialist, RG 33, NARA/Fort Worth, Texas.

[38] Ibid.

[39] Ibid.

[40] Ibid.

[41] 1926 Annual Narrative Report, Phillips County HDA, RG 33, NARA/Fort Worth (for example).

[42] 1929 Annual Narrative Report, St. Francis County HDA, RG 33, NARA/Fort Worth, Texas.

[43] Lu Ann Jones. *Mama Learned Us to Work*, 172.

[44] Ibid., 171-183.

[45] 1920 Annual Narrative Report, Negro District HDA, RG 33, NARA/Fort Worth, Texas.

[46] 1932 Annual Narrative Report, Mississippi County Local HDA, RG 33, NARA/Fort Worth, Texas.

[47] 1927 Annual Narrative Report, Saline County HDA, RG 33, NARA/Fort Worth, Texas.

[48] 1927 Annual Narrative Report, Union County HDA, RG 33, NARA/Fort Worth, Texas.

[49] Ibid.

[50] 1924 Annual Narrative Report, Washington County HDA, RG 33, NARA/Fort Worth, Texas.

[51] 1923 Annual Narrative Report, Saline County HDA, RG 33, NARA/Fort Worth, Texas.

[52] 1927 Annual Narrative Report, State HDA, RG 33, NARA/Fort Worth, Texas.

[53] 1933 Annual Narrative Report, St. Francis County Local HDA, RG 33, NARA/Fort Worth, Texas.

[54] 1927 Annual Narrative Report, Lee County HDA, RG 33, NARA/Fort Worth, Texas.

[54a] 1920 Annual Narrative Report, Southeast District HDA, RG 33, NARA/Fort Worth, Texas.

[55] 1927 Annual Narrative Report, Saline County HDA, RG 33, NARA/Fort Worth, Texas.

[56] Ibid.

[57] 1927 Annual Narrative Report, St. Francis Local HDA, RG 33, NARA/Fort Worth, Texas.

[58]1927 Annual Narrative Report, Saline County HDA, RG 33, NARA/Fort Worth, Texas.

[59]1920 Annual Narrative Report, North Central District HDA, RG 33, NARA/Fort Worth, Texas.

[60]1927 Annual Narrative Report, Saline County HDA, RG 33, NARA/Fort Worth, Texas.

[61]1921 Annual Narrative Report, Negro District HDA, RG 33, NARA/Fort Worth, Texas.

[62]1927 Annual Narrative Report, Eastern District HDA, RG 33, NARA/Fort Worth, Texas.

4

1927: Year of Destruction

Digital pictures of records from four Arkansas Delta counties during the period 1926 through 1933 were made for a project at the University of Arkansas at Little Rock. As the records were transcribed, they revealed an amazing glimpse at a brief piece of Arkansas women's history. Although the story is concentrated in only four counties—and there were other flooded counties in the state—the story is so wonderful it had to be included in this book about Arkansas's women. First, however, the Union County agent's experience is shared.

Just as home demonstration members and agents were participants in efforts to alleviate suffering caused by the Great War in Europe and the influenza epidemic of 1918, some also participated in the aftermath of the historic tornado at Strong and the Great Flood of 1927. Some agents penned amazing eye-witness accounts of the devastation. For Myrtle Watson, Union County agent, her account of the historic tornado at Strong in 1927 included great personal grief. Her flood account provided a wonderful human interest story as well. Both accounts follow:

On the afternoon of May 10th, a storm struck our little town of Strong, and almost wiped it away. Twenty-seven people were killed. Out of the number, nineteen were my personal friends and acquaintances, and some were close friends. The wounded, and the bodies of the dead were brought to El Dorado. The undertakers' parlors were full, and the hospitals were overrun. There had been a storm at Norphlet too, and so there were wounded ones coming in from that direction too. All hands did all they could to relieve the suffering and to take care of the dead bodies. I closed my office to all other duties, and for about two weeks gave assistance in whatever [way] I could do at Strong and at the El Dorado hospitals.[1]

During the spring months when the whole Mississippi Valley was under water, we suffered less than many of our neighbors. In fact, no lives were lost here, but some parts of the county were covered by water for several weeks, and there was considerable damage to property, and inconvenience to the people. Two of our towns, Calion and Felsenthal, on the Ouachita River, were flooded for weeks. I went to Calion during the time, and rode all over the town in a boat. The people of the town sat on their porches or roofs, rode up and down the streets in boats, helped each other and asked for no aid from the outside – the happiest people in the world, and just thankful that it was no worse – the finest example of pure optimism I ever saw. It was a great lesson to us all."[2]

In the Delta

Accounts of flood relief work by eight agents in four Arkansas Delta counties provided a look into one aspect of their work that very few Arkansans are likely to know. These responsibilities were assigned to the agents by their counties' governing authorities because of their expertise in nutrition and foods work and their affiliations with either the University of Arkansas at Fayetteville or its African American branch at Pine Bluff that became Arkansas AM&N. Each agent reported on how she, the women with whom she had been working, and home demonstration women throughout the state responded to the emergency. Excerpts from the 1927 *Helena World* newspaper have been interspersed among text describing some agents' accounts, as follows:

Memphis, Tenn. April 14: Reports of three levee breaks added to the alarm over flood conditions in the valley of the Mississippi River and its major tributaries. . . .Livestock and other moveable property affected by these stages should be moved by or before the dates given and preparations made for possibly higher stages. . . .the village of Jacksonport, near Newport, Ark., has been abandoned, according to a telephone message received here from Newport today. . . .Water—called the most uncontrollable of the elements—menaced the Mississippi Valley today as one of the most damaging floods in the history of the Mississippi River became more and more apparent, in the opinion of experienced flood fighters.[3]

Phillips County

Friday, April 15: 50 families housed in box cars on the Mo Pac railroad at Elaine were to be removed this afternoon into the vicinity of Barton Crossing while a train left Lexa early this morning for Wynne and Forrest City to obtain additional box cars to house refuge[e]s driven from their homes in the Elaine vicinity. Following the excessive rainstorm last night, along with the flood conditions affecting the White River and the backwater conditions in the southern part of Phillips County, Elaine began today to experience its first trouble of the present high water. Where water was reported appearing in only ditches yesterday, a rise of 1 foot, flooding parts of the town, was reported this morning.

Numerous families of the town were preparing early today to vacate their homes, some coming to Helena to seek protection behind the 60 foot levee which assures safety in this city. Others will leave their homes this afternoon and some will be housed in boxcars or National Guard tents as the water situation grows active due principally to the swollen condition of the White River which is unable to empty into the flooded Mississippi.

Rains last night and today also increased the state of the backwater in the Mellwood and Elaine sections. Red Cross officials who visited Elaine yesterday reported the conditions as far as refugees are concerned to be good and ample. Facilities for care for them were available with Mo Pac sending in additional box cars while 100 additional National Guard tents were requisitioned from Little Rock headquarters.[4]

Sunday, April 17: Elaine people are moving rapidly to Helena, elsewhere
Motor trucks from Helena transfer organizations and private trucks were being pressed into hard service yesterday in completing the evacuation of Elaine as backwater conditions became more acute in the little town in the southern part of the county. Water was reported to be rising rapidly, making motor traffic difficult at many points along the highway between Helena and Elaine. One stretch of a mile was reported under water yesterday afternoon with the rise fairly rapid.[5]

Monday, April 18: Special trains move refugees from Wabash and Elaine backwaters
90 families of refugees housed in Mo Pac box cars in the vicinities of Wabash and Elaine were ordered removed this morning as the backwater condition in the southern part of the county became more acute. Evacuation of Wabash plantations was started yesterday when the water was reported to have covered plantation no. 1 and to be entering plantation number 2 of the Howe Brothers property. Special trains from Lexa and Helena were ordered into the Elaine and Wabash sections to move the families as well as those others who were not yet quartered in box car or tent homes.

Helena is to become a refuge camp with hundreds of families from Whitehall, Wabash and Elaine districts coming here to be encamped in the hills back of the city. Between 75 and 100 were expected from the Saint Francis River country where the break in the Whitehall levee early Saturday morning caused inundation of thousands of acres of land, driving many away from their homes into Marianna, while others sought refuge on ridge territory or the levee top until aid could be sent to them. Tenants of Wabash plantations began early yesterday morning in moving their household effects and stock up the Oneida road, fleeing before the rapidly rising backwater.

6,000 refugees

A government survey of the flood condition . . . found that approximately 1000 box cars were in service in the county, there being from six to 12 people in each car. The number of refugees so housed had been placed at 5,000, with probably 1,000 additional refugees housed in National Guard tents. Planters are still caring for their tenants wherever possible and few cases of distress were found.[6]

In her "Flood Report of the Work in Phillips County," Carrie W. Moore of Phillips County noted that the first of all the refugees came by boatload at midnight. After three days, more than 1,000 (unclear) were housed in the Eliza Miller High School in West Helena as well as in churches in the area. Upon the refugees' arrival, 1,000 cups of soup were served to them at Moore's direction, along with dry clothing provided by the Red Cross.[7]

Feeding the refugees proved to be a dilemma for the nutrition-minded agent. Because the African American refugees were not accustomed to eating scientifically balanced meals, they did not adjust well to the food provided them. Thus, for breakfast they were instead served grits, gravy, and bacon, coffee for adults, and milk for children. Dinner consisted of cabbage with salt pork, sweet potatoes, beets, and rice pudding with sauce for dessert. Similar meals were served each day to 500 individuals, using only one cook stove at the school. Two meals were served daily, with sufficient leftovers for a lunch at supper time.[8]

The county health nurse, Miss Freeman, was responsible for most of the work among the sick refugees housed at Eliza Miller School. Freeman appointed Moore to plan and serve meals to the sick at regular hours and to give orders for their baths. Those cared for at the school included five women with new-born babies, nine cases of tuberculosis, two of small pox, and five of rheumatism. After the patients were settled in, they were taken to West Helena for their tests. Moore noted that all patients were given good care.[9]

At a meeting held in Helena on April 21, County Judge John C. Sheffield worked on plans to aid the refugees. Extension agents were asked to devote as much time as possible to the emergency work. They learned that 125,600 acres of cultivated land was under water and that 17,000 people in the county had become refugees. The damage was estimated at $1,400,000 (difficult to read). Mary Alice Larche of Phillips County initially visited various refugee camps and was eventually assigned to the Helena camp. She gave out clothing, maintained office files, and made lists of things needed. During the following weeks, she worked day and night, seven days a week. Once the damages were assessed, rehabilitation could begin. In Phillips County, 3,000 units of garden seed were given out. The workers were discouraged that some individuals (pulled up and) ate the vegetables as soon as they came up, requiring replanting. Since the seeds were freely given, the people planted again.[10]

Larche realized there was a need for food preservation work, but she also recognized that most families had lost their canning jars and bottles. So she asked the Red Cross for more up-to-date equipment to carry on the work. "Our Red Cross Relief worker," Larche opined, "was a man of good sense, and wanted the people to have all that he could give them."[11] So he provided ten sets of steam pressure cookers, Burpee seals, and 10,000 containers. Larche noted that the equipment was divided with the local agent.[12]

St. Francis County

Friday, April 22: 8,000 flood refugees arrive from town near Forrest City
8000 flood victims are being cared for in camps established here and world war nurses are being recruited from these sections to aid in combating diseases which have broken out among refugees. For the past 3 days refugees have been pouring into Forrest City at the rate of 1000 a day, taxing the facilities available for caring for them.

Widener, Heth, Hughes, Whitmore and Round Pond, with a total population of about 4000 are completely under water and their citizens are being driven here for food and shelter.

Madison and Palestine are expected to be submerged by the end of the week. Appeal for funds said $1000 a day is needed to feed the refugees here. Leading women of the city have moved from Bridge tables to hospital work. They have established a hospital of their own to care for the stricken refugees.[13]

St. Francis County is due west of Phillips County, which borders the Mississippi River. In her 1927 annual report, Bird Tatum, St. Francis County agent, noted that she was unable to carry out the regular program of work because of the floods in April. The rains and storms continued for weeks; then, for the next three months all work ceased as the agents turned their attention to the flood sufferers. As 10,000 refugees were thrust upon the workers in a few days, Tatum worked night and day—in rubber boots and rain coat—wherever she was needed. Her work included getting emergency hospitals furnished and providing milk for children.[14]

The Red Cross director appointed Tatum as chairman of clothing distribution; the base was located in the Episcopal parish. Tatum called a meeting of presidents of women's clubs and church organizations and asked that each group provide two women every day to issue clothing. As carloads of clothes came from everywhere, the women served 300 to 500 refugees daily for over three weeks, including Sundays.[15]

Tatum continued, "I got to where I couldn't eat or sleep, doctors ordered me to bed. After two days rest I worked in the camps — the emergency was over."[16] She gave demonstrations to refugees in making rugs from tow sacks, with materials provided by local businessmen. She also gave demonstrations in canning beans and talked with groups of refugees about healthy eating and its relationship to good health; she stressed correct diets for children. As the refugees returned to the bottoms, she accompanied the Red Cross nurse in making the rounds to finish vaccinating against typhoid. As she visited the homes, Tatum helped with the sick and advised family members of sanitary precautions and how to use lime for whitewashing. She was among a group of agents called to Little Rock to meet with Red Cross directors, Secretary of Commerce Herbert Hoover, and others to work out plans for Extension agents to assist in rehabilitation work in the flooded areas.[17]

As Lugenia Christmas, local home demonstration agent in St. Francis County, completed her annual report, which was due to the state office in Little Rock during December 1927, she noted that she was still working with the Red Cross in distributing clothing to those who lived in the flooded areas. The General Mission Board of the Presbyterian Church contributed eighteen boxes and barrels of clothing, shoes, and hats. The Royal Circle of Friends, a black fraternal organization in Arkansas, contributed sixteen cartons. Communities not in the flood area contributed 1,296 pieces of clothing. Following the closing of the Red Cross distribution headquarters, 9,347 articles were distributed.[18]

African American home demonstration club members—
both women and girls—prepared 785 bowls of soup,
distributed 688 bottles of milk for mothers and
infants, and planned and served seventy-seven meals
in the emergency hospital as well as 289 meals for
those who were not hospitalized. Mrs. Henrietta E.
Ankrum of Forrest City, both a junior and adult home
demonstration leader, was in charge of the management
of the emergency hospital for twenty-one days, during
which time she cared for sixty-eight bedfast patients.
Christmas noted—true to home demonstration agent
form—that the floods provided opportunities to stress
lessons in proper selection, planning, and preparation
of foods.[19]

Mississippi County

Gardens on a whole were good, although late.
Some had to plant twice and even more than
that in sections where there was deep water.
The people seemingly were determined to have
gardens as they thought that was their only
hope of living."[20]

In Mississippi County, local agent Cora Lee Coleman
took charge of dietetics in the emergency refugee
hospital after meeting with the county judge. The
hospital was financed by the national and local
Red Cross; doctors donated their time. At one point
the hospital had eighty-nine patients. The prevailing
diseases were pellagra, other dietary diseases, typhoid
fever, malaria fever, whooping cough, and pneumonia;
the hospital also cared for maternity cases. Gertrude
Conant, state nutrition specialist, traveled to the county
to help Coleman work out diets for each of the patients.[21]

Coleman and Conant were especially interested in the pellagra cases. They found that in each case in which appropriate diets were administered, the patients improved. The diets included milk, fruits, vegetables—especially tomatoes—and red meat twice each week.[22]

In the late spring, the county Extension agents distributed 8,000 packages of family garden seed provided by the Red Cross. Each package contained a combination of bean, cabbage, tomato, carrot, corn, onion, lettuce, kale, beet, parsnip, radish, and turnip seeds. Seed potatoes and sweet potato clips—along with feed for livestock—were distributed according to the number of family members. At the seed distribution points, instructions were given in planting and canning.[23]

Through the National Red Cross, fifteen 25-(gallon) steam pressure cookers, several thousand tin cans and thirty gross of glass quart jars were distributed. The County Council of Farm Women and the Junior County Council—i.e., the leadership of home demonstration work within Mississippi County—met and set up community canning schedules. For each all-day canning meeting, two or more communities in the same school district were brought together. Publicity was provided by newspapers, local pastors, schools, handbills, and the council members. Everyone was invited to come and bring whatever vegetables they had. The girls and women canned all day and prepared a picnic dinner, while the men and boys whitewashed houses, outhouses, and the school. A steam pressure cooker and Burpee sealer were left in each community to be circulated among households.[24]

Coleman stressed to the women the importance of a canning budget—i.e., storing up enough food for the family's needs—as well as sharing any excess vegetables left in the garden with neighbors who had no gardens. Coleman commented, "Adversity draws us together."[25] Fifteen hundred cans of tomatoes were turned in to her to be distributed to the pellagra patients. Miss Marcelle Phillips' club women provided 220 cases of canned milk and six cases of tomatoes. The National Red Cross provided two county nurses for sixty days. Coleman assisted the nurses as they held clinics in communities throughout the county. She took the opportunity to talk about Extension work, sanitation, and proper food habits, and to distribute government pamphlets and offer the county agents' assistance and cooperation in all farm or home problems. One result of the Extension employees' work was a wider acceptance throughout the county. Communities in which Coleman had been unable to make an inroad or find an audience had come, received instructions, and followed them. Some voluntarily sent representatives to the quorum court to tell of the value of the agents' instructions. "It means," said one man, "a winter's supply of food for our family."[26]

Coleman summarized the work as follows:

> 3500 cases of pellagra were treated during the flood and the months that followed. I feel that the intensive campaign put on for "Family Gardens" and "Grow Food for your Live Stock" and the Canning Campaign that followed this is one of the best pieces of work that I have put across since I have been in Mississippi County. More pantries are stocked with varieties

of canned foods and more people are following
Better Food Habits than I ever knew. . . .
I realize that the year has been filled with
disappointments but I think the extension
workers schedule of work met the emergency
called for and without these agencies working
together it could not have been accomplished.[27]

Coleman's overall narrative backed up her statement of
accomplishments as she reflected on the year's work.

Although Coleman provided detailed descriptions and
thoughtful insight into her work during the flood, the
annual report of Mary J. McCain of Mississippi County
did not include her flood work as part of her annual
report. In her discussion under the "Home Gardens"
heading, however, she made a telling statement:
"Gardens on a whole were good, although late. Some
had to plant twice and even more than that in sections
where there was deep water. The people seemingly were
determined to have gardens as they thought that was
their only hope of living."[28]

Lee County

After the floods receded, the problem of Home
Beautification was a real one, or rather it was
a question of being able to [inhabit] the home
at all. Nearly every club member planted more
flowers.[29]

In Lee County, local agent Annie L. Smith was busy day
and night working with flood refugees. Smith was put
in charge of the hospital kitchen, looking after the diet
and preparation of meals for the patients. The Red Cross

gave her the responsibility to purchase and distribute sweet milk for the babies each day. A local community club furnished ten gallons of buttermilk every other day for the refugees. Under Smith's supervision, black home demonstration club members organized a soup kitchen. Much of the makings for the soup were furnished by Captain Eugene Hamilton (difficult to read) from army or regular government supplies as well as by the Negro Flood Sufferers Relief Committee.[30]

At Smith's request, Captain Hamilton had a cook tent erected at the camp. The tent was equipped with ten long tables, two stoves, two (?) of army pans, wood, water, jars and cans, sugar, salt, and a spray outfit for killing flies—all made possible by the Red Cross. There were two steam canners and two Burpee sealers, one set belonging to Smith and the other loaned by a community club. All home demonstration club members not within the flooded area were called in for a meeting. The women were organized into four groups of canning club units, with each assigned to a certain part of the camp.[31]

At a meeting called by the Red Cross, the women were told that Mr. C. E. Yancy would furnish wagons to carry the refugees out to pick blackberries for canning. The berries, along with any other vegetables or fruits, were to be brought to the canning headquarters and worked up under the home demonstration agent's instruction. The Red Cross provided green beans. The people were pleased to get something canned for their shelves during the winter. The agent provided eight canning demonstrations of berries, peaches, and greens. Smith noted that they worked night and day when necessary to get the berries put up before they became stale. As a result, women and girls were instructed in operating the steam pressure canners and sealers, and quarts of fruits and vegetables were canned.[32]

Sewing demonstrations were also given in the camp. The women were interested in remodeling clothes since many of the garments sent to the camp needed to be modified. The girls did quite a lot of cutting down or enlarging garments. Through the work in the camp, four home demonstration clubs were organized for women in various sections of the county where the people had not been reached previously. Smith's annual report covered the period December 1, 1926 through only June 30, 1927. She resigned when the flooding was over.[33]

Flora A. Ferrill, home demonstration agent in Lee County, reported flood emergency activities similar to those of other agents. She supplied scraps of material to elderly women (she called them old ladies) for piecing quilts, gathered children together on Thursday afternoons for storytelling, helped get milk for the young children and babies, and made sure each person had a dry change of clothes. When Annie Smith resigned toward the end of the flood period, Ferrill took responsibility for organizing canning for the black clubs in the bottoms. The Red Cross had furnished ten steam pressure canners and 2,600 cans for this purpose. She asked the local farm agent to get the club leaders to her office one Saturday morning for training. She met with the club leaders several times. She later received from the leaders a report of a successful canning program.[34]

Better Homes Week was an annual contest in which communities cleaned up roads, downtown areas, and individual homes as they vied for recognition. Ferrill's comment regarding Better Homes Week follows:

> Many of the homes and the outhouses in the bottoms had to be whitewashed to make them livable. Better Homes Week came during the flood, when those who were not refugees were busy taking care of those who were. After the floods receded, the problem of Home Beautification was a real one, or rather it was a question of being able to [inhabit] the home at all. Nearly every club member planted more flowers.[35]

Ferrill made a statement that perhaps summed up the writer's thesis for this chapter: "The Red Cross has done a wonderful work for our people in the bottoms—and the Red Cross has received quite a bit of assistance from the Home Demonstration Agent."[36]

The Englewood Farm Club, Lee County

The Englewood Farm was seven miles from the Whitehall break in the Mississippi River levee. The two-year-old club was made up of the planter's wife and nine tenant wives. When the levee broke, they fled for their lives, leaving all their worldly possessions behind. They stayed in the Marianna refugee camp for four weeks; before that, they had not seen land for three weeks. While the members were in the camp, Ferrill met with them regularly to study how they would manage when they returned to their homes. When the Red Cross made it possible for the women and their families to return home, they found dead fruit and fruit trees, along with gardens that refused to grow until very late.

Later in the year, in preparing for her annual report of home demonstration work, Ferrill asked the president of the Englewood Farm club for a report of the year's work. The president's response—which may have indicated a sense of incredulity that Ferrill made the request—follows:

Dear Miss Ferrill,

In reporting the activities of the Englewood Club for the present year I will say that the club members have canned 1600 quarts in tin and about the same amount in glass. This consisted of figs, [unreadable], tomatoes, pickles, chow-chow, catsup, etc. . . .

As you know, the early flood about April 16, destroyed our gardens, lots of our furnishings and all of our plans. The homecoming would make a Chinese Stone Bed weep. Destruction everywhere. The many little things in every home around which cluster affectionate memories and the little tokens of endearment were gone. In their place was MUD, SLIME, and FOUL SMELL.

It took courage to go on, but most of the people met it nicely, showing that they were game. They planted gardens, rebuilt fences, cleaned up, and burned the debris, rebuilt chicken houses and had this going fine when about the 10 of June the water came back, destroying all that had been done. Many could hardly muster courage to tackle the job again.

This, however, many of them did and owing to the lateness of the season and the hot sun, being unseasonable, and yet the ground being water-[unreadable] below the surface it harbored cutworms to such an extent that it was with the greatest difficulty that any kind of crop could get started off.

I think that it is wonderful that we gathered so much through such trying times. We could never have accomplished so much, had we not done like Alexander the Great who had a fiery horse that was afraid of its shadow. Alexander always rode him facing the sun, keeping the shadows behind.—and we [unreadable] kept the sun of hope before us.

Wasn't it Walt Whitman who said: "The other side of every cloud is bright and shining, and so I turn my clouds about and always wear them wrong side out to show the lining."

Thanking you, Miss Ferrill, for your interest, care, fine work, and splendid inspiration even in the darkest hours, we are,

Yours very truly,

Englewood Club
Winnie F. Noonan [unclear], President[37]

The following letter in the *Helena World* did not mention home demonstration agents or members:

Sunday, May 1: Women aid Red Cross Relief Work—play active part in work of aiding the refugees brought to Helena: Sewing Rooms
Official praises ladies for their work during present crisis affecting the Delta Regions.

Women through every agency in Helena and Phillips County have assisted in the relief work for the refugees—hearts, heads and hands. Scores of women labored all day making thousands of practical garments to clothe those in need. Scores of other women have been busy in distributing this clothing to the refugees. Singer Sewing Machine Company loaned large numbers of machines and motors for sewing rooms at court house, high school, and Catholic Club. Repaired all old machines for service—free of charge.

Members of Retail merchants' association have sent a generous supply of wearing apparel. Helena citizens have given wearing apparel and many dug deep into pockets to help clothe the needy.

Over 500 mattresses and pillows made by women of Helena . . . laboring all day long to make a comfortable bed for the night for those who had lost household goods. New South Oil Mill contributed cotton linters with which mattresses were made.

Women helping to establish two emergency hospitals—one for men and one for women.

Camps at West Helena, Barton, Lexa, Marvell and Helena Crossing road have organizations doing wonderful relief.

Colored people, at their churches and school have given shelter and clothing to 1000s and hot food served to the hungry.

Relief kitchen maintained for several days at River Terminal for hungry refugees coming by barge loads from the stricken areas.

Signed: J. T. Hornor, Chairman, Red Cross[38]

Letter to Agents in the Flooded Counties

State agent Connie Bonslagel kept in close contact with agents working in the flooded areas. Her letter regarding their clean-up responsibilities completes our look at this wonderful piece of history.

810 Federal Bank & Trust Building
Little Rock, AR
June 14, 1927
HD Agents in Flooded Districts:

In many cases the Red Cross is making grants for home furnishings. We have prepared a list of household goods that seem to be necessary and which can be had for the small amount that the Red Cross is able to allow each family. This list may be helpful to you. The prices you may be able to get in your county may not be the same but there will not be a great deal of difference.

In addition to the goods listed here, we agreed that it would be well to ask for a few glass jars for each family. I am taking for granted that you have been giving canning demonstrations so as to have the people ready to take care of the surplus from their gardens. It might be well to concentrate on a soup mixture of corn, tomatoes, and okra, as the main product to be saved. Canning of tomatoes and beans, you will, of course, give. Mr. Martin also suggests that a grant of $10 or more be [made] for tools – hammer, saw, nails, etc., so that the men, at their leisure hours, can help with making the homes more habitable. Pens of chickens—five hens and a rooster—are being allowed by the Red Cross in each of the counties.

We are hoping that when the grant is made for barns, fences, and outhouses, you will see to it that an acceptable toilet is one of the first outhouses built. I believe that this emergency, disastrous as it is, gives us an opportunity to raise standards of living among some people that we might otherwise not touch. We should not let this opportunity go by.

Cordially yours,
Connie J. Bonslagel, State Agent[39]

1 laundry stove	$4.50
1 kitchen table – 4 ft.	2.00
4 double-cane seat chairs	3.92
1 iron bed	4.50
1 bed spring coil	3.00
1 mattress – all cotton, 45 pounds	4.00
1 wash tub	.71
1 wash board	.50
1 wash boiler – copper bottom	2.35
1 safe	3.50
6 white hotelware plates	.15
6 white hotelware cups and saucers (6 for 25 cents)	.25
2 white hotelware 6-inch vegetable platters	.25
6 knives (6 for 12 ½ cents)	.12
6 forks (6 for 12 ½ cents)	.12
6 spoons (6 for 12 ½ cents)	.12
6 tablespoons (6 for 12 ½ cents)	.12
1 9-inch steel frying pan	.20
1 wood bread bowl	.25
1 [?]-cup grey enamel coffee pot	.10
1 grey enamel dish pan	.15
1 aluminum 2-quart pitcher	.19
1 grey enamel preserving kettle	.15
1 paring knife	.08
1 bread pan	.25
Total	$31.50

Endnotes

[1] 1927 Annual Narrative Report, Union County HDA, RG 33, NARA/Fort Worth, Texas.

[2] Ibid.

[3] *Helena World*, April 14, 1927, Arkansas Historical Commission State Archives (used by permission of the *Helena Daily World*, 2012).

[4] *Helena World,* April 15, 1927, Arkansas Historical Commission State Archives (used by permission of the *Helena Daily World*, 2012).

[5] *Helena World*, April 17, 1927, Arkansas Historical Commission State Archives (used by permission of the *Helena Daily World*, 2012).

[6] *Helena World*, April 18, 1927, Arkansas Historical Commission State Archives (used by permission of the *Helena Daily World*, 2012).

[7] 1927 Annual Narrative Report, Phillips County Local HDA, RG 33, NARA/Fort Worth

[8] Ibid.

[9] Ibid.

[10] 1927 Annual Narrative Report, Phillips County HDA, RG 33, NARA/Fort Worth, Texas.

[11] Ibid.

[12] Ibid.

[13] *Helena World*, April 22, 1927, Arkansas Historical Commission State Archives (used by permission of the *Helena Daily World*, 2012).

[14] 1927 Annual Narrative Report, St. Francis County HDA, RG 33, NARA/Fort Worth, Texas.

[15] Ibid.

[16] Ibid.

[17] Ibid.

[18] 1927 Annual Narrative Report, St. Francis County Local HDA, RG 33, NARA/Fort Worth, Texas.

[19] Ibid.

[20] 1927 Annual Narrative Report, Mississippi County HDA, RG 33, NARA/Fort Worth, Texas.

[21] 1927 Annual Narrative Report, Mississippi County Local HDA, RG 33, NARA/Fort Worth, Texas.

[22] Ibid.

[2] Ibid.

[24] Ibid.

[25] Ibid.

[26] Ibid.

[2] Ibid.

[28] Ibid.

[29] 1927 Annual Narrative Report, Lee County HDA, RG 33, NARA/Fort Worth, Texas.

[30] 1927 Annual Narrative Report, Lee County Local HDA, RG 33, NARA/Fort Worth, Texas.

[31] Ibid.

[3] Ibid.

[33] Ibid.

[34] 1927 Annual Narrative Report, Lee County HDA, RG 33, NARA/Fort Worth, Texas.

[35] Ibid.

[36] Ibid.

[37] Ibid.

[38] *Helena World*, May 1, 1927, Arkansas Historical Commission State Archives (used by permission of the *Helena Daily World*, 2012).

[39] 1927 Annual Narrative Report, State HDA, RG 33, NARA/Fort Worth, Texas.

5

The Early School Lunch Work

Women's historians have called the late nineteenth and early twentieth centuries "a veritable golden age of women's organizations, which multiplied rapidly in both number and membership and among every class, race, ethnicity, and region."[1] In fact, home demonstration club membership grew so rapidly in Arkansas during the mid-1920s that Connie Bonslagel was concerned the increase was merely a symptom of growing socialization among women through organized club work. Bonslagel directed the agents to poll members and was obviously relieved to find the women who joined home demonstration clubs actually participated in the projects. Within the context of rapidly growing women's club membership, Bonslagel's concern was surely justified.[2]

Leading women activists at the turn of the century—such as Elizabeth Cady Stanton and Jane Addams—penned their own histories for posterity and thus provided a rich cache of records for historians to analyze in future decades. Although the earliest scholars examined white, middle-class women's activism, a second group delved into the organized activities of working-class, immigrant, African American, and rural women.[3]

Both groups of scholars recognized a trend toward women's involvement in so-called "Progressive Era" causes. (The Progressive Era of the late nineteenth and early twentieth centuries was a time of amazing social change in which women in particular were encouraged to look outside their own walls and to contribute to the betterment of their communities.) Scholars thus worked to determine the extent of this involvement and to demonstrate how women contributed to progressive social change in the United States, particularly changes that led to the federal government's social programs of following decades.[4]

An important way in which home demonstration club women looked outside their homes and reached out to their communities was obviously through the school lunch program. Early reports, some of which are shown below, tell us that home demonstration agents were encouraging better nutrition for school children from almost the very beginning of the work.

> [1919:] In Desha County a special drive was put on for increasing the amount of milk being drunk by school children. Accurate charts showing weights and measurement and improvement in school work are kept.[5]

> [1920:] In Chicot County the agent is placing hot lunch equipment in the schools. The Junior Red Cross furnished the money.[6]

[1920 state report:] 242 public demonstrations in child feeding, including school lunches, were conducted by agents.[7]

[1920 Negro district report:] Nutrition work included 212 demonstrations in school lunches.[8]

A review of the school nutrition program in Saline County provides a sense of how slowly the work sometimes progressed:

[In 1920, the agent reported] two schools using more milk, in one of which every child has been weighed and measured.[9]

[1923:] Three schools are serving a hot dish in the noon lunch during the cold months and milk is taken by the pupils from home during the warm days. The teacher in each school has cooperated with patrons and the home demonstration agent.[10]

[1927:] Foods work has included hot lunches in two schools and an attempt to establish the habit in other schools.[11]

Members took up the cause as a natural outgrowth of their clubs' educational activities. They learned about nutrition and perfected safe canning practices. The next step was for them to share of the abundance of their labors with the community's most vulnerable population—and they took that step. Mary Ray commented in her 1926 district report that just a few years earlier, Negro members knew almost nothing about the meaning of the word "nutrition." By 1926, however, club members had seen demonstrations in preparing better school lunches and were practicing what they had learned.[12]

The Take-from-Home School Lunch

Women's responses to the need for better childhood nutrition took two routes. First, numerous demonstrations were given in selecting and packing children's lunches. At the annual Farmers' Week in Fayetteville, a demonstration of a poor school lunch was given by Bethel Grove twins and 4-H members Polly and Dolly Rouse. The poor school lunch included a slice of pie, mashed apple pie, biscuit sandwich with a fried egg, and another biscuit with cold fried meat. In contrast, the ideal packed lunch included sandwiches wrapped in oiled paper, a ripe tomato, and fruit. The twins encouraged mothers to keep small, cold-cream-type jars on hand to fill with jelly or fruit.[13]

In her 1927 state report, Bonslagel included a detailed account of the school lunch work done by the agent in Hot Spring County. She noted that other counties had put on programs that were equally complete. The story follows in full:

> January 1 the children of the Malvern school and of five rural schools who are undertaking the work in nutrition were weighed and measured to determine which were under-weight and in other ways not up to their best efforts in school work. In each case instructions were given to the children, to the teachers and the parents in better food habits. The results of

the demonstration seemed to prove that these instructions were followed.

[The second paragraph talked about the number of children weighed and the number who were under-weight. The numerals in the paragraph were unreadable. However, the final result was that 101 children had brought their weight to normal in three months.]

These young people had followed the home demonstration agent's instructions and were— most of them—drinking a quart of milk a day and were bringing to school sandwiches which their mothers were making according to their home demonstration agent's suggestions. Raw carrots and raisins were conspicuous among the foods used for sandwich fillings. The parents were forming the habit of giving the children candy as dessert at meal time instead of letting them eat it between meals. Many of the children stopped [the agent—name unclear] on the street to tell her that they had quit eating candy. A large number of these pupils are still using the food selection score cards with a view to checking up on their food habits—increasing the use of milk and fresh fruits and vegetables in the diet and decreasing candy between meals, coffee, cocacola [sic.], etc.

The people of Hot Spring County are hopeful that the interest in this work will result in their securing a public health worker in the near future. Five schools in the county put on this same demonstration. At Rockport results were outstanding. Twenty four out of the [two-digit number but unreadable] children in school were underweight at the initial weighing and measuring. During the first month every child gained from one to eight pounds and 14 brought their weight up to normal. During the second month four more brought their weight to normal, making 18 out of 24. They were ambitious to make it 100 per cent by the close of school. This group of children with their very able teacher as leader made a practice of sitting at lunch for [unreadable number of] minutes each day. They tell stories and otherwise entertain each other during the lunch hour. Every child brought a bottle of milk to school and they agreed to bring boiled eggs instead of fried eggs so often found in the school lunch. Each child also included one fruit in the lunch. Those who were badly under-weight drank a mid-morning and mid-afternoon glass of milk.[14]

The Hot School Lunch

The Department of Agriculture traces the beginnings of hot school lunch programs as far back as the mid-nineteenth century. However, none of the individual programs gained enough momentum to become permanent. The Department credits the 1904 book *Poverty*, by Robert Hunter, a self-described sociologist, with wielding a strong influence on the United States' effort to feed hungry, needy children at school. Hunter argued that compulsory school attendance was to no avail when children were hungry and thus unable to do the work.[15]

Beginning in the early 1900s, rural schools attempted various methods of providing hot lunches—from large stew pots filled with meats and vegetables donated by school families—to the pint-jar heating method described below. The Department of Agriculture credits teachers, parent-teacher groups, philanthropic organizations, school-oriented associations, school boards, and groups of mothers with providing support for the program. County home demonstration agents of the University Extension Service were noted as "extremely helpful to rural schools in devising plans for providing some supplementary hot foods and in drawing up lists of suggested 'menus' in advance."[16]

In Arkansas, club women and agents were concerned because children took cold lunches to school during winter months. One agent provided a detailed description of her plan to provide a hot lunch for children. The plan follows:

> Each child should bring in a fruit jar containing something he likes to eat. That dish may be a vegetable or soup left from the day before or something prepared especially for the lunch. A large vessel with a lid should be provided. A rack of some kind should be placed in the bottom of the vessel. About eleven or eleven-thirty o'clock in the day one pupil should put enough water into the vessel for the water to be about one inch deep. Place all the jars on the rack and loosen the jar-lids. Place the cover on the vessel. At noon the food is hot and each child can get his jar. The poor preparation that is often done at school is avoided. The dish washing does not

take up the playtime as each child carries his jar and spoon or fork home with him.[17]

Home demonstration women took the work a step further to try to guarantee a hot lunch at least part of the time. After preserving enough food for their families' needs, they canned any remaining vegetables, often as soup mixture, and donated them to the local school. The account of the Elaine club, which follows, is surely representative of what was happening all over Arkansas.

In the area of Phillips County in which much of the flood work was done, the people had shown little interest in home demonstration work. But, as agent Mary Alice Larche noted, "[A] little leaven leaveneth the whole."[18] One woman in Elaine had wanted a club, and due to her interest, the work had progressed rapidly. The newly organized club had met only two times before the flood in April and May. Elaine residents had expected two feet of water, but their town was inundated with ten feet instead. By July, Larche and a small group of club members and those from a nearby town were able to meet.[19]

The idea of establishing a cafeteria for the Elaine school—which had been discussed before the flood—resurfaced. Since there was now an abundance of vegetables, the women decided to can soup mixture for the school. They met three times for this purpose and canned 150 no. 3 cans of soup mixture. By September, the women were unable to find tomatoes for additional soup. Larche asked for and received 200 cans of tomatoes from the Red Cross. The tomatoes had been canned by home demonstration club women in northeast

Arkansas for women in the flooded area. The soup was to be served free to children who brought their lunch on cold days. When the soup supply ran out, the women planned to provide additional mixture.[20]

Larche provided a stunning account of the club's work, which follows:

> The Elaine Club entered its second year in February, and it had been a good one. As stated in last year's report, it was the plan of this club to open a free cafeteria in the school, giving the children hot soup and crackers on cold bad days during the winter. The club took for its study for the year, Nutrition, and it was studied intensively.
>
> The weather became very severe the first week in January, and the cafeteria was opened that week. As there was no Home Economics equipment in the school, it was necessary to purchase cups, spoons and a stove. In order to secure the money for this equipment, it was decided to have a Community dinner. The equipment was ordered, wholesale, received and used and the dinner was given the 25th of the month.
>
> The club made nearly $100.00 on the dinner, and therefore paid for the equipment, and had a good surplus. It was used later, in buying crackers for the soup, oil for the stove, meat, potatoes and etc. for the soup.

The cafeteria was run by volunteer committees from the club, under the leadership of the President, Mrs. Lacey. There were approximately 275 children served each time, with one or two cups of soup, on an average of four times a week for three months. No doubt, it helped to prevent much illness among the children, as there were many who would not have had a sufficient amount of food during those hard months following the flood.

In addition to this, the Health Unit Nurse and I visited the school weighing them and giving health talks to all the children from the Primary to the High School, every two weeks, and after weighing the children, and checking up on them, we found 70 that were undernourished and underweight. We then appealed to the Red Cross, and were given a pint of fresh milk a day for each of the children. It was sent down by bus every morning from the creamery in Helena for three months. This was of inestimable value to the children, and made others interested in drinking milk. Some extra bottles were always added. The principal of the school cooperated with us in these things, and said that the scholarship of the children had been increased and he wished that it was possible to continue the work longer. The children kept health score cards in all of the grades, and were very much interested in the project. They improved in personal appearance at once, *and some of them began to look more "human" after a few weeks* [italics added].

With the work being done along the line of better nutrition in the school and the club, there is no wonder that the cases of Pelagra [sic.] and other deficiency diseases are becoming scarce.[21]

It is clear that home demonstration women in Elaine—along with home demonstration members throughout Arkansas—were active participants in a national, Progressive Era movement to find a remedy for a significant social problem. Although early goals of home demonstration work did not include activism and public outreach by its members, women embraced their newly found capabilities and used them for the common good. They indeed looked outside their four walls and accepted their responsibility for the community of children just outside their doors. Professional home demonstration agents definitely took the lead in the effort; however, Mary Alice Larche's account of the Elaine club clearly illustrated a grass-roots effort by the women.

The school lunch program gained momentum during the 1920s and took on even greater significance during the Great Depression of the 1930s. During that decade, many states and municipalities adopted legislation—some including appropriations—to enable schools to serve a noonday meal to children.[22]

Endnotes

[1]Kirsten Delegard, "Women's Movements, 1880s-1920s," in *A Companion to American Women's History*, ed. Nancy A. Hewitt (UK: Blackwell Publishers, 2002), 328.

[2]1927 Annual Narrative Report, State HDA, RG 33, NARA/Fort Worth, Texas.

[3]Delegard, 328-331.

Ibid.

[5]1919 Annual Narrative Report, State HDA, RG 33, NARA/Fort Worth, Texas.

[6]1920 Annual Narrative Report, State HDA, RG 33, NARA/Fort Worth, Texas.

[7]Ibid.

[8]1920 Annual Narrative Report, Negro District HDA, RG 33, NARA/Fort Worth, Texas.

[9]1920 Annual Narrative Report, Saline HDA, RG 33, NARA/Fort Worth, Texas.

[10]1923 Annual Narrative Report, Saline HDA, RG 33, NARA/Fort Worth, Texas.

[11]1927 Annual Narrative Report, Saline HDA, RG 33, NARA/Fort Worth, Texas.

[12]1926 Annual Narrative Report, Negro District HDA, RG 33, NARA/Fort Worth, Texas.

[13]1927 Annual Narrative Report, Washington County HDA, RG 33, NARA/Fort Worth, Texas.

[14]1927 Annual Narrative Report, State HDA, RG 33, NARA/Fort Worth, Texas.

[15]Gordon W. Gunderson. "The National School Lunch Program Background and Development," National School Lunch Program website, accessed November 28, 2011. http://www.fns.usda.gov/cnd/lunch/AboutLunch/ProgramHistory_2.htm#EARLY, np.

[16]Ibid.

[17]1924 Annual Narrative Report, Saline County HDA, RG 33, NARA/Fort Worth, Texas.

[18]1927 Annual Narrative Report, Phillips County HDA, RG 33, NARA/Fort Worth, Texas.

[19]Ibid.

[20]Ibid.

[21]1928 Annual Narrative Report, Phillips County HDA, RG 33, NARA/Fort Worth, Texas.

[22]Gunderson, n.p.

6

Keeping the Work Going: Hiring, Retaining, Continuing the Funding

Hiring Agents

Meanwhile, back in Little Rock, Connie Bonslagel was struggling with the realities of hiring and retaining well-qualified home demonstration agents for the counties. One major problem was the fact that the fairly new field of home economics had not yet been refined to meet the needs of Arkansas's rural women. In 1929, Bonslagel commented that some new agents came with advanced degrees, and all came with a special interest in a particular line of work, usually foods, clothing, home management, or child care. They rarely were adequately prepared, however, for the more fundamental but necessary categories of food production, poultry, gardening, and home dairy work.[1]

She stressed the importance of not letting the rural women know of new agents' "ignorance"[2] in areas the women considered crucial to their lives. Noting that a "restraining, guiding hand has been necessary to bring about a balance"[3] between what the new graduates wanted to do and what the women needed, she continued, "They were early taught the fundamental principle of Extension's work, namely, that the farm women's real needs and not the new agent's likes are to determine the program."[4]

Throughout the early years, the district agents spent a great deal of their time in training new employees, who were often fresh from college. As the program expanded yearly, it became obvious there was a need either for more than one agent in many counties—or for more experienced, seasoned ones. The work was simply too varied for one new college graduate to successfully navigate. As a partial solution, by the late 1920s and early 1930s, some new college graduates were placed as assistant agents—sometimes without pay—in order to gain needed experience.

Retaining Agents

Retention of the young agents was another problem. One clue to the situation was a 1929 report that eight young women had resigned to be married, with two or three having no intention of staying throughout the year when they came to the position. On the other hand, a 1928 listing of agents included ten for whom the term "Mrs." preceded the first name.[5]

The inconsistency was created by a policy change within the U. S. Department of Agriculture at some point in the early 1920s. The policy—which is alluded to in various histories of home demonstration work in other states but could not be located—banned married women from working as agents. As a result, one wide-spread criticism of early Extension work was that married women were not allowed to work as agents, even though the women with whom they worked were married. Those married women who were already working were apparently grandfathered in and allowed to remain employed.[6]

The policy was typical of the era and was similar to the one for public school teachers. One of several theories concerning such policies pointed to a widely held belief that married women were not the principal breadwinners and were simply working to have extra money to spend, i.e., the "pin-money theory," which assumed that most women did not have to work because they had someone to support them. As the Great Depression deepened, working women were accused of taking jobs away from men. In such an atmosphere, college women of this generation were thus deeply conflicted about marriage versus a career. Choosing a career often meant foregoing marriage and motherhood, which led to disapproval from family and society.[7]

Continuing the Funding

And then there was the matter of paying the agents. Although obtaining funding from the state's counties had been a constant concern for management from the beginning, it should go without saying that the Great Depression made the situation critical. In several reports, it was noted that much of the time of the district agents (supervisors)—both men and women—was taken up in making sure the counties actually paid the agents.

Bonslagel commented that in 1934,

[i]t was necessary to discontinue cooperation in some few counties due to the county falling behind as much as three months in payments to agents, but in each some plan of financing

has been developed in the county to make the payments and the service has been restored within a very short time. County judges and other [?] have generally given excellent cooperation in the financing of the counties' part of the salary of county agents and county home demonstration agents.[8]

By 1935, it was noted, "in 23 counties, county scrip is below par, as low as 60 cents on the dollar in some."[9]

Realizing The Power of Organization

In 1929, during Farmers' Week at Fayetteville, the Arkansas State Council of Home Demonstration Clubs was formed. In 1933, Pearl E. Perkins, state president, and Fern Salyers, state chairman, Legislative Committee sent the following letter to the counties:

Do you know a bill has been introduced in the House of Representatives at Little Rock to abolish your branch experiment station – the Fruit and Truck Station at Hope, the Rice Station at Stuttgart, and the Cotton Station at Marianna, and that it is rumored that one may be introduced to abolish all Agricultural Extension work. Do we want this to happen?

This situation calls for immediate action on the part of the Home Demonstration women over the state. Every member of the legislature, and the Governor, must be told that the farming people of the state want their support for this work.

Please have the presidents and officers of your clubs to write, and a majority of members to write letters at once to your Representative, your Senator, and to the Governor, asking them to support both measures. Just write to these men as you did to your Justice of the Peace in November, for the situation is just the same. If this is to have the desired effect, it is necessary to get the letters out at once.

Very truly yours,

Mrs. F. C. Perkins, President
Mrs. E. L. Salyers, Chairman,
Legislative Committee[10]

The above letter indicates the women's realization of the power of numbers and organization. Bonslagel commented in her 1933 report that "the state legislature met early in the year, and effort to secure adequate and permanent state funds for the support of Agricultural Extension and Experiment Station work received time and attention."[11]

Providing Needed Support to Relief Efforts

Despite funding problems, the home demonstration work continued full force in its contributions to the relief efforts, as is illustrated below:

Late in the summer, the State Relief Agency purchased a limited amount of canning equipment to be allocated where and as the county home demonstration agents recommended. By December 1, 207 canning centers were equipped, and four field canning kitchens and 70 [unreadable] and sealers were ready for use. Canning schools were held to train supervisors for these kitchens. These supervisors in turn taught 13,220 men, women, boys, and girls the canning process.[12]

A circular, *The Arkansas Food Supply Plan*, was widely used among people on or near the relief rolls [?]. Demonstrations on low cost, adequate diets were carried in nine counties. Hot lunches were planned and supervised in 270 schools, affecting 11,077 children. Home demonstration agents trained leaders in this work which will be greatly expanded. Instructions in the preparation of simple, easily grown, easily stored foods were furnished in circular form and in demonstration meetings.[13]

The importance of lay leaders to the home demonstration program cannot be emphasized too strongly. Although club women had been instructed as county and community leaders from the very beginning of the work, they came into their own during the 1930s. In 1933, Bonslagel praised their work and its contribution to the overall program during the time of Arkansans' greatest need:

The leadership of strong, dependable farm women, many of whom have been home demonstration club members for ten and fifteen years and the "esprit de corps" developed in the clubs has been a major factor in keeping up the morale and standards of many farm families. This [unreadable] leadership and organized effort have also enabled the home demonstration agent to give less personal supervision to the carrying out of the demonstrations under way and more time to initiating home demonstration practices among people heretofore strangers to the work. The setting up and operation of canning centers on plantations and in outlying communities is an example, and the supervision of gardens grown by people on relief from seeds furnished by the RFC is another.[14]

Home demonstration women and their families joined the leaders in making significant contributions to the relief operations:

Because of the general poverty and because of the large numbers of unemployed families who are being moved into the country, the thrifty farm families find themselves with an unaccustomed responsibility in taking care of the needy. Home demonstration clubs are doing much social, economic, and educational welfare work. Where they are, they teach the new comers to garden and can. Where they prove unteachable, club women can for them; many demonstrators including one or more hundred quarts for charity in their budgets.[15]

Reaping the Rewards of a Good Reputation

The writer was not able to delve into all the factors that influenced a positive change in the funding for county agents—and the continuation of the Extension programs. However, the overwhelming indication from the records is that the various directors of Depression Era relief programs saw the immense contribution of the home demonstration women—both agents and lay leaders—in helping farm people survive, especially through their garden demonstrations and the government-provided community canning centers. Bonslagel summed up the situation, as follows:

> Relief activities of all regular agents aroused citizens of neighboring unorganized counties to their need. The state director of relief influenced sentiment for home demonstration appropriations in all counties. He found the home demonstration agent invaluable in certain live-at-home phases of the relief program and in helping families from becoming subject to relief.[16]

Continuing the Work

In 1933, forty-nine counties supported home demonstration agents. In 1934, all of the forty-nine renewed appropriations for agents. In fact, only nine counties did not "carry the work"[17] for 1934. The growing support for home demonstration work throughout the state thus led to additional "opportunities" for Bonslagel and the district agents: hiring qualified persons to fill twenty-seven positions! (There were indications that some emergency agents were hired with funds provided by the relief agencies.)

It should come as no surprise that—by 1934—fresh college graduates were not among those hired to fill most of the positions. Instead,

[t]he matter of securing qualified persons for 27 positions has provided no small problem. 20 graduates of the University of Arkansas, all 34 years old or over, but only one with any previous Extension experience, were placed. Others were offered positions but would not give up their teaching positions. Two additional Arkansas girls, honor graduates of the State Teachers College, were employed. Five mature women from other states, two of them with Extension experience, were placed. One Arkansas woman and one from outside the state have married and left the force. Both were replaced by graduates of the University of Arkansas.[18]

Although all of the new hires were home economics graduates, twelve of them had either special Extension work training or experience as agents. It is apparent from the above discussion that some of the new employees had likely been school teachers.[19]

As an expected sign of the times, agents' salaries were described as so low that the women were barely able to maintain a "passable standard of living."[20] Many were "forced to give up life insurance, use their savings, let school debts go unpaid, and borrow money in order to maintain themselves and buy and operate their cars."[21]

Endnotes

[1] 1929 Annual Narrative Report, State HDA, RG 33, NARA/Fort Worth, Texas.

[2] Ibid.

[3] Ibid.

[4] Ibid.

[5] Ibid.

1928 Annual Narrative Report, State HDA, RG 33, NARA/Fort Worth, Texas.

[6] Lynne Anderson Reiff, "'Rousing the People of the Land': Home Demonstration Work in the Deep South, 1914-1950," (PhD diss., Auburn University, 1995), 228.

[7] Barbara Harris. *Beyond Her Sphere: Women and the Professions in American History* (Westport, Conn.: Greenwood Press. 1978), 117.

[8] 1934 Annual Narrative Report, State HDA, RG 33, NARA/Fort Worth, Texas.

[9] 1935 Annual Narrative Report, State HDA, RG 33, NARA/Fort Worth, Texas.

[10] 1933 Annual Narrative Report, State HDA, RG 33, NARA/Fort Worth, Texas.

[11] Ibid.

[12] Ibid.

[13] Ibid.

[14] Ibid.

[15] 1932 Annual Narrative Report, State HDA, RG 33, NARA/Fort Worth, Texas.

[16] 1933 Annual Narrative Report, State HDA, RG 33, NARA/Fort Worth, Texas.

[17] 1934 Annual Narrative Report, State HDA, RG 33, NARA/Fort Worth, Texas.

[18] Ibid.

[19] Ibid.

[20] Ibid.

[21] Ibid.

7

The Work Goes On

With the residuals of the Great Depression bearing down on rural women, it is surely surprising to learn that normal home demonstration work continued at something of a fast pace—perhaps even a sprint! There was one caveat concerning the work, however:

> It was necessary throughout the year to adjust and readjust but never to change in principle home demonstration teachings because of the fact that farm families had less and less money to put into family living. Maintaining rather than raising standards became the objective in many cases.[1]

Household Management

Mrs. Ida Fenton, Extension economist, household management, described several emphases in her 1934 report. She began with the five-year farm water systems step-by-step plan—a complete plumbing plan for rural families:

The Five-year Farm Water Systems Plan

First year: Kitchen sink, drain board, and pipe drain.

First or second year: Hand operated pump, with piping from well to storage tank.

Second year: Hot water tank and water heater.

Third year: Plan bathroom, install tub and lavatory, with drain pipes.

Fourth year: Build septic tank (homemade), with sewer line, overflow [?].

Fourth or fifth year: Install flush toilet, and hire plumber to put all piping and connections in proper condition.

Fifth year: Should have hot and cold running water, septic tank disposal, and complete bathroom.

At any time: Install electric pump if electricity is available. Gasoline engine may be used to pump water in storage tank.[2]

During the plan's first year, 175 women had undertaken to carry it out. The following agreement, typed on a card, "gave a business-like aspect to the demonstration and secured complete cooperation in the family"[3]:

We agree to use this amount of the farm income for home improvement the year of 1932: $10___; $15___; $20___; $25___; $50___; $75___; $100___. I will make this improvement first: Sink___; hot water___; septic tank___; bath___; cold running water___; other improvement___.

We will use the following farm crop or livestock for earning this money:

Crop_____   Amount_____

Livestock_____   Amount_____

Other income_____   Amount_____

Husband_____

Wife_____ [4]

Fenton mentioned the Arkansas County home demonstration organization, where a federal housing survey found that only 191 houses had running water, even though the county had above-average housing in the state. The agent was a "splendid organizer"[5] who presented the water systems project in "a very convincing way."[6] Fenton continued:

> It is always a mystery how some women manage. One woman installed complete plumbing, except running hot water, for $2. The materials were all obtained by collecting discarded materials around the farm. This included a storage tank, sink made from a gas tank, bath tub and lavatory.[7]

Monday is Wash Day

In both the North and South divisions of Sebastian County, Fenton provided two-day leader training in laundering. The two lessons were planned around wash day and ironing day, respectively. The six-point lesson plan for wash day:

Wash Day Demonstration

1. Locate clothes line out of view from highway and front of house.

2. Arrange for benches and tubs to be located at proper height.
3. Remove stains before laundering.
4. Soften hard water.
5. Bleach clothes by recommended methods.
6. Practice day-before preparations for wash day.[8]

Followed, quite naturally, by the six-point plan for ironing day:

Ironing Day Demonstration
1. Use approved methods of starching.
2. Arrange for use of ironing board at the proper heights, one for sitting and the other for standing.
3. Dampen clothes overnight (if possible).
4. [unreadable] iron by using more cord.
5. Proper pads for ironing different materials and articles.
6. Proper ironing, folding, and airing.[9]

Fenton also touted the kitchen improvement demonstration, which was planned to extend over a two- or three-year period. This plan was made up of six steps as well:

Kitchen Improvement Demonstration
1. **The cheerful kitchen:** A discussion of backgrounds, windows, color schemes, the outlook and a general view of the kitchen.
2. **The comfortable kitchen:** Light, ventilation, rest corner[?], heights of working surfaces, heat control.

3. **The sanitary kitchen:** Cleaning methods, dishwashing, control of pests, disposal of waste, cleaning kit.
4. **The convenient kitchen:** Arrangement, refrigeration, storage spaces.
5. **The well equipped kitchen:** Store management, small equipment, how much and how to select it, and home safe equipment.
6. **The kitchen routine:** Methods and plans of work, short [unreadable], information file.[10]

Can She Bake an Apple Pie?

The following description of a kitchen arrangement demonstration is guaranteed to exhaust even the fittest reader!

Kitchen improvement work was stressed in Yell County when the specialist visited that county during the summer. We emphasized good arrangement as an improvement which can be made at no cost.

We asked the entire group of women to bake an apple pie and count the steps or measure the distance traveled from the time the pie is begun until it is on the dining table ready to be served. They were to answer roll call at a club meeting giving the distance traveled. The comparison of those distances is an interest getting line.

Mrs. Apple, the woman who took the most steps, walked one-sixth of a mile to make and place the apple pie on the dining table. The agent helped her arrange her kitchen by moving the dining unit to one side of the room. She set up a circular arrangement, beginning with the stove as a fixed piece of equipment. The storage cabinet and work table were moved to the left of the stove. To the right was placed a serving table and a supply of condiments which are used in the final seasoning and garnishing of foods before sending them to the dining table.

These improvements reduced Mrs. Apple's travel from one-sixth of a mile to [fewer than 100] steps. The apple pie furnished only one food on her table for dinner. It was estimated that Mrs. Apple traveled at least one mile to prepare her dinner every day, and about one-half to three-fourths of a mile to prepare the other two meals. This was a distance of 2 1/4 miles in preparation, and 1 3/4 miles to clear away after the meals. This meant four miles of travel each day for preparing and clearing away the meals—130 miles per month and 1,460 miles per year. Quite a marathon and yet the sweeping, dusting, making of beds, washing, ironing, care of children and housecleaning have not come in for their share of time and travel[!][11]

From a Ford Gas Tank

One last vignette from Ida Fenton's report:

In a rather isolated, mountainous community in the northern part of Conway County, a demonstration has been located which is so outstanding that it is a pride and joy. This community has so long been isolated that our Extension program has been slow. Mrs. Alma Stroud built in a cabinet with a sink made from a Ford gas tank. She placed two half-windows in the wall above the sink, and put an ivory and green linoleum on the floor. This decided her color scheme for her, so the cabinet and other woodwork are enameled ivory and green. This nice demonstration is sure to act as a contagion in this community.[12]

Finally, Fenton recommended an easy-to-do kitchen improvement idea: Make doilies or lunch cloths for the family to use at least once each day. She suggested making them from flour sacks, sugar sacks, or gingham. She described the project as "good pick-up work for this winter instead of so many quilt tops."[13]

Nutrition Update

In marking the twentieth anniversary of the 1914 Smith-Lever Act, which funded demonstration work, Gertrude Conant celebrated accomplishments in nutrition. Conant, who joined the Extension in 1918, reminisced that with the advent of the World War, emphasis was placed on food production and preservation. In 1918, instructions were given in food selection and preparation, with bread making contests to add interest. In 1934, over 4,200 women and girls entered this contest.[14]

During the early years, there was no mention of corrective feeding for dietary deficiency diseases. However, in 1934 agents from thirty-seven counties reported 5,123 individuals adopting diets for such health issues as pellagra, constipation, anemia, and rickets. The number of women serving balanced family meals in 1934 totaled 14,174.[15]

A major nutrition emphasis in 1934 was Child Feeding and Care (Parent Education)—especially for clubs having a large number of preschool children. Conant reported that Logan County's child nutrition work had culminated in a Better Babies Club, with 145 babies enrolled in 1934. Following two baby clinics held in the county for non-club members' children, additional mothers joined the club. By 1935, thirty-one counties had clubs reaching 2,581 babies through work with 1,820 mothers in 167 clubs.[16]

Other counties reported over 2,000 mothers who were carrying on child feeding demonstrations. Searcy County reported that one baby's life was saved because the mother followed Extension recommendations for child feeding.[17] One mother's success story is repeated below:

> Mrs. Bill Swan of Forrest City who enrolled her three month old baby, William Bruce Swan, last year, reports that at 15 months he weighs 32 pounds. This child was very nervous and restless, they could find no food which seemed to agree with him. Miss Conant recommended his feeding schedule. She included in the diet juice from an onion wrapped in brown paper and baked, and an extra amount of raw egg until he could take a whole egg in his milk.[18]

Food preservation continued to be extremely important during the various droughts and years of the

Depression. In 1935, the emphasis was on budgets and quality. (A budget was a predetermined number of jars or tins of food that the member put up for her family in order to meet its needs during the entire year.) Farm women placed on their pantry shelves 9,452,357 quarts of fruits, meat, and vegetables, at a value of $5,675,608.[19]

"... a Poem as Lovely as a Tree"[20]

In 1932, in each of forty-two counties, as many as three communities were working on a five-year community landscaping demonstration, which began in 1930. In addition, home demonstration work was expanded to include an unexpectedly impressive project, which is shared below:

> Two years ago, as a further [unclear] of interesting farm people in home grounds and as a means of giving Arkansas a better face for tourists, we selected one cross-state highway, no. 71, and set out to have every home along that highway cleaned up, painted, and planted. Nine counties were involved, and a fairly good job is under way. [We] added highway no. 3, which diagonals the state, involving 13 counties. Considerable improvement is apparent. 464 miles of highway were cleared of junk and generally cleaned up; over 1,000 miles were graded, 10 miles of embankment were terraced, and over 400 miles of fence rows and roadsides were cleaned. 85 communities in 30 counties are doing highway beautification.[21]

The work came just in time for the George Washington Bicentennial Celebration throughout the nation. Although Washington's Birthday had been celebrated for many years—including the Centennial Celebration in 1832—the 200-year anniversary was an extremely important occasion. Gilbert Stuart's famous painting of Washington, which has surely hung in untold public schools, was rendered for the celebration. There was—and is—a George Washington Bicentennial March, penned by John Philip Sousa. The march was premiered by the combined military bands of Washington, D. C., and conducted by Sousa himself.

Connie Bonslagel had been appointed to the Committee on Landscape Planning and Planting of the President's Conference on Home Building and Home Ownership. She had attended two meetings in Washington with leading landscape architects. Her reporting of the Bicentennial Home Grounds and Tree Planting work follows:

> We were asked to encourage the farm people cooperating with us to take part in the George Washington Bicentennial Celebration. We made our plans to correlate the tree planting done with the home grounds work under way. Of the 29,000 plus trees planted in the three month campaign, 14,912 were shade trees and 6,000 plus of these were planted on or near home grounds. 1,911 on school grounds, over 500 on church grounds, 817 [unclear] in cemeteries, and over 400 in parks and along parkways. Also along highways, and the rest around filling stations, courthouses, stores, gins, and railroad

stations. 19,000 plus shrubs were also planted to the memory of George Washington and to the advantage of farm homes; 7,000 plus of the trees and 6,000 plus shrubs came from the woods of Arkansas.[22]

To Market, To Market

Rural women's historians have found that, traditionally, American farm women sold their wares for many years before home demonstration work began. Products included butter, eggs, and fresh vegetables. In 1932, fourteen counties reported that demonstrators in gardening, poultry, and home dairy marketed their products individually. In addition, fourteen counties reported some form of cooperative marketing underway.[23]

Curb markets were doing business in five counties: Phillips, Sebastian, Jefferson, Union, and Pulaski. The women who sold on the curb market in Union County had a curb market home demonstration club.[24]

Ten roadside markets were operated in five counties: Pulaski, Sevier, Union, Franklin, and Greene. Those on a cross-state highway in the fruit section of the state were more profitable than others, even though they may have operated only during the summer. Nine of the roadside markets were owned and operated by individuals or families. One—in Franklin County—was a cooperative market built and operated by twelve women. It was noted that "[d]efinite requirements and standards have been set up for Roadside Market demonstrators." So-called "home demonstration markets" seem to have been what we call a "farmers' market." Details follow:

Home demonstration club women in five counties are operating home demonstration markets. This type of market is found to succeed in towns of five to ten thousand people. Towns under 5,000 are as a rule rather small for a market of any kind to thrive, while the town of more than 10,000 is more likely to support a curb market.

An average of 20 women sell on these markets. 10 women in Greene County have sold on the home demonstration market in Paragould products amounting to $1,000 since the market opened in April.

17 women selling on the Pope County home demonstration market in Russellville have taken in over $700 since June. The Johnson County market in Clarksville has netted over $900 [difficult to read].

The market at Fayetteville, in Washington County, does the most thriving business. They opened in February, and have made sales amounting to 8 thousand plus dollars.

A definite home demonstration marketing association is organized so as to insure a businesslike and lasting organization. All home demonstration markets reported are organized after this plan.[26]

Home Industries

Although there were early comments concerning women's making and selling crafts, the general tenor seemed to indicate that these activities were tolerated rather than condoned or recommended. However, with the difficulties of the Great Depression, the position of Extension specialist in home industries was created in May, 1934, "to handle standardization and marketing of handicrafts and other home industries."[27] Miss Etna McGaugh was appointed to the position. Although actual sales figures were unreadable, the state report noted that "the economic situation of many farm families has been materially strengthened through improved income from various home industries."[28]

Items made and sold (and referred to as handicrafts) included rugs, quilts, baskets, vases, and pieces of furniture. A home demonstration market for these special products was attempted for the first time—and with satisfactory results—in Hot Springs (Garland County).[29]

The 1935 report was much more exciting. In early December the first state home demonstration market was established in the historic Majestic Hotel gift shop in Hot Springs! Eighty-two home industry demonstrators' products had been approved by the board of standards, and the women were eligible to sell on the state market. Inventory in the shop included approved homemade rugs and mats (hooked, braided, crocheted, and woven); baskets made of Arkansas native split oak, pine needle, honeysuckle, and buckbush; woven articles, woodcrafts, linens, homemade toys, and even more![30]

Mattress Making

In Sebastian County, farm women who worked in a mattress factory made their own mattresses with cotton they had grown. They shared their knowledge with other women in the area. In 1926, Rosie L. Wolfe, who may have been the state clothing and household specialist at that time, came to Sebastian County and studied the women's technique. She began teaching women in other counties how to make their own mattresses, using home-grown cotton. By 1935, 2,630 were reportedly made in 54 counties. An average of $3.00 was spent for materials to make each mattress. In fact, the following chart provides the figures for the years 1932 through 1937:[31]

Year	Counties	Mattresses Made
1932	15	375
1933	37	1,225
1934	52	2,497
1935	54	2,630
1936	63	5,965
1937	69	4,556

The Greene County agent reported that forty leaders in the various clubs had been trained in mattress making. The club members of Consolidate No. 1 Community had made mattresses for themselves and had also taken orders for five additional mattresses from individuals outside the club. The women used the money they earned to apply to the cost of a kitchen they had recently added on to their club building. The agent commented that by using cotton grown on their own farms, the women had taken advantage of just one more means of living-at-home.[3]

Although mattress making was a real boon for home demonstration women and their families, perhaps the most important factor was the women's cooperation in the emergency relief centers. In 1937, twenty-five counties established emergency relief mattress factories that made 6,902 mattresses. Home demonstration agents, trained leaders, and the household furnishings specialist provided the training. The lay leaders were well versed in the process and were comfortable in their roll and rarely asked for assistance from the agents.[33]

In evaluating the program in 1939, Connie Bonslagel listed several reasons for the rapid expansion of mattress making in the state, as follows:

- Low incomes throughout Arkansas, which prevented families from replacing worn ones
- Farm families' surplus of low-priced cotton
- Prevalence of low grade mattresses, which created a desire for good cotton ones
- Leaders trained over an eight-year period who were available to teach the process
- Proven worth of the homemade mattress, established over the years[34]

In March 1940, Clay, Crittenden, Jefferson, Madison, and Columbia counties initiated a mattress demonstration program, apparently as a community outreach. The program spread to the remaining seventy counties within a month.[35]

By the end of 1940, 137,477 mattresses had been made: 7,772 of home grown cotton, and the remaining vast majority were made of Federal Surplus Commodities

Corporation (FSCC) cotton. In addition to 7,244 women leaders, 4,323 men assisted with the program. The average cost per family was $.28—for needles, twine, and thread. These were high-quality, all-cotton mattresses made with eight-ounce ticking, worth $15 each.[36]

Bonslagel addressed issues other than just the physical act of mattress making. She noted, for example, that only low income farm families were eligible for the mattresses—so that mattress manufacturers would not be hurt by the program. She also found the mothers in about 20 percent of eligible families were home demonstration club members. Thus, she was able to emphasize that the home demonstration program was serving the lowest-income farm group as well as the average- and higher-income groups.[37]

Bonslagel completed her study of the mattress-making phenomenon as follows:

> Every effort has been made to keep high
> standards in mattress making in all counties.
> This fact has helped to eliminate criticism which
> might have come from mattress manufacturers
> or small town merchants who sell mattresses.
> Arkansas farm families have had twelve years[']
> experience. [There are] trained leaders in most
> communities. 12 years had demonstrated that
> homemade mattresses will hold up. With
> low farm income, many couldn't replace old
> bedding. Farm families have been made aware
> of the possibilities of the cotton mattress
> demonstration program.[38]

Surely the extra work created by the mattress program was a strain on home demonstration agents, lay leaders, and members.

Clothing Update

In 1939, the clothing program reflected farm families' needs as the decade of hardships ground to an end. For the first time, sewing machines were mentioned. In fact, by then the machines were in need of repairs. Reports indicated, once again, the importance of lay leaders out in the counties. Following are some updates on the program, all bundled under one endnote for 1939:

A number of factors affected the clothing program for 1939. Although the farm income was somewhat better for farm families as a whole, few families considered it good economy to purchase very much new clothing except as a very necessary replacement. Clothing of former years, often of good quality but out of date, was in need of remodeling and repairs. Sewing machines in all counties were badly in need of a more intelligent care, and often in need of definite repairs or replacements.

Lawrence County reports a typical clothing program. In this county there are 26 leaders in clothing who assist the home demonstration agent in forwarding the clothing program. These leaders are brought together once or twice each year for definite training in clothing work. In 1939 they were given demonstrations in clothing construction and wardrobe planning at those training meetings. These leaders are given a subject-matter file of all clothing information, are held responsible for the clothing contest, assist fellow club members with clothing problems and give method demonstrations in clothing to both home demonstration club members in home demonstration clubs and to 4-H members in 4-H clubs. They keep a pattern file of children's self-help clothing. [Self-help clothing was designed so that small children could dress themselves.]

Results indicate the extent to which the teachings were carried by agents and local leaders. Sewing machine clinics were held in two communities; 20 demonstrations were given in dry cleaning, spot removal and pressing by leaders in clothing. Two communities had a clothing contest with 31 women entering from the Clover Bend [difficult to read] Community. Twenty-six families carried wardrobe planning demonstrations.

[Returning to statewide information:] For clothing contests, the Danish system of judging was recommended, and fashion operettas were suggested as a medium for presenting models. This was a cooperative piece of work for the clothing, music, and recreation leaders.

Wardrobe planning: Eighteen home demonstration club members carried a family wardrobe demonstration in Columbia County during 1939. Mrs. Lura Jarvis of the Waldo Rural Club said, "I didn't realize that I had so many clothes on hand, or that I spent so much for clothes. From now on I'm planning to buy quality instead of quantity."[39]

Care and repair of sewing machines: In Craighead County more than 200 sewing machines have been cleaned following demonstrations given at club meetings. Cleaning involved taking the machine apart and cleaning each part thoroughly with white gasoline applied using a small stiff brush. Then tensions and stitch lengths were adjusted.

Care and repair of clothing: In Clay County, care and protection of clothing has been a slogan in the clothing program during 1939. Mrs. E. L. Ecmon [difficult to read] of the Blue Home Demonstration Club showed the women of her community that closets could be built with no extra cost. From scrap lumber two closets were constructed, canvassed inside and out with old dresses and other materials, and then papered to match the interior of the rooms.[41]

The following quotation, from the report of the Clinton Home Demonstration Club meeting, was published in a local newspaper: "The demonstration Miss Mary Britman gave on cleaning sewing machines was of great interest to the entire group. We consider this one of the greatest services she has given our county."[40]

Expanded Better Babies Program

The Better Babies Clubs, begun in Logan County during the early 1930s, grew somewhat exponentially as programs relevant to helping mothers cope with virtually every aspect of a child's life were added. By 1938, 74 percent of the counties boasted clubs, with 4,341 "healthy and happy youngsters"[42] on the rolls of 357 clubs. The 1938 report, which follows, reveals what we would call an interdisciplinary program:

Being a Better Baby is no small obligation. The work originally started as an outgrowth of nutrition projects of home demonstration clubs under the direction of Miss Gertrude E. Conant, Extension nutritionist. But nowadays, being a Better Baby calls for the right kind of clothes, the right kind of toys, low shelves and books in the closet, and the very best of manners, as well as milk and cod liver oil.

The mothers of children of the pre-school age, are enlisted by leaders in the home demonstration clubs, frequently before the baby arrives. Literature concerning prenatal care, proper feeding, and general care of the baby is supplied to the mother. 266 baby clinics were sponsored by the home demonstration clubs and the county health service gave mothers in 35 counties an opportunity to check up on the physical progress of their babies in 1938.

A special shelf in the pantry, full of tiny jars of purees and fruit juices canned especially for the baby, is found in hundreds of homes where the Baby Canning Budget is rigidly followed. The nutrition leader in the home demonstration club is ready with information on what the baby should eat from the time he gets his first drop of milk until he trudges off to school with a lunch box full of vitamins and minerals.

Clothing for the Better Baby is under the direction of Miss Sue Marshall, Extension clothing specialist. Self-help garments so the child can know the satisfaction of independence as he learns to dress himself, roomy [unclear] to keep pace with his rapid growth, and the choice of materials and colors come under this program. Patterns are made available to the mother through clothing leaders in the home demonstration clubs.

Homemade toys and play equipment are included in the Better Babies program, and are a part of the responsibility of home industries leaders under direction of Miss Sybil Bates, specialist in home industries. Stuffed dogs and cats, play pens and teeter-totters are made at home to keep the baby busy and happy.

Recreation leaders working with Miss June Donahue, community activities specialist, will be taught suitable games, exercise, and hobby interests in 1939.

Child development in the way of manners and general behavior is the responsibility of home management leaders and Mrs. Ida A. Fenton, home management specialist. Low hooks and shelves so the child can put away his own clothing teach habits of orderliness and helpfulness, and young parents are encouraged to teach unselfishness, kindness to pets, courtesy, and obedience from the very first day, by example as well as precept.

Better Babies leaders do not stop with the mothers in the home demonstration clubs. Whenever there is a baby, or one on the way, in the community, the leaders offer advice and counsel. County training schools are held for the leaders in order to keep them up to date in child development information.[43]

Forestry Program

In 1939, home demonstration women in the state initiated a tree-planting program in which demonstration forests were established in nine counties on idle farm lands. The initiative was an impetus to the federal land-use program as the acres were leased to the county home demonstration councils for a period of time to allow seedlings to grow into trees for logs or fence posts. Plans for the program were developed the previous year by the Extension forester and a county home demonstration agent. The plan was presented to the State Home Demonstration Council in August of 1938 for its approval. The report continued, as follows:

Two points of popular appeal in this program were the pride of ownership in the educational and financial enterprise, and the personal participation of each club member in planting her own seedling.

Cross County Home Demonstration Council sponsored the second home demonstration forest planting in the state. A 40-year lease was given to the council on an acre of land located 4 miles east of Wynne on Highway 64. Since the Tulip poplar is native of Crowley's Ridge (but practically extinct except for a few valued shades) the council decided to adopt this variety. Seedlings were obtained from Ohio through the Extension forester. One thousand seedlings were planted. The purpose of this planting [was] fourfold: (1) to encourage the planting of similar forests throughout the county; (2) to encourage the study by 4-H and farm and home organizations of forest management; (3) to use as a highway beautification project; and (4) to be used by 4-H and farm and home organizations for picnic purposes.[44]

No mention of this apparently short-lived program was found in later reports.

Rural Electrification

Connie Bonslagel noted in 1939 that—through the Rural Electrification Administration program—the Extension Service had one of the "greatest opportunities for serving rural people ever given them."[45] She continued, as follows:

The attitude of the Arkansas Extension Service has been that electrification is a part of the modern standard of living which should be made available to all farm people in the state as fast as it is economically feasible. Keeping its position as an educational organization, the Service has given out information on how electrification can be obtained and how it may be used to greatest advantage. The actual development has been left to organizations of rural men and women.

The allotment for the first rural electrification cooperative in Arkansas was made just 1 1/2 years ago. At that time, of the 252,319 farm homes in the state, only 2,943 were being served with electric power.

Many a home demonstration club woman trudged up and down the hot dusty roads of summer the past 3 years signing up families and getting easements. Home demonstration agents met with committee groups at night holding inspirational REA meetings and pointing the way to better farm life through the use of electric power.

[Perhaps as an example of what could be done with electricity in the homes,] [i]n Arkansas County this year 30 washing machines, 1 mangle, 7 electric sewing machines, 13 vacuum cleaners, 31 irons, 6 ranges, 4 roasters, 6 water heaters, 32 radios, 25 refrigerators, 9 water pumps, 30 fans, 2 food mixers, and 15 pieces of miscellaneous equipment have been purchased.[46]

Despite all the activities and "busyness" during the 1930s, the decade was also one of reflection and change.

Endnotes

[1] 1933 Annual Narrative Report, State HDA, RG 33, NARA/Fort Worth, Texas.

[2] 1934 Annual Narrative Report, Home Economist, Household Management, RG 33, NARA/Fort Worth, Texas.

[3] Ibid.

[4] Ibid.

[5] Ibid.

[6] Ibid.

[7] Ibid.

[8] Ibid.

[9] Ibid.

[10] Ibid.

[11] Ibid.

[12] Ibid.

[13] Ibid.

[14] 1934 Annual Narrative Report, State Nutrition Specialist, RG 33, NARA/Fort Worth, Texas.

[15] Ibid.

[16] Ibid.

[17] Ibid.

[18] 1933 Annual Narrative Report, St. Francis County HDA, RG 33, NARA/Fort Worth, Texas.

[19] 1935 Annual Narrative Report, State HDA, RG 33, NARA/Fort Worth, Texas.

[20] Joyce Kilmer, "Trees," 1913.

[21] 1932 Annual Narrative Report, State HDA, RG 33, NARA/Fort Worth, Texas.

[22] Ibid.

[23] Ibid.

[24] Ibid.

[25] Ibid.

[26] Ibid.

[27] 1934 Annual Narrative Report, State HDA, RG 33, NARA/Fort Worth, Texas.

[28] Ibid.

[29] Ibid.

[30] 1935 Annual Narrative Report, State HDA, RG 33, NARA/Fort Worth, Texas.

[31] 1932 Annual Narrative Report, St. Francis County Local HDA, RG 33, NARA/Fort Worth, Texas.

1935 Annual Narrative Report, State HDA, RG 33, NARA/Fort Worth, Texas.

Thomas Wayne Copeland, *Good Neighbors: Agents of Change in the New Rural South, 1900 to 1940* (Ph.D. Diss.,The University of Mississippi, 2011), 197. (Citing "Mattress Making." Arkansas Extension Service, No Date circa 1940, File 1-9, Box 1, University of Arkansas Special Collections, Fayetteville, Arkansas.)

[32] 1937 Annual Narrative Report, State HDA, RG 33, NARA/Fort Worth, Texas.

[33] Ibid.

[34] 1939 Annual Narrative Report, State HDA, RG 33, NARA/Fort Worth, Texas.

[35] 1940 Annual Narrative Report, State HDA, RG 33, NARA/Fort Worth, Texas.

[36] Ibid.

[37] Ibid.

[38] Ibid.

[39] 1939 Annual Narrative Report, State HDA, RG 33, NARA/Fort Worth, Texas.

[40]Ibid.
[41]1939 Annual Narrative Report, State HDA, RG 33, NARA/Fort Worth, Texas.
[42]1938 Annual Narrative Report, State HDA, RG 33, NARA/Fort Worth, Texas.
[43]Ibid.
[44]1939 Annual Narrative Report, State HDA, RG 33, NARA/Fort Worth, Texas.
[45]Ibid.
[46]Ibid.

8

A Time for Evaluation and Change

The sources of misery seemed to have no end during the 1930s. In the Northwest, thirty-four counties suffered a severe drought during 1936 and were declared drought relief counties. Agents and club members participated in intensive canning activities to save the remaining food supplies and conducted a fall garden campaign. On August 20, "a state-wide Drought Recovery Day was devoted to giving information as to fall planting of food and feed, fall canning of meat and vegetables, and other information which would be needed as soon as rains come."[1] Throughout the years, reports indicated that animals were often slaughtered and canned because there was no feed for them.[2]

Broadening the Home Demonstration Program
Even as catastrophic conditions continued and funding throughout the state remained tentative, home demonstration agents met at Fayetteville in March 1936 for their state conference. We are indebted to someone— whose name was not given—who provided a detailed summary of each of the speeches by rural economists and sociologists. Miss Etna McGaugh had become interim state agent while Connie Bonslagel apparently took a leave of absence. McGaugh included the

various summaries in the 1936 state report. Dean Dan T. Gray of the University of Arkansas made the introductory remarks, which set the tone for the program of reflection and moving forward:[3]

Economic and Social Forces Affecting Rural Life

Dean Dan T. Gray in his introductory remarks showed us how as home demonstration agents our training has been limited to the physical affairs and we have failed to receive training in the social and economic side of life, which has to do with life and living itself.

Today the farmer must know more than merely farming. The farmer cannot exist long if he follows the old ideas in farming – every man for himself. If he is a good farmer and knows farming only, he is an easy [difficult to read] to organized society. The farmer must know how community organizations, taxes, transportation, tariffs, the church, schools, markets, and in fact every form of organized society bear upon his life.

Our homes are not poor and standards of living low just because our people wish it. We find many people of high ideals living in poor surroundings and no way of making the conditions better. Many of the [state's?] good farmers have lost their homes through different types of losses. Today, as Agricultural workers, the challenge is ours to help find a solution to their problem.[4]

Other speeches included insights into rural life, the new role the government was taking in agriculture, the need for a strong forestry program, and the toll that soil erosion was taking on the state's economy. The following is a portion of McGaugh's wrap-up summary of the entire program:

> Miss McGaugh traced the growth of home demonstration work from 150 members in 1914 to 45,780 in 1936. She stated that even though our program had started with physical things and had dealt largely with food, shelter, and clothing, we have experienced rapid and persistent developments. We are now thinking about home standards; we will soon be able to see how a planned agricultural program can help us to realize these high standards we are now only thinking about.
>
> Women should realize the strength of 45,000 in number. They should see beyond their community and county groups. They should see what their help can mean to future farm programs.[5]

The overall theme of the conference was that it was time for home demonstration workers and agricultural workers to work together as the overall emphasis became a strengthening of the entire rural family.

A Look at Some Programs

State reports for 1939 provided a wonderfully rich evaluation of the various programs as they stood toward the end of the Great Depression. In fact, the entire

1930s were overflowing with insights and information. Several of the programs have been summarized below in bulleted form. It is important to read the reports with an understanding of the economic and social philosophies offered at the 1936 training conference. By doing so, it should become evident that the women's program was embracing the entire household as it stretched to meet the needs of the women and their families.

The Live-at-Home Program: The program is summarized below, as follows:

- Incomes were still too low to buy food and feed in amounts needed.
- "Hard times" had taught its lesson: Conserve.
- The outlook for 1939 was bright only for families showing thrift and who would produce and conserve food and feed.
- Past experience showed that many families who did not produce food and feed did without with resultant health hazards.
- A need for protecting the cash income of the farm by the live-at-home practices was evident.
- County agricultural committees, composed of a farm man and a farm woman from all political townships, met in February of 1939.
- Practically without exception in all seventy-five counties, the committees stressed the value of the live-at-home program and urged that it be the basis for the Extension program for the year.
- Farm incomes were too low to allow for adequate housing if labor and materials were paid for in cash.[6]

The Gardening Program: The following points were stressed by leaders and agents in the average county gardening program, as follows:

- Planning the home garden to meet the needs of the family.
- Planting successively throughout the growing season.
- Implementing improved cultural practices.
- Fencing the garden to protect it from livestock and chickens.
- Making the garden more accessible to the house.
- Controlling insects.
- Utilizing more and better varieties of plants.
- Saving seed where practical and possible.[7]

Home Dairy Work: Interest in home dairy work was stimulated by the following factors:

- An Increase in general livestock production.
- A total of 65,726 farm families without cows.
- An urgent need—from a nutritive standpoint—for two cows per farm family to freshen at different seasons.
- Relatively poor standards in sanitation, housing, feeding, and butter/cream-making.
- Idle acres taken out of cotton.
- Improved pastures resulting from various relief programs.

Although intangible, the greatest result was in the improvement of health through the consumption of cleaner milk and of greater quantities of milk and milk products.[8] (From the 1940 report comes this word: "Plans for the home dairy program were dispensed with by all county and home demonstration agents at their semiannual district conference. The chief reason was that so many families didn't own a dairy cow; [the reason] is that they do not have feed, pasture, or facilities for keeping one.")[9]

Homemade Homes: The homemade homes campaign, which was begun in 1937, arose from the need to assist farm families in constructing their own homes and farm buildings. Arkansas's per capita income was $139 in 1939; low incomes were the major cause of five out of every six farm homes in Arkansas needing to be repaired or replaced. Years of drought, floods, low prices, and reduced incomes generally had delayed normal building and repair work on farms throughout the state. By 1939, the following evaluations were made:[10]

> Farm people are now planning for better homes, just as always in the past they have planned farm crops. The building of comfortable attractive homes is recognized as an essential part of farmstead operations. . . .

> A journey through any part of the state discloses many instances where through the use of home labor and native materials, homes have been built which far surpass those erected at higher cost where such wealth was not to be had.

> Farm labor has been found to be worth more in home construction than if it were devoted entirely to crop production.[11]

The Poultry Work: As we recall that poultry work was given number one priority in home demonstration work in 1922, we find growth throughout the years. In 1927, a club woman wrote to her district agent. Part of that letter is included below and may be contrasted with reports that follow:

> My Agent instructed us in a new way of raising poultry, do away with the mixed flock and get pure breds, so I did. With a small insulator and 14 Barred Rock hens, I hatched 263 chicks. From my chick[s] and garden, I added to the family income $53.20, which was a wonderful help. May such 'God sent Faries' as our Agents live forever.[12]

> In 1934, fifty-one members of the Ellmore[?] Club in Newton County raised 20,000 broilers.[13]

> [In 1934,] 64 hatcheries, practically all the commercial hatcheries in the state signed the hatchery code which was sponsored by the Extension Poultryman in cooperation with county and home demonstration agents. Through this work, better contacts with commercial hatcherymen have been developed on the flock improvement program. Much progress has been made in the hatchery industry in Arkansas in the past 20 years. Prior to 1919 there were no commercial hatcheries in the state. Now there are 897.[14]

> Poultry work in Arkansas in 1937 was conducted largely through organized groups and

local poultry leaders. The Arkansas Poultry Improvement Association with 461 members representing 25 counties has sponsored the National Poultry Improvement plan. 64,000 birds were qualified as A. S. approved in 1937, which represents nearly a 100% increase over last year. Hatchery participation increased from three to fifteen. This organization was largely responsible for securing legislation to prevent poultry theft.[15]

The above programs reflect a much broader outlook than was previously seen in the work. The fact that each one was included in the home demonstration report indicates cooperation between the home demonstration work and the agricultural work in providing for the entire family. Home building, growth of poultry cooperatives, and the live-at-home program were important to both the farmer and his wife.

In 1938, Connie Bonslagel referred to the new philosophy as one of the outstanding factors of the year, as follows:

[One factor] is the disposition of the Extension Service as a whole to look on all progress, projects, and farm enterprises as designed not for the land's sake nor for the livestock's sake, but for the farm family. The farm and home considered as a unit or the farm family approach as the accepted Extension Service policy is a factor which makes for more than formal cooperation between the two Extension agents in a county. In word and act they develop a joint program through the close correlation of the various phases of the Extension program into one county program with better homes and better family living for Arkansas farm families as the objective.[16]

In 1939, Bonslagel evaluated the new cooperative program in a slightly different way. Again, she praised the changes:

> Cooperation between Agriculturalists and Home Economists; Family approach to program: A closer cooperation and understanding on the part of the county and home demonstration agents has developed over a period of years. This fact, together with a feeling on the part of the whole farm people that the program is a family farm and home program and is not separated into agricultural and home economics sections, makes our work take on the whole family approach more completely each year. This has resulted in more joint conferences of agricultural and home demonstration agents and more joint training schools for men and women leaders, and in strengthening of our farm unit demonstrations.[17]

No doubt, by the end of the Great Depression, home demonstration work had a broadened focus.

Endnotes

[1] 1936 Annual Narrative Report, State HDA, RG 33, NARA/Fort Worth, Texas.

[2] Ibid.

[3] Ibid.

[4] Ibid.

[5] Ibid.

[6] 1939 Annual Narrative Report, State HDA, RG 33, NARA/Fort Worth, Texas.

[7] Ibid.

[8] Ibid.

[9] 1940 Annual Narrative Report, State HDA, RG 33, NARA/Fort Worth, Texas.

[10] Ibid.

[11] Ibid.

[12] 1927 Annual Narrative Report, Negro District HDA, RG 33, NARA/Fort Worth, Texas.

[13] 1934 Annual Narrative Report, State HDA, RG 33, NARA/Fort Worth, Texas.

[14] Ibid.

[15] 1937 Annual Narrative Report, State HDA, RG 33, NARA/Fort Worth, Texas.

[16] 1938 Annual Narrative Report, State HDA, RG 33, NARA/Fort Worth, Texas.

[17] 1939 Annual Narrative Report, State HDA, RG 33, NARA/Fort Worth, Texas.

9

All Work and No Play: Having Fun, Getting Together, and Reaching Out

But enough of so much seriousness! Rural women and their families needed to have fun and socialization.

Extension Specialist in Community Activities Appointed

In 1935, an Extension specialist in community activities was appointed. The purpose for the position—added during the very heart of the Great Depression—was to provide leadership in organizing a recreational program in every county in Arkansas. The following summary indicated the anticipation with which the position was received:

> The average farm family life is not complete without the opportunity for self-expression to be provided through drama, music, games, and other forms of community recreation. The appointment of an Extension Specialist in Community Activities in 1935 was welcomed as a step toward a definitely organized recreational

program in all counties in the state. Her
organization was a ready-made one for 57,000
farm women, members of home demonstration
clubs, working in 1,800 home demonstration
clubs in the state, [who] had already selected
a leader in recreation for each particular club.
Also waiting were 72,668 4-H club members
and 38,000 men who were members of farm
organizations.[1]

By 1939, the community activities program could boast
of the following statistics:

- 1,457 rural communities under guidance of
  7,752 local leaders
- [?] communities with a "Neighborhood Night"
  plan of regular entertainment
- 217 community choruses
- 129 community orchestras
- 2,075 plays and pageants
- 46 counties in state-wide drama tournaments
- 8,162 families that followed a program of home
  recreation
- 176 communities that were assisted in
  obtaining library facilities[2]

Fortunately, the following narrative reports were
included in the 1938 and 1939 state reports:

In Chicot County the Empire Community under
the leadership of Mrs. Dewitt Hill has organized
a chorus of 18 voices. They meet twice a month
for practice. The nucleus of the County Chorus
made its first appearance at the county council

meeting singing Sweet and Low, Polly Put the Kettle On, Little Brown Church in the Vale, and Love's Old Sweet Song for the clothing revue.[3]

In making the family recreation hour her project for this year, Mrs. Ollie Crook of the Round Pond Home Demonstration Club in St. Francis County, is finding it works wonders in keeping her family of nine happy and congenial.
Their family recreation activities consist of radio programs, homemade games, and family reading. The favorite games of the children include checkers, both Chinese and otherwise. At certain time the boys have a special radio program. Any member of the family may listen in with them or if they desire they may carry on some special game in another part of the house. Then at a different time of the day the girls get their favorite radio program. Two hours participated in by all the family are the reading hour and the music hour. The father spends some time reading to the entire group. It is always the privilege of any member of the family who does not desire to spend his time this way to do any activity of his own interests in another part of the house. Another interesting feature is the music hour. The mother plays the piano and the rest of the family join in singing.[4]

Twenty-two clubs reported sponsoring 53 community nights for whole families. The kinds of parties listed were picnics, ice cream socials, basket dinners, meetings in parks with outdoor cookery, weiner roasts, watch parties, Valentine parties, Fourth of July celebrations, farewells and homecomings, taffy pulls, egg hunts, cake walks, and orchestra practices.[5]

Realizing the need for reading material, both educational and entertaining, the Mountainburg Home Demonstration Club, Crawford County, under the direction of Mrs. E. F. Bruce, president, decided to work with the WPA [Works Progress Administration] in sponsoring a community library. They secured a vacant room in one of the store buildings and built shelves for the books. People in the community donated 246 books which were approved by the State Library Board. There are approximately 300 books in all now and the Board is planning a number of entertainments to raise money to buy more books.

Approximately twelve of the best magazines [such] as American, Readers' Digest, Better Homes and Gardens, Good Housekeeping, Ladies Home Journal, etc., are on file. Mrs. Harrison Peters, Librarian, reported that 38 people checked out books the first day the library was open. The total expense was $15.39 for lumber, supplies, tables, etc., to start the project.[6]

At our Fall Festival last weekend, one of the most popular booths was our recreation center booth. Young and old stopped to examine, play with, and ask questions about the homemade games. These games – at least ten different ones – were all made by Mrs. Greta Canbill [unclear], who attended Camp Robinson and gained the homemade game inspiration there. Upon her return to Jonesboro, she has been a very enthusiastic champion of homemade recreation.[7]

45 county home demonstration rest camps with an attendance of 2,743 were held and 36 4-H club camps with 3,358 attending.[8]

The Greene County Home Demonstration Chorus, made up of the three best singing voices from each of the 39 home demonstration clubs, and which has held bi-monthly practice periods for more than a year, has merited the attention of the Paragould musical organization. The chorus has appeared on various county-wide programs and gave a special radio program of Easter music.[9]

Although some of the undertakings seem quaint, the community activities program was surely one step toward providing additional support for the entire rural family—both socially and emotionally. Two relevant comments wrap up the discussion of the recreation program:

The family approach is used in community activities work particularly in the recreational features. The two county Extension agents [male and female] are jointly responsible for the program with adults, young people, and children. All ages, from the grandfather to the pre-school tot participate in "neighborhood nights" which are a part of the recreation program in 477 communities.[10]

Cultural possibilities in rural living hitherto somewhat overlooked even by farm people themselves are being seen in a new light. Big, little, old and young Arkansas farm people have found they like to play.[11]

State Home Demonstration Camp, Camp Pike, Arkansas, August 26, 27, and 28, 1935

Connie Bonslagel provided the following description of one of the legendary state encampments at Camp Pike/ Camp Robinson in her annual report for 1935:

The Seventh Annual meeting and the Third Camp meeting of the Arkansas State Council of Home Demonstration Clubs was held the last week in August. At this time there were 1523 home demonstration clubs represented in the state with 37,408 members. This year the camp attendance has increased. We began our State Camp in 1933 when there were 1040 women present, in 1934 we had nearly 1200 women in attendance and in 1935 there were 1533.

The National Guard of the State of Arkansas furnishes camping equipment, camp ground, and facilities with a fine building for meetings and a swimming pool wonderfully clean, clear, cool. Thirteen mess halls and an Officers' Mess Hall and an Administration Building where exhibits can be put up.

While the camp only accommodates 1200, the National Guard officers with many of their men brought in extra equipment to accommodate the overflow of women at camp this year. A week before camp opened there were 1804 women who had signified their intention of attending and this number had to be reduced by phone, so that the campers would not be uncomfortable due to the crowded conditions.

The success of the Camp was due to the splendid organization and cooperation of all who were interested, including the National Guard Officers, the home demonstration staff and county extension workers, and the officers and many individual women of the State Council of Home Demonstration Clubs.

1363 1/2 inches of publicity and space for 37 cuts was given in the state and out of state papers, and farm magazines. Clippings have been made from the Arkansas Gazette, Arkansas Democrat and Commercial Appeal, Arkansas Farmer, Farmer's Wife, Kansas City Star and Progressive Farmer. 47 army cooks and a steward prepared the meals which were served in 13 mess halls, and in officers' mess.

Special committees were appointed to take care of the meals and hospitality, transportation, press, pictures, registration and exhibits, aid tent, home industries contest, quilt contest, state cotton dress contest, song contest, and one of the men from the state office took all the worry of electric lights, loud speaker, spot lights, etc., on his shoulders so that we would not need to consider that angle at all.

Miss Vera Knook, the librarian for the city of Little Rock, put up an exhibit of about 400 books suitable for use in a rural community library.

307 women were entered in the various contests during the camp.

The program which opened on Monday evening with a band concert by the 153rd Infrantry band with educational, inspirational and recreational features, was largely participated in by home demonstration club members themselves. Special music by several of the counties and dances added to the program.

Some of the outstanding speakers were Brigadier General E. L. Compere who gave the Welcome; Miss Druzilla Kent who spoke to us on Homemaking in Denmark; Mr. T. Roy Reid and Mr. E. B. Whitaker with the Rural Resettlement Administration, and of course, we had an address from our own State President, Mrs. E. H. Casner. Dr. Hedger [?] of the McCormick Memorial Fund gave four lectures which were the high lights in the whole program: "What the Community Owes the Child," "How to Tell a Well Baby," and "Positive Health for Farm Women" [were three of the lecture titles]. Other speakers were Miss Mae Creswell, state home demonstration agent for Mississippi and Miss Sallie Hill of the Progressive Farmer and Southern Ruralist, and Governor Futrell. Afternoon group meetings included topics such as child care, home industries, rural library, art and home life, and officer's round table, home community planning and improvement, and home community recreation and housing.

A water carnival completed the program on Wednesday night and on Thursday morning after breakfast the group got into their cars and made a tour of Little Rock.

The oldest woman attending camp was Mrs. Hulen, who was 77 years old.

Recreation consisted of swimming and archery, and entertainment included in addition to the songs and dance numbers, an accordion solo and eight living pictures posed by the women themselves such as "Song of the Lark," "The Whistler's Mother," "The Pot of Basil," and "The Madonna of the Sacred Coat."

The women attending were allowed to bring their own food stuff from home and pay 50 cents registration or pay $1.50 for their meals and 50 cents registration. Most of them paid the entire amount.[12]

Reaching Out to Communities

Expecting home demonstration women not to reach out to their communities would be the equivalent of asking the sun not to come up in the East! Examples of the women's generosity have already been seen over and over again. Three additional examples of their willingness to give are included below:

Annually, contributions, which would amount to several thousand dollars in value, are made which help to cheer or provide physical comforts for people living in their communities, and even to foreign countries. But these people do not always have money to give, so they share what they can of products of their own labor— food grown on the land where they live or articles of clothing or household furnishings, fashioned by their own hands from home grown products or purchased through sale of them. All contributions made are voluntary and are given directly to the recipients or through an organization.[13]

In Carroll County, the old-fashioned methods of caring for the needy have not been forgotten. Reports on community charities were given by 24 clubs. Club women helped 12 storm victim families in West Concord, Shady Grove, and Berryville communities replenish their bedding and linen supplies and gave them some clothing. They helped families who had lost their homes through fire with bedding, household linens, rugs, food supplies, and even furniture. They sent gifts and gave special programs to inmates of the County Home, provided funds to send sick to hospitals, supplied clothing to needy school children and sent Christmas baskets where prospects for gaiety seemed few.[14]

Wherever there is a need, seemingly home demonstration club women find a way to meet it. From the Luna Landing Home Demonstration Club in Chicot County comes this report: $1.00 cemetery fund; $1.00 Red Cross; $2.50 to band; 4 pairs pajamas to children sent to State Tuberculosis Sanitarium; fruit juices, baskets of food, linens and soft cloths to sick and needy; one woman gave six weeks lodging to a woman in search of work; 30 dozen fruit jars, cans and extra jar tops and rubbers to canning kitchen for school lunch room; paid tuition for three grammar school children; and $1.00 bus fare for bus going to Luna Landing from Lake Village to bring people to church in town.[15]

Home demonstration women continued the tradition of community service begun many years before.

Endnotes

[1]1939 Annual Narrative Report, State HDA, RG 33, NARA/Fort Worth, Texas.

[2]Ibid.

[3]Ibid.

[4]Ibid.

[5]Ibid.

[6]Ibid.

[7]1938 Annual Narrative Report, State HDA, RG 33, NARA/Fort Worth, Texas.

[8]Ibid.

[9]Ibid.

[10]Ibid.

[11]1939 Annual Narrative Report, State HDA, RG 33, NARA/Fort Worth, Texas.

[12]1935 Annual Narrative Report, State HDA, RG 33, NARA/Fort Worth, Texas.

[13]1940 Annual Narrative Report, State HDA, RG 33, NARA/Fort Worth, Texas.

[14]1939 Annual Narrative Report, State HDA, RG 33, NARA/Fort Worth, Texas.

[15]1940 Annual Narrative Report, State HDA, RG 33, NARA/Fort Worth, Texas.

10

Learn and Live
by Claudia Cranston

*Connie Bonslagel's 1938 state report mentioned that
a* Good Housekeeping *feature writer had penned an
article about the women's annual encampment at Camp
Robinson. The article was found on the Cornell University
Home Economics Archives website. Since the article was
not old enough to be in the public domain, a letter was
written to the* Good Housekeeping *editorial offices in New
York, asking for permission to reprint it. The written
answer was that, although Hearst Communications, Inc.,
and* Good Housekeeping *would not object to our use
of the material, the entities no longer possess the
reprint rights because of the time that has elapsed since
publication.*

One word of caution: Be prepared to be delighted!

> Under the stars the city of tents stood row on
> row. On the oak-fringed lawn in the moonlight
> twelve hundred women in their light-colored
> cotton dresses knelt or sat. The Army Band
> played "Arkansas."

It was the Lawn Party. The first evening of the annual four-day encampment of the Arkansas Council of Home Demonstration Clubs at Fort (sic.) Robinson. Twelve hundred farm women delegates were on the lawn of the Officers' Mess—representing fifty-three thousand farm women back home.

The Lawn Party—when the Army Band played "Arkansas," and the Army Adjutant welcomed the women to the Fort—was the last the Camp saw of the men for four days. And in the stillness under the pin oaks and the white oaks when the blare of the Army Band had died away, the singing of the twelve hundred women on the moonlit lawn was as much like flowers as sound. It seemed to me I could see the sound of their voices—pastels and white—pink crepe myrtle, and pale Cape jasmine.

"There's a gold mine in the sky,
Far away.
And we'll find that long lost gold mine—
Some sweet day."

And when, between the songs and the costumed folk dances, the delegates discussed their camp theme, "Recognizing and Developing Our Rural Resources," and discussed their coming programs of demonstration lectures— Better Light For Better Sight, Land Use And Architecture, There Is No Drudgery Where There Are Dreams—I could see the fifty-three thousand farm women back home with their faces all

turned one way—toward our encampment at
Fort Robinson! Waiting for their delegates
to return and tell them about the latest
lectures on home building and decoration. The
latest fashions for their daughters, the newest
vocational training for their sons, the balanced
foods from their farms for their tables.

Fifty-three thousand women waiting for reports
on the demonstrations of electricity for their
kitchen equipment, electric power for their
poultry brooding, refrigeration, irrigation.
Reports on the better shoes for their families'
feet; the better light for their families' eyes;
the better books and the better magazines; the
best reading for home economics, for art and
etiquette and entertainment; the best stories of
travel, adventure, and love.

Fifty-three thousand farm women waiting to
plant the season's seeds of civilization in fifty-
three thousand farm homes. A great rural
culture rising from its own roots, planted solidly
in its own soil instead of scattered from a thin
veneer of sophistication at the top!

These women of the Arkansas Home
Demonstration Clubs—under the direction of
the Extension Service of the Agricultural College
of the University of Arkansas, and with the
cooperation of the United States Department
of Agriculture—offer the nation an object
lesson in organization. Their annual Home
Demonstration Camp at Fort Robinson, near

Little Rock, is the "Showcase" of that organization.

Two factors have made the progress of the Arkansas Home Demonstration Clubs stand out above that of other states. These two factors are, first, their personal leader, Connie Bonslagel, State Home Demonstration Agent—and, second, their annual Arkansas Army Camp "Showcase."

The leader thought of the Army Camp, and the Army Camp showed the women how to organize. Took the burden of "the housework" off the women's shoulders, so that for the first time in their lives they can put their minds on their minds!

The Army tents, the Army cots, the mattresses, the mess halls, the administration buildings, the auditorium, the swimming pool, the shower baths and toilets are furnished by the Camp— just as they stand permanently for the National Guard. The farm women pay $2.50 each for their food for the four-day encampment—and from that there is a surplus in the treasury every year!

Counting $2.50 for food, it would seem that $5 would be a liberal estimate of the total expense of each delegate to the Camp, as transportation is really the only other expense. And the transportation is arranged by a second stroke of genius comparable to that of using the Army Camp in the first place.

The majority of the twelve hundred women
gather at central points, and the school buses
pick them up for the trip. They carry their
Army kits in their arms—their blankets, and
their knife and fork and plate, and their cup
and saucer and spoon. They are required to
use the regular school-bus drivers, for safety
to themselves and the buses. And they are
required to pay for the gas and oil and the
driver's expense.

Up until the Army idea in Arkansas the
farm women's Home Demonstration Clubs have
usually met with the men's farm organizations—
the women spending practically their whole time
cooking for the men, just as at home! Having
their Home Demonstration interest shouldered
out of programs, or crowded into a few
hours. Imagine, then, the emancipation of
an Army Camp! Where no men or babies
are allowed—much less waited on—and where
the Army stewards do the work! With every
woman already registered at the Administration
Building—sure of her tent, her bed, and her
breakfast—there was no hurrying to make ready
for the first night. Instead there was group
meeting group under the oaks of the Officers'
quarters and down the avenues of the Army
tents. The happy shouts of the women from
the far-distant farms who seldom see their
acquaintances.

The streets of tents were laid out like long city
blocks on one side of the big paved boulevard

down the middle of the Camp, always full of khaki-covered Army trucks delivering provisions to the mess halls. Every street had a number, and every tent had a number, and every occupant of every tent was registered. In some tents there were only two women, in others as many as five. In three minutes any woman in the Camp could be located from the Administration Building. There were regularly appointed "pages" to run errands between the tents, and "captains" responsible for "tent runners."

"Say, you!" I heard a coloratura soprano captain call out as a figure sneaked from a tent and hung a brassiere on a tent rope. "The Army regulations say do not heap garments on outside tent ropes."

There was a suppressed snickering from under the censured canvas, and the furtive figure sneaked out and took the brassiere in. I walked to the turned-back flap of the tent door and stood in the light from the electric bulb hanging in the middle. There were five Army cots in that tent, and five women sitting on them in different stages of nightiness, all giggling like boarding-school girls set to talk, and in high good humor over the brassier incident.

"Come in! Come in!" called out a young woman in pink pajamas.

It turned out I had dropped into a "poultry contingent" tent. The five women came from neighboring counties in the poultry-raising district.

"On our place we hatch out eight thousand chicks, all together on the same day," the young woman explained when I asked questions. "And they are every one white!"

"Every year?" I asked.

"Sometimes twice a year," she said. 'We are deciding now," she went on, "whether to heat the brooders by electricity or not."

"How will you decide?" I asked, curious to know. "How will you know what is best to do?"

"Oh, we test that out!" an older woman said. "That's what these Home Demonstration meetings do for us."

"You see," the younger woman explained, "tomorrow, when the groups of poultry raisers from all over the state come together, we will elect a couple of women in different localities to experiment this coming year. In a small way they will try out heating brooders by electricity. Then next year, when the poultry raisers meet here again, the experimenters will report the results. Then we shall know whether to take it up or not."

And there I had a spotlight on the practical way the details of farm methods improvements are worked out cooperatively by the women of the whole state. I found that this "discuss, test, try, then adopt" system was the women's rule about every sort of new method or machine—for canning, preserving, dairying, sewing, dyeing, cooking, kitchen gardening, as well as poultry raising. Certain expert women, or groups, are selected to experiment for the whole fifty-three thousand club members. For, of course, a farm—a farm home—is not built in a day. A long-time program is required for all recognition and development of rural resources, and a year is a short time to test a big, important investment and report upon it.

When I left the poultry-raising contingent I passed a group of thirty, maybe fifty, women, sitting on long, low wooden benches under trees a little secluded from the tents. The women were reciting something, and I stopped to listen. They were reciting the Home Demonstration Women's Creed—all together like a litany—their voices like young soprano choirboy voices in the mysterious stillness of the oak grove:

"I believe in the open country and rural life in the country;

"I believe that through working together as a group we can enlarge the opportunities and enrich the life of rural people;

"I believe that the greatest force that molds character comes from the home, and I pledge myself to create a home which is morally wholesome, spiritually satisfying, and physically healthful and convenient;

"I believe in my own work as a homemaker, and accept the responsibilities it offers to be helpful to others and to create a more contented family and community life, so that in the end farm life will be most satisfying."

As the women finished and the sound waves of their treble recitative ebbed away, the Camp bugler began the Camp taps. Pure silver. Bugle silver. In the cool tenderness of a Southern night after the simmering heat of a long Southern afternoon—

"Day is done.
Gone the sun
From the lake,
From the hill,
From the sky.
All is well,
Safely rest—
God is nigh."

And practically the next thing I knew was that same bugler blowing the reveille!

The morning "executive" meetings of the different divisions of the Club Councils began each camp day. There was a major seriousness and scope about these Council meetings, at which resolutions were arrived at affecting the entire club membership. For example, it was concluded at one of them to instruct each and every Home Demonstration Club in the state to make a study of and report on Problems in the South that Have a National Influence.

In addition to the early morning Club Council meetings, there were the demonstration lectures on Adventures in Self Improvement—the reviewing of the model dresses made by different club members for morning, afternoon, and Sunday; the exhibitions of textile weaving, hooked-rug making, quilt piecing; the rehearsal of an operetta; the drama tournament; the assembly singing; the meeting at the fun center where all sorts of games were played; the meetings at the Bookmobile.

One of the most popular of the many lectures, and a good example of the practical demonstration that is included in lectures, was the foot clinic at the Red Cross tent. After lectures on foot care and correct and attractive footwear, six chiropodists were busy giving treatments to the farm women who poured into the tent to have their "hurty" feet relieved!

One day during a hot rest hour right after the noon meal—it was 100 [degrees] F. in the shade if you could find any shade—I went visiting. In a tent on the far outskirts of the canvas city I talked to a woman from up around Siloam

Springs who had changed over from raising chickens for her "allowance money" to raising pigs instead, and was making a big profit.

"And what do you think of the Home Demonstration Clubs?" I asked her.

She was a woman of middle age, who must have weighed well over two hundred pounds. The Army cot sank under her. Every line of her features recorded deep experience of living—reality, work, frustration, hope. She fanned with a small, futile fan, the perspiration streaking in beads and rivulets down her face, as it did down mine.

"What do I think of the Home Demonstration Clubs?" she repeated after me. "First comes my religion," she said. "And next comes my Home Demonstration Club! That is what I think."

With all this evidence spread all day before my eyes—vital, broad, brilliant, the actual operation of the centuries-longed-for ideal of adult education—it was only after taps at night and before reveille in the mornings that I even had time to learn about my own tentmate—a rice farmer. To learn such startling things as that on her husband's farm the bill is $200 and $300 a month for electricity to flood the rice fields! I sat up on my Army cot and stared at her across the tent, practically stunned, when I heard this.

But I didn't have any more time to be amazed over the water for the rice fields, because she remarked casually right after that that she had canned one thousand quarts of fruits and vegetables in her kitchen from her garden and orchard!

And while I was still thinking that over—and wondering how I could get back to Arkansas to her rice farm before that thousand quarts was gone—she said she canned chickens, too, and bacon! And she said she knew a woman who was expert at canning meat, who could can a whole cow for you—everything a cow has except horns and hide—for two dollars!

Well, I didn't say I didn't believe any of these tales my tentmate told me at odd moments after taps and before reveille. But I did say I'd like to see them!

But something I did see that would not be imaginable to any world except our own there at the Fort was the last camp night. Those twelve hundred farm women wouldn't go to bed at all the last night!

After the lectures and the planning, and all the serious business—after the water carnival at the big pool—after the taps and the lights out, away off on the edge of the tented city five women crept out of one tent in their nightgowns. They were as silent and as white as ghosts under the great gold moon that was as round as a golden apple, bigger than any cartwheel, and so close above the peaked tents in the Southern air its light was of incomputable watts!

Those first five women in their white nightgowns became the head of a curious procession. For from tent to tent they were joined by others until in and out among the streets of the city of canvas a strange and wonderful apparition wound, a thousand strong, finally taking in the last tent and bursting into song to wake the dead, had there been any dead—

"There was a frog lived in a pool—
Doo-dah, doo-dah.
His home was damp and nice and cool—
Doo-dah, doo-dah, day!"

With that as a start, everybody can believe what went on the rest of the night. The cool, delicious night of the Southland, after the day's heat of the day. The white procession broke up into groups, laughing, jostling, organizing and disorganizing games. And after the games they danced the picturesque square dances of Arkansas and Texas.

Did I say picturesque? Fancy the farm women from a thousand farms, tall and short, young and middle-aged and very old, high, wide, and handsome, hopping in the moonlight in their nightgowns like children!

In vain the swift hours fled, the moon fell down
the sky, the captains called their cohorts to their
tents, and the bugle boy repiped his plaintive
"Day is done, gone the sun."

A thousand women were having a night out.
The only night out many of them had ever had,
or ever would have in their whole lives! They
shouted in derision:

"Early to bed and early to rise
Makes you healthy, wealthy, and wise.
But I found out, and I know it's true,
A whistle does much more for you.

Yoda—layee—ee!"

And not until their mass will was totally
exhausted, in the last hour before the pale
pre-dawn, did those thousand women quiet
down. Quiet down too soberly, as the Southern
temperament is likely to do. For as I turned
on my Army cot to sleep, I wished that they
wouldn't sing, as they marched to their tents,
the song that, for many of us, is too true:

"Still all my song shall be
Nearer my God to Thee,
E'en though it be a cross
That raiseth me."[1]

Endnote

[1]Claudia Cranston, "Learn and Live" in *Good Housekeeping* magazine, Volume No. 108, No. 4, April 1939. Retrieved from the Cornell University online Home Economics Archive: Research, Tradition, History, on February 23, 2012.(http://hearth.library.cornell.edu/cgi/t/text/pageviewer-idx?c=hearth;cc=hearth;q1=Claudia%20Cranston;rgn=full%20 text;idno=6417403 1409 004;didno=6417403 1409 004 ;view=image;seq=203;node=6417403 1409 004%3A5.57;page=root;size=s;frm=frameset;).

(Written notice received on April 11, 2012, that neither Hearst Communications, Inc., nor *Good Housekeeping* magazine had retained the copyright to the article because of its age, although neither would object to the reprint of the article.)

11

The War Years

The attack on Pearl Harbor on December 7, 1941,
followed the close of the Cooperative Extension Service
reporting period, which ended on November 30.
Therefore, the years 1940 and 1941 have been combined
to discover the home demonstration work immediately
before the war began for the United States. The chapter
then moves seamlessly into the actual war years.

The Nation Prepares for War

By 1940, the nation was preparing for war and
responding to the war already being fought in Europe.
The National Defense Program had directed farm
women's thinking toward (1) increased emphasis on
the production of a well-planned food supply for all
farm families; (2) increased home consumption of cotton;
and (3) improved standards of citizenship among farm
families. Home demonstration agents had taken the
lead in making registers of all home economists in their
counties and in listing their areas of expertise, so that if
home economists were needed for special activities, the
agents would be able to name well-qualified individuals
for foods, housing, or sewing work.[1]

A Strong Live-at-Home Program

The Preparedness Committee of the State Home Demonstration Council met in September 1940 and determined that food was the first line of home defense. Home demonstration clubs' Committees on Preparedness made live-at-home inventories in their home communities. In Stone County—one of the two or three most remote mountain counties in the state (according to the report)—Mrs. Myrtle Fulks was chairman of the County Committee on Preparedness. Connie Bonslagel considered Fulks' presentation so remarkable that she included the entire speech in the state report. We agree and have done the same:[2]

National Defense in Relation to Our Farmers' Present Economic Situation

In thinking of National Defense, our first problem is, perhaps, to determine just what we mean by National Defense as related to the work-a-day farmers and other citizens of Stone county, Arkansas. National Defense, according to my idea, is anything that makes the nation stronger, that protects its people, and helps us to withstand an enemy – whether that enemy be an army or a smaller-than-normal income.

We all know that lowered farm incomes are bound to develop from the loss of our foreign markets. Due to present war conditions across the Atlantic, and [?] the Pacific, too, it is either impossible to ship our goods, or they could not be accepted by former buyers if we could ship them. England was one of our major markets, and now the great danger of shipping from deep-sea mines, torpedoes, submarines, and other things not so easy to understand, makes it impossible for us to sell our cotton and other goods to this market. Germany formerly also purchased much cotton, but for obvious reasons is no longer buying from us, or more properly – we are not selling to her. Now you can readily see that if this continues, we will lose a great source of our national income.

We might look at the matter this way, the nation as a whole is in much the same position that you would be in if, for instance, you were selling a pound of butter a week to your neighbor. That pound of butter sold for 25 cents, the only cash you took in, and with this cash you bought a dime's worth of sugar and 15 cents worth of coffee each week. Suddenly your neighbor could no longer buy the butter from you and there was no one else in the community who could afford to buy the butter. Obviously, you would have to do without the sugar and coffee you had been buying with the income from the butter!

However, you still have the butter on hand, or the raw cream. For the sake of economy you cannot destroy the cream, or if it has been churned, the butter. What would you do? I can tell you: You would seek ways to use the butter in your cooking at home. Haven't you housekeepers, or homemakers, done that very thing many times? Well the nation is trying to find ways to use the cotton they cannot sell. In your own mind now, can you not see that just this is a form of defense? Then, too, our leaders are finding other things for us to plant instead of the cotton. They are suggesting new ways to use cotton in the home. Many of them so practical that it amuses us that we, ourselves, have not thought of them earlier. So, it is we must decide to use the most of the cotton grown at home, either in things we make or things factories make for us and that we find in the stores.

Now to me, National Defense is as much a part of the farmer's duty as it is the soldier's duty. It is our work to so plan our living that it will not be necessary to sell so much to get our money with which to buy other things. In other words, the part our Stone county farmers have to play in the National Defense is to "Live-at-Home" in the true sense of the words. Stone county is an integral part of the nation, just as each of us is a part of the county. We must so plan our farming and our living that the fact of the predicted lowered farm income will not hurt us, lower our living standards, nor cause us to go hungry.

It is very true that a nation is no stronger than its people. And we cannot be strong as a nation or as individuals unless we have the proper food. Whose duty, but the homemaker's and the farmer's, is it to see that we are properly fed? The homemaker must plan her living so that it can be raised at home. The farmer must see that she has what she needs grown on the farm. This is the essence of a Live-at-Home program. This can be done only through a planned program, much as many of us have carried out in the past. This means raising and canning vegetables and fruits and meats enough for a full year's supply, raising poultry and seeing that the family owns at least two good milch cows [this term is correct and is even in the dictionary] that will keep them in milk and butter the year round. It means encouraging the men to raise their own feed and to build trench silos for the winter's feed supply.

Our part of the National Defense is not only to see that our own families carry out this program of living at home but to preach it and to tell it at every community gathering, whether it be home demonstration club, community night, or what-not. Our leaders will seek to find new markets for our products, to protect our incomes, and to help us in all ways, but in the meantime, we must help ourselves. We must live as happily as possible and as comfortably as possible. We are fortunate here in Stone county that the garden is easily grown, the season long, and the people of the county already familiar with the plan of living-at-home from what we grow.

We must develop a stronger community spirit. Petty differences must belong to the past, for we are now a part of the National Plan and there is no room for internal strife, whether in club, community or county. These points, then, are what we must consider in the future.

We must use our cotton at home.

We must plan our living so that we can grow practically everything at home.

We must not only practice these things, but teach others to do the same.

We must so plan our families' meals that we will develop strong bodies and alert minds.[3]

A Well-Planned Food Supply

By 1940 gardens were being planted according to Agricultural Adjustment Act (AAA) requirements. Home demonstration agents estimated that "13,243 good farm gardens were planted and tended this year as a result of AAA payments. One good garden practice resulting from the AAA requirements was to keep the garden free from insects and weeds in the planting of hairy vetch in more garden plots than usual."[4] This discussion brings to mind an interesting development during the 1930s and into the 1940s: the increased cooperation and collaboration with various governmental agencies set up to meet the needs of families during such difficult times. The acronyms and agency titles lend an unexpected flavor not found during the earlier years.[5]

Feeding the Children

As home demonstration women accepted the call to live-at-home, they turned once again—or simply continued—to ensure a proper lunch for the school children in their communities. Home demonstration club women had shown concern over the underweight children in their communities and had for many years planted extra vegetables, canned extra quarts, and then had given of their time in preparation of the hot dish that the school children might have a nourishing hot lunch. By this time, in most counties the women cooperated with government agencies. The following examples are shared as a tribute to women throughout the state who were doing the same work:[6]

One example is the Accident Home Demonstration Club in Benton County that is serving a hot lunch to each one of the fifty children enrolled in this rural school. Mrs. Harvey Graham, president of the club makes the following report: In the late autumn we gathered enough vegetables to can 250 no. 3 cans for our school lunch project. This winter we met and canned 122 pounds of beef. This canning was all done at the club house by members of the home demonstration club with the help of several men. Beginning with January each child has had a hot lunch and they are given all that they can eat. We find that the children have better health, fewer colds, a noticeable increase in weight as well as a marked improvement in grades.[7]

In Jackson County, 500 children have been eating hot lunches in two of its schools for the past two weeks. This project shows what cooperation between rural and urban clubs can accomplish. While the hot lunch project was being established in the Tuckerman and Swifton schools the home demonstration club women and PTA women met and agreed that the urban women would raise the money to buy sugar, crackers, cocoa and other staples. The rural women are going to furnish canned foods to supplement these and the Surplus Commodities and the Welfare Offices furnish the ingredients to make soup or stew.[8]

In Johnson County, 18 of the 25 hot lunches being served in as many schools are sponsored and 13 partially supplied by Surplus Commodities. Eleven of these centers have paid WPA workers. The Ozark community has just finished a 20 x 10 building. New equipment included two large cook stoves, $125 worth of cooking utensils, pots and pans, and several aluminum cold pack cookers. The 16 by 3 feet serving table covered with steel has storage shelves built underneath. There are six tables covered with linoleum which will seat 96 children. The unit has electricity and a sink. One hundred children are fed in this unit. Five pigs are being fattened from the garbage for use in the hot lunch project.

In Spadra [Johnson County], Mrs. Ruby Matlock, 4-H club leader, is the project supervisor. One hundred and fifteen children are fed daily. The Surplus Commodities furnishes lard, meal, flour, beans, tomatoes, canned grapefruit, rice, eggs, and wheat cereal. The project raised a garden and canned over 300 quarts of beans and tomatoes. Two pigs are being fattened and are to be used as meat for the children. The children state, "We're thinking of how good those back bones are going to taste this winter."[9] The project buys food from the children, ten cents per quart of sweet milk, ten cents for one-half gallon of buttermilk. Some eggs and canned goods are bought from the children at market price. The food is used to pay the five cents a day for the meal. There are 20 children eating free. No food or money is given. The children who are able to pay do not know the other children do not pay. Below are two samples of the meals that the children receive the year round: (1) Meat loaf, gravy, creamed potatoes, English peas, cranberry congealed salad, hot rolls, pumpkin pie, cocoa; (2) baked beans, candied sweet potatoes, lettuce salad, cornbread, grapefruit, oatmeal cookies. Mrs. Matlock commented on watching the children gain weight and improve in their studies after a month or two. She also noticed most an improvement in their dispositions—less fussiness on the playground.[9]

The Lamar [also Johnson County] project was the first hot lunch school project in the county. The PTA sponsors this project that served over 300 children a hot lunch consisting of two vegetables, bread, fresh or canned fruit and a hot drink each day. Mrs. Florence Sparks, a home demonstration club member is in charge of the project. At the beginning, 30 children were underweight. Not one of these 30 children was underweight at the end of the school term. During an influenza epidemic all of the schools in the county were forced to close except Lamar. The PTA attributes this to the hot lunch program. The Surplus Commodities supplies the project with cornmeal, flour (graham and white), beans, fruits, potatoes, and some cabbage. The remainder of the food is contributed or brought from home by the children in exchange for their lunches. They raised a garden and canned food for their hot lunch program.[10]

In ten Lincoln County schools the home demonstration clubs sponsor the hot lunch, affecting about 900 students. All of these schools use the surplus commodities and two use WPA workers. In all of them home demonstration club members have cooperated with the PTA where one exists and have had definite influence in making the lunch possible. One home demonstration club has selected hot lunches for their year's project. One 4-H club is sponsoring one hot dish lunch. They do the preparation and the Surplus Marketing Administration furnishes the materials.[11]

In Baxter County, six of the eight hot lunch projects at schools were sponsored by home demonstration clubs. These are: Buford, Cassville, Oakland, Crispence, Three Brothers, and Fluty.

The Buford hot school lunch, which has been in progress three years, was started by the home demonstration club, and the first year the members took turn about in cooking. The last two years they have had a WPA cook, and the last year they also had a WPA garden. However, they still donate food, and they gave their club house to be used for the lunch room.

The Cassville project was sponsored by the East Cotter Home Demonstration Club. They helped raise money to buy the equipment and a WPA cook was hired.

The Oakland Home Demonstration Club sold a quilt at a pie supper and raised twenty dollars to buy lumber to build a house for the lunch room. Men in the neighborhood donated their labor to build the house. The school teacher, Mr. Tanner, said he can tell a big difference in the students, who seem more alert and less restless than when they had only cold lunches to eat.

The Crispence club raised money to section off a part of the room and build a cabinet for their school.

The Three Brothers club helped buy part of the equipment and donated the rest. They have also helped furnish food.

The Fluty club raised money by selling quilts to build a lunch room on the side of their school.[12]

More schools were interested in serving hot lunches as more home demonstration club women took over such projects. The following figures, which were taken from the state reports for 1938 to 1941, show the number of schools following recommendations for a hot dish or hot lunch:

1938	1939	1940	1941
355	117	1,005	1,711[13]

Preparedness in Foods and Nutrition

Preparedness leaders in foods and nutrition played a vital role in their counties and communities. The men specialists in food production, poultry, gardens, dairy, and beef production aided the nutrition specialist and district agents in training the women. Preparedness leaders were already dairy, poultry, gardening, canning, foods, and nutrition leaders. They were selected to make live-at-home surveys on food production and food and feed on hand in their neighborhoods.[14]

Often, the women were surprised to find families who produced little of their own foods. A summary of the survey sheets was used as a basis for discussing neighborhood needs. Then the leaders went back into the homes with Family Food Supply Charts in order to help the families determine the amount of food the family should raise in order to be well fed.[15]

Canning budgets were planned, and each family member was given a food selection score card to help build better food habits. Each Preparedness leader gave many days to receiving training and to getting out into the homes to help inspire farm families to do a better job of food production. One club president reported the following:[16]

> Three families in our community were assisted in planning their garden. Our club foods leader took her pressure cooker to their homes and taught them to can. These three families are as proud as our club is that the shelves which were

bare last year are all full of canned vegetables and fruit for this winter.[17]

Home Dairy Update: Although home dairy work was suspended in 1940 for lack of families with milk cows, the work was intensified during 1941 as a result of the defense activities undertaken in all counties. Census figures showed that Arkansas had a serious shortage of dairy animals. Although 161,154 families had dairy cows, 26 percent or 35,518 families had none. The estimated amount of milk needed in Arkansas was 1,636,635 pounds. In 1940 milk actually produced in the state amounted to 296,034 pounds.[18]

Increased Home Consumption of Cotton: A Cotton Christmas

As has been mentioned previously, the South continued to produce cotton even though demand and prices had fallen. The cotton mattress-making programs were a means of using up surplus cotton. In 1940, the Cotton Christmas program—sponsored by the Agricultural Extension Service and the Arkansas Council of Home Demonstration Clubs—became a part of the year-round cotton utilization program. The program included proclamations by the governor, several mayors, and a few county judges; demonstrations in making cotton gifts and in wrapping them in bright cotton materials; and pledges by home demonstration club groups to give cotton gifts, decorate doors, windows, and trees in cotton, and wrap gifts in cotton![19]

County agents reported the following Cotton Christmas activities:

In one county, all home demonstration women's husbands received cards saying, "Your wife would like to have a 108 inch good grade cotton sheet for Christmas."

Members of a 4-H club, after hearing a talk on the cotton situation, wrote notes to their parents, asking for cotton gifts in their stockings this year.

In another county, home demonstration club women agreed to try to popularize the wearing of cottons both summer and winter by buying better cotton materials and by tailoring them more beautifully. They also agreed to talk to their merchants about stocking the nicer fabrics.

Home demonstration agents furnished speakers to civic clubs, including Lions, Rotarians, Elwanians, and Chambers of Commerce.[20]

Cotton Garments for Europe: "Hands-Across-the-Sea" Program

In addition to making garments for members of their own families, home demonstration women and 4-H girls and Junior Adult Club girls made garments for 21,826 children in war-torn European countries. The program, known as the "Hands-Across-the-Sea" project, was the first organized project by rural women for aid to Europe's war victims. Items included dresses, boys' suits, shirts, overalls, nightgowns, slips, panties, and robes and dressing gowns for preschool children.[21]

The women chose cotton because it was Arkansas's principal farm product, and cotton fabrics held up well for children's wear and frequent launderings. Each member provided the material for the garment she made. Many of the women who were unable to buy the material used feed or flour sacks. The Red Cross recommended patterns, and usually all members of one club used the same pattern. Requirements included front openings to make children's dressing and undressing easier. The long sleeves were required because of the moist, damp climate of most European countries.[22]

To simplify the distribution of garments, an age label was sewed into the neck of each one. All garments were made with deep hems and large seams to make alterations possible. A needle, thread, and all remaining scraps of the material were packed with each garment.[23]

Cotton Comforters

The home industries specialist reported on state-wide local leader training in cotton comforter making in 1941, with 34,251 made. The specialist found comforters to be much superior to handmade quilts. She noted that although the quilt had held first place in the farm woman's bedding improvement scheme, quilts took a great deal of time and many were poorly made. And besides that, they did not provide warmth. She encouraged women to make fewer quilts and to make them real works of art—and then to make cotton or woolen comforters for warmth.[24]

The Cotton Mattress Program: Growing Weary in Doing Good

Surely there is no doubt the cotton mattress-making project—for families who were on the relief rolls—was an amazing accomplishment. During 1940 and 1941, home demonstration agents had trained 12,639 mattress and comforter leaders, who had supervised the making of 385,850 mattresses and 34,251 comforters! No leader had been paid for her work. However, Connie Bonslagel's 1941 report indicated friction among agents, lay leaders, and club members.[25]

Bonslagel alluded to agents' not having enough time to train the leaders adequately—and not being able to ensure the leaders' sufficient interest to come out to the meetings. The agents were stressed (and stretched) by the training requirements of the Defense program and the educational work of the various Department of Agriculture and Department of Defense agencies that relied on their help.[26]

Then there were the club women who did not understand the agents' inability to attend club meetings—even though each agent had thirty or so clubs to oversee as well as the additional responsibilities added because of the economic situation. There were losses of many long-established home demonstration clubs along with increased numbers of members' complaints—more numerous than ever before.[27]

Added to the mix were relief families who blamed the agents when they were not able to receive a mattress! As Bonslagel commented,

Supervisors have spent considerable time in protecting conscientious and capable agents from unjust accusations of favoritism and other machinations in connection with the activities of certain mattress centers, with the certification of families for mattresses and with disappointments resulting from cotton and ticking shortages, inferior cotton and the like.[28]

Overwork, fatigue, and stress had taken a toll on the organization during its twenty-seventh year under the Smith-Lever Act. Arkansas's agents were being asked to take on more and more responsibilities in addition to the educational work that was vital to their positions. Lay leaders—considered the mainstay of the home demonstration program—were not able to keep up with the demands placed on them.

And yet the home demonstration program continued to grow. During 1941, seventy-seven county home demonstration agents, two full-time assistants, and four apprentices enrolled 64,863 home demonstration club members in 2,224 community or neighborhood organizations that met once and sometimes twice each month, twelve months in the year.

The graphic of enrollment and number of clubs from 1914 through 1941 on the following page provides a snapshot of the organization's continuous growth. (The figures are for white members only. Black membership figures were retained separately and inadvertently were not copied from records at the National Archives.)[29]

Year	Enrolled	Clubs
1914	130	--
1915	800	17
1916	1,619	--
1917	2,083	159
1918	6,234	291
1919	3,042	252
1920	2,541	189
1921	1,392	239
1922	2,484	357
1923	4,526	220
1924	6,613	376
1925	8,034	425
1926	7,732	422
1927	8,748	446
1928	10,300	557
1929	12,929	658
1930	14,095	675
1931	20,087	877
1932	21,566	923
1933	22,599	1,128
1934	30,689	1,309
1935	42,351	1,663
1936	45,072	1,762
1937	46,732	1,783
1938	55,670	1,952
1939	59,948	2,056
1940	63,163	2,138
1941	64,863	2,224[30]

The Nation is at War

Conservation at the Heart of All Programs

By 1943, conservation was the keyword of the family clothing and household furnishings program. The state plan included the following statement:

> Since war needs have taken over many textiles and household furnishings formerly used by civilians, it becomes increasingly necessary for civilians to conserve and use to the very best advantage possible all of those materials and articles on hand. This problem will include (1) care of clothing, (2) renovating and remodeling clothing, and (3) care and repair of household furnishings. The matter of choosing substitute materials and articles also becomes a big problem in the life of the consumer.[31]

Sue Marshall, clothing and household arts specialist, noted that special war-time leaflets and miscellaneous publications were prepared and distributed. Two of the leaflets were titled *Remodeling Garments into Victory Clothes* and *Mend Your Clothes*. Samples were provided of steps used in making various types of patches for mending. The specialist provided leader training meetings on remodeling and mending, washing knitted garments, and dry cleaning and storing woolen garments. The leaders asked for additional help in 1944 on tailoring and remodeling. Marshall's report included the following vignettes:[32]

> Mrs. C. A. Brock of Poinsett County reports that she cleaned eight garments for 33 cents and has

taught other women in her club how to dry clean garments. Mrs. Brock says it is more convenient to clean garments at home than to send them out of the county by parcel post to be cleaned.

In Carroll County, the agent gave demonstrations on making and blocking sweaters for home demonstration and 4-H groups. She made a cardboard form for shaping sweaters while they dried. Demonstrations on care of shoes were given by many of the agents in the state this year.

Clothing leaders used the Red Cross sewing program as a means of teaching improved sewing practices. There is a revival of interest in the use of dress forms as an aid to home sewing.

The state totals in numbers of garments made are lower for 1943 than in 1942 in every case except infant garments. Perhaps people have been influenced by the pledge "Buy only what you need" and have refrained from purchasing so many garments as they have in previous years. The shortage of materials for work clothes and children's school clothes may be another factor in reducing the number of garments made this year. Increased time given to food production may have left too little time for doing clothing instruction.

Sewing machine schools have been important as the specialist continued her plan to reach sixteen counties each year. Lawrence County reported, "As a result of a circular letter sent to home demonstration club members, inviting them to attend a sewing machine school at Strawberry, July 7, 18 women came from three nearby clubs and brought fourteen machines to be cleaned and adjusted.[33]

Marshall prepared a letter for agents to send to county clothing leaders that included a list of patterns of work clothes for women. Although the term "work clothes" was vague, the context indicated the discussion was about clothes for women to wear when working outside in the field or garden. The letter encouraged women to buy and make durable garments that would not require frequent replacement. During the war, many rural women who had not previously worked in the fields had to perform the tasks normally done by the men in the family.[34]

Conserving Household Items

Things seemed to change quickly during this time. In 1941, women were encouraged to buy cotton products during the Cotton Christmas campaign. By 1943, cotton household items were becoming scarce. The Farm and Home Radio News Service, Thursday, November 11, 1943, bulletin on "Hints for Homemakers on Extending Life of Household Cottons" is printed in its entirety, as follows:

Fayetteville, Ark.—Household cotton may become as scarce and precious as the tires and tubes on the family car!

In issuing this prediction this week, Miss Sue Marshall, Extension specialist in clothing and household arts, pointed out that sheets, pillow cases, hand towels, wash cloths, bath towels, and even dish towels are becoming more and more difficult to replace.

This situation makes it necessary that the best possible care be given supplies on hand, Miss Marshall said. She advised that the life of household cottons can be extended by observing the following practices:

Loosen all sides of sheets from under the mattress before removing them from the bed, rather than to yank them off by one corner. Hang sheets on the line by the two hems rather than lengthwise. Distribute the wear on sheets by placing the end of the sheet with the narrow hem, instead of the wide one, at the top of the bed. When ironing sheets, plan to make creases in different places from time to time to distribute wear.

Try to select still, sunshiny days for wash day, rather than a windy one, to save unnecessary wear on materials. Take clothes off the line as soon as they are dry if the day is windy.

Wash garments and household articles before they become badly soiled to avoid hard rubbing or the use of strong bleaches. Depend upon bright sunshine to bleach white materials, rather than strong commercial bleaches.

Iron such things as sheets and towels as little as possible because ironing wears out material as much as washing or wear does. By ironing only the hems, then placing them on the bottom of the stack each time, most of the wrinkles will have disappeared before they are used.[35]

Food Conservation

Gertrude Conant, long-time foods and nutrition specialist who began her work in 1918, retired from the Extension Service on June 30, 1944. During her last years in the work, she served part-time as specialist in child development and family life. In the meantime, Mary E. Longhead was named specialist in foods and nutrition, with Blanche Randolph as assistant specialist. For 1943, a well-planned and executed live-at-home program for every farm family continued to be the food and nutrition program's contribution to the nation's wartime agricultural activities. The food conservation program encompassed every possible means of preserving food, including freezer lockers, dried fruits and vegetables, brined vegetables, and stored potatoes, in addition to the amazing amount of food preserved in glass and tin containers, as follows:

1943 Canning Statistics:

	Rural	Urban	Total
Glass containers			
At Home	16,000,000	2,000,000	18,000,000
At Comm. Ctrs.	270,000	40,000	310,000
Tin containers			
At Home	77,000	18,000	95,000
At Comm. Ctrs.	48,000	34,000	82,000[36]

As can be seen above, the demand from urban women for information on canning was quite great. Urban leaders were invited to attend leader training schools given by Extension workers and home demonstration club leaders. In Pulaski County, thirty-five specially trained home demonstration club leaders in food preservation held thirty meetings in the greater Little Rock area. At these meetings, 596 city women were taught to can by the steam pressure cooker method as well as by the hot water method. Most of the meetings were held in churches.[37]

Longhead's report on the war-time food preservation program follows:

> Victory gardeners, particularly in urban areas, sometimes found when canning time came that they lacked equipment, time, or the know-how. Food preservation centers, pressure cooker sharing, canning on the shares, all helped to solve the problem. Maintaining pressure canners was an important part of the canning program. There were 7,316 gauges tested during the past year, and 1,200 of these found to be needing adjustment were either replaced or repaired.
>
> Since it is not so easy to replace food lost through lack of proper storage facilities, that phase of the food preservation program is being taken more seriously. Storage structures built this year include cellars, earth mounds, underground barrels, above ground structures.

The quick freezing program could not be expanded very much this year. Locker plants already established were filled to overflowing, and new plant construction was halted or slowed up because of lack of materials.

Making American cheese, which has aroused only passive interest in the past, took on added interest this year with cheese rationing going into effect. Home demonstration agents reported holding 26 leader training schools, with an attendance of 336, and 178 method demonstrations with attendance of 2,603.

Food selection and meal planning were carried along with other work on food utilization. The Basic Seven food chart proved a stimulus in interest in meal planning.[38]

Home demonstration women provided major support to the government's Share-the-Meat campaign that opened late in 1942. (Apparently the campaign was an educational program to limit the amount of meat used by consumers so that more would be available for the armed services and allies. It may have been a precursor to meat rationing.) Neighborhood leaders—set up by the Extension to carry out special wartime activities in rural areas—were the counterpart to block leaders in urban areas. In Lincoln County, for example, fifty-two neighborhood leaders, seventeen home demonstration club leaders, and thirty block leaders were furnished information on the campaign through circular letters, leader meetings, and home visits. The leaders then passed the information on to 1,061 homemakers through seventeen home demonstration club meetings, four called meetings, and 235 home visits.[39]

The War Ends

On August 14, 1945, Japan surrendered to the allied forces and thus ended the war. The formal document of surrender was signed on September 2, 1945.

As they had throughout the decades, Arkansas's home demonstration women contributed invaluable support to the war effort. Through the live-at-home program, women conserved clothing, textiles, home furnishings, and food—and they made sure their neighbors did the same. It seems appropriate at this time to revisit a portion of Myrtle Fulks' 1940 presentation in Stone County:

> In thinking of National Defense, our first problem is, perhaps, to determine just what we mean by National Defense as related to the work-a-day farmers and other citizens of Stone county, Arkansas. National Defense, according to my idea, is anything that makes the nation stronger, that protects its people, and helps us to withstand an enemy – whether that enemy be an army or a smaller-than-normal income. . . .
>
> We must develop a stronger community spirit. Petty differences must belong to the past, for we are now a part of the National Plan and there is no room for internal strife, whether in club, community or county. These points, then, are what we must consider in the future.

We must use our cotton at home.

We must plan our living so that we can grow practically everything at home.

We must not only practice these things, but teach others to do the same.

We must so plan our families' meals that we will develop strong bodies and alert minds.[40]

Well done, ladies.

Endnotes

[1]1940 Annual Narrative Report, State HDA, RG 33, NARA/Fort Worth, Texas.
[2]Ibid.
[3]Ibid.
[4]Ibid.
[5]Ibid.
[6]Ibid.
[7]Ibid.
[8]Ibid.
[9]1941 Annual Narrative Report, State HDA, RG 33, NARA/Fort Worth, Texas.
[10]Ibid.
[11]Ibid.
[12]Ibid.
[13]Ibid.
[14]Ibid.
[15]Ibid.
[16]Ibid.
[17]Ibid.
[18]Ibid.
[19]Ibid.
[20]1940 Annual Narrative Report, State HDA, RG 33, NARA/Fort Worth, Texas.
[21]1941 Annual Narrative Report, State HDA, RG 33, NARA/Fort Worth, Texas.
[22]Ibid.
[23]Ibid.
[24]Ibid.
[25]Ibid. (The author has not attempted to reconcile any discrepancies in figures concerning the cotton mattress-making campaign. Figures that seem inconsistent with earlier reports may be due in part to the difficulty in reading numerals on the digitally photocopied carbon copies from the archives.)
[26]Ibid. (without the note)

[27]Ibid.

[28]Ibid.

[29]Ibid.

[30]Ibid.

[31]1943 Annual Narrative Report, State Family Clothing and Household Furnishings Specialist, RG 33, NARA/Fort Worth, Texas.

[32]Ibid.

[33]Ibid.

[34]Ibid.

[35]Ibid.

[36]1943 Annual Narrative Report, State Foods and Nutrition Specialist, RG 33, NARA/Fort Worth, Texas.

[37]Ibid.

[38]Ibid.

[39]Ibid.

[40]1940 Annual Narrative Report, State HDA, RG 33, NARA/Fort Worth, Texas.

12

After the War

A Time to Reevaluate, Regroup, and Move Forward
More than 17,000 Arkansas farm families left their
homes during the war. The 1945 census showed that
the number of farms decreased by 10,147, although
nineteen counties showed gains in the number of farms.
The trend, however, was to fewer and larger farms.
During the war, club women were found in school
rooms, local stores, and sometimes driving school buses.
Those who remained in the home worked in the fields,
assisting with planting, cultivating, and harvesting
food crops. County agents found that during 1945
home demonstration women were returning to their
communities, and fewer women were being employed
outside the home.[1]

Entire families who had moved to war plants and to
other states were gradually returning home. This was
especially true for families who still owned their own
farms. During 1945, 104 home demonstration clubs
were organized while there was a loss of 182 clubs.
Agents were optimistic that the loss of 3,323 members
would be regained in 1946.[2]

The State Home Demonstration Council held a seminar
on policies and problems in adult education in which

participants discussed the need for Extension workers to recognize and study the many ways in which Arkansas's rural living had been affected by the war. Families were classified as war veteran families, families away from Arkansas during all or part of the war, newcomers, and families who remained in Arkansas permanently.[3]

It was noted that women had been out of contact with home demonstration work for numerous reasons. Some moved with their families to war plant areas or moved about the country as their husbands went from military camp to military camp. They may have assumed extra duties at home while other members of the family were absent in service or in war industry or harvest. They may have dropped out due to low morale in a few cases or continued to be nonparticipants as they had been in peace time. Younger women may have grown up with city war jobs and returned home or started homes of their own. They may have moved from other areas and had not made contact with the local organizations. On the other hand, many had remained active in clubs and other community activities while emphasis had turned to the war effort on the home front.[4]

The following discussion provided rich insights into the needs of those families returning home:

> More than 17,000 farm families have left their homes during the war period. Those returning will have had new experiences and will have changed attitudes and many new ideas. There will be some eager to come back to rural living, some reluctant, some wanting to do their work more like the factories (with greater

precision), some wanting more free time, some wanting greater conveniences, such as lighting, ventilation, storage, water, air conditioning, and other goods and services, some wanting more cultural materials within reach, such as books, art, music, and opportunities for cultural contacts, some wanting communications and transportation improved, others wanting health protection facilities, and still others wanting richer school and educational experience for young and old. Those who have stayed at home will have been looking forward to "after the war" for many better things, also. Newcomers usually have similar reasons for their relocation.[5]

Changes for Rural Families

Throughout 1945 Arkansas's farm families continued to supply men and women to war plants and to the armed forces. With increased incomes, many families were able to pay off old debts and to buy bonds with the definite purpose for future buying. Families were planning to remodel old home and farm buildings with lumber from farmsteads. The Extension provided building schools for those who were planning to build.[6]

Rural electrification lines had been increased by 22,112 miles to serve 47,436 customers. Fifty-nine farm families participated in live-at-home demonstrations in nineteen counties. Special emphasis was given to food production, conservation, and better nutrition. "Except for sugar, some fat, and cheese, many Arkansas farm families hardly realized that a point system was in effect."[7]

There was a trend toward improving rural health conditions. With so many doctors and nurses gone, farm families realized the need for a health program. Subjects to be considered for home demonstration work in 1946 were home sanitation, sanitary toilets, screens, and prevention of household pests. Club members assisted in organizing and attended Red Cross nutrition and nursing classes.[8]

Women were also concerned about local matters. They realized their rural schools were inadequate and that many boys and girls had left school to work in war plants. In some cases, they took action to improve the school lunch, assisted in fundraising, and worked to improve school grounds.[9]

In looking toward 1946, it was anticipated that wartime activities would decrease. The 4,034 women who assisted with the rationing program would not have this task for another year. Women would not find it necessary to be actively involved in Red Cross fund drives and production work. Home demonstration women would continue, however, to collect fat, adding to the 50,435 pounds already collected.[10]

The women's world views had expanded. They planned to continue discussions on "Keeping-up-to-Date."[11] With young people from their communities in all parts of the world, it was natural for women to plan programs and discussions to learn more about far away and often unheard of places. For example, in Craighead and Baxter counties, club women exhibited articles sent from various countries by sons and daughters, husbands and fathers in the armed forces. Other examples follow:

Madison County members studied Hawaii, the Philippine Islands, New Guinea, India, China, Italy, Russia, and North Africa.

In Lonoke County, by coincidence, a ceremony called "Authors of Democracy" was presented on V-E Day.

There have also been pageants, book reviews, UN and Pan American flag displays, quiz programs, musical programs, films, and panel discussions.[12]

Citizenship had taken on more meaning for members. They wanted to stay informed. Home demonstration councils had continued to buy war bonds. During each bond drive in 1945, club women carried on campaigns to encourage home demonstration members, neighborhood clubs, and county councils to buy bonds. Because the purpose of buying the bonds was "to help the boys get home,"[13] they opened up the campaigns to entire communities. They sponsored white elephant sales, pie suppers, and auctions. The results were two-fold: community bond sales went "over the top,"[14] and entire communities enjoyed a day or evening of surely much-needed recreation.[15]

Planning for the post-war years included the following concerns, which have been summarized, as follows:

• Needs of returning service men and women, families returning from work in war plants, and small children moving with their parents to rural areas

- Food production changes to meet post-war needs
- Hazards of land speculation and further inflation
- Requirements for improved roads, rural electrification, and new equipment
- Negative effects of individuals' desires to purchase new but unproven equipment[16]

Because membership had fallen off each year for the past four years, the decision was made to recommend that the vice president of each county council and each home demonstration club, as membership chairman, put on a membership campaign. Local club committees visited members who had not attended in some time, long-time non-participants, and newcomers. As a result, fifty-five counties reported 184 newly organized clubs, and 3,497 new members were added in seventy-one counties. During the same year, however, seventy-one counties reported the loss of 3,710 members to do war work or to accept positions of some kind in larger population centers.[17]

The Remainder of the Decade

By 1947, the demographics of the work were definitely beginning to change. Young women, urban dwellers, wives of veterans—so-called "G.I. wives"—and women who worked outside the home were given special attention as innovative approaches were taken.

The Urban Work

Urban women, especially young homemakers, were demanding more help. Reports for 1947 showed that several clubs had been organized in urban centers. Of the total home demonstration membership of 39,421, 31,302 were farm women, 4,818 were rural non-farm women, and 3,301 were urban women. To meet the needs of town and city women, plans were being worked out for leaders of existing clubs to receive additional training from agents and specialists.[18]

The Consumer Speaks program would be offered to urban women. In Arkansas, this national project was headed up by the state subject-matter specialists. Areas studied in 1947 were clothing, foods, household equipment, and home furnishings. Thirty discussion meetings in each of the subjects were conducted by county agents. This "systematic type of group discussion [was] an excellent Extension teaching method."[19]

Telephone service, similar to what was already being done, would be provided also. Advertisements in local newspapers would give the topics as well as the telephone number to call. Additional work to be developed included night classes for working women; special work with women members of small income groups; and consultant services, with a home demonstration club leader in charge, one afternoon a week.[20]

Special-interest group meetings for urban families were held in most of the larger towns where freezer locker plants were to be established or were already operating. Demonstrations on preparation of food for freezing were held, and freezer locker plants mailed thousands of Extension Service leaflets on the preparation of fruits, vegetables, and meats for the freezer locker.[21]

In Little Rock, classes in clothing and millinery were held for young women residing at the Young Women's Christian Association (YWCA). The county handicraft leader and an assistant met with nineteen young women to make Christmas toys.[22]

The Work with Younger Women

In nearly all counties, the young wives of veterans were invited to join home demonstration clubs or to form groups exclusively their own. One group was organized in Terry Village, the married student housing complex on the University of Arkansas campus in Fayetteville, following two open meetings on food preservation. A second group of wives, called the Dames Club, met with the home agent for demonstrations on kitchen efficiency and making educational toys.[23]

In Waldron, the agent worked with forty-one G.I. wives, demonstrating yeast bread making, furniture refinishing, clothing construction, and slip-cover and handicraft making.[24]

At the State College at Jonesboro, G.I. wives who lived in a trailer camp were provided four classes—in low-cost, nutritious meals and in child care.[25]

In Independence, Craighead, and Calhoun counties, as well as in many other counties, the agent met with young women and girls who were above the 4-H club age and had not studied home economics. Participants were interested in meal preparation, clothing work, personal improvement, and various homemaking skills.[26]

One long-time club in Monette, Craighead County, organized a daughter and daughter-in-law club for their married daughters and their sons' wives.[27]

Younger housewives and girls who had grown beyond the 4-H club age provided the greatest increase in membership. Former 4-H girls were welcomed as outstanding community and home demonstration club members.[28]

The war years had definitely had a devastating effect on the work. Despite the efforts mentioned above, it must be noted that in 1941, 64,863 Arkansas women were members of home demonstration clubs. In 1947, the number was 39,421. Would that number grow, remain the same, or decrease in the coming years?

The Program

During the second half of the decade, there was a trend toward broadening the base of interest in home demonstration clubs' programs and activities away from home economics and homemaking. In 1947, 1,505 clubs in seventy-seven counties held discussions on health; 1,057 clubs in sixty-nine counties discussed school problems; 1,042 clubs in sixty-one counties had programs on citizenship; and 1,446 clubs in seventy-five counties discussed safety.[29]

However, there were trends indicating interest in purely homemaking activities that seemed to balance out the program. In seventy-two counties, 36,283 families followed the Arkansas Food Supply Plan. An estimated value of $11,260,612 was placed on the food produced by these families at an average of $310 for each family.[30]

Connie Bonslagel made the following assessment of the outlook for 1948:

> Local and county home demonstration subject-matter leaders are again coming out to training meetings in sufficient numbers to make their efforts really important in spreading the influence of Extension teachings in the counties. The promise for home demonstration leadership in 1948 is good. The outlook for a program, practical but not hide-bound, to reach and influence a larger cross-section of the state's rural people is good.[31]

The Work in Sevier County, 1948

Our work in the National Archives at Fort Worth included copying records from six representative counties throughout the state. Sevier County was selected from the Southwestern corner. As it turned out, the state reports were filled with rich insights and examples from throughout Arkansas that precluded—for the most part—use of the county reports. However, a look at one county agent's report for 1948 seemed appropriate to provide an understanding of how the changes throughout preceding years—changes in rural life, Extension philosophy, club membership—had affected the work. Sevier County was chosen because—of the six representative counties—it had received the least mention in the narrative reports.

As she completed her annual narrative report during December of 1948, Miss Ovita Oakley, Sevier County home demonstration agent, had just finished her first twelve months in the county. She noted that interest remained about the same as during the last two or three years of the work. She commented, "Apparently, there is a general upheaval of people in every walk of life which affects home demonstration work as well as other phases of civic affairs."[32] In her county, 75 percent of home demonstration members were farm women, 20 percent were non-farm rural women, 5 percent were urban. Leadership training was difficult due to lack of transportation. Because the report followed a prescribed list of topics, the headings have been included as pertinent subjects are discussed.[33]

Factors and Methods: Oakley indicated that although the farm was of greatest importance to the family from the production standpoint, "the home is equally as important for the wellbeing of the family, so naturally this necessitates the two being considered as a unit in planning a successful program."[34]

Functions of Local People in Developing the Program of Work through County Agricultural Committee: Oakley provided the following explanation of the county structure of home demonstration work:

> The Executive Committee of the Home Demonstration Council assists in developing the program of work throughout the year by discussing and making decisions of importance; they give guidance to the Board of Directors, and to the home demonstration agent in developing the program. County wide problems receive consideration through the Board of Directors and the Executive Committee.

Subject matter leaders keep informed on their particular phase of the program through Extension literature, and in turn give this to women in their community. It is [each leader's] duty to present a part on the program when her subject comes up for study; to attend leader training meetings on her phase of the program and bring to the community the training which she received.

[The] farm and home organization leaders make possible the development of the county program. The majority of community programs and activities of any kind in the county are sponsored through members of these organizations. People in general have learned the value of getting results through organized groups and therefore make use of organizational practices in every possible way.[35]

Influence of the Family Food Supply Demonstrators: Oakley reported that it was difficult to get families to follow the program. Although people had slowly begun to show interest toward a systematic process for conserving the family food supply, a high percentage did not actually follow the recommended plan. She stated that the county goal was "to help people become more conscious of the world wide critical food situation, and thereby interest them in a better home supply, and that a 'pattern' or system is valuable in health of the family."[36]

Gardening: Oakley found, once again, a lack of planning and managing for a balanced food supply the year round. She reported that 250 women planted something different in their gardens during the year. For the most part, they were pleased with the results. Most of the reports from the homemakers said something like "the family liked the vegetable because it was different, or made for variety."[37]

Poultry: Teaching methods included demonstrations in culling hens for egg production, insect control, group discussions, and monthly "Poultry Reminders" from Extension poultry specialist, W. S. Pollard.

Home Grounds: The DeQueen Garden Clubs cooperated with the Horatio home demonstration clubs in building a roadside park, conducting a spring clean-up campaign, and attempting a city beautification project.

Food and Nutrition: The work included six discussions on planning balanced community meals. Two were for rural fellowship meetings with the Chamber of Commerce in Wright's Chapel and Beacon Hill. Some 300 people enjoyed the results demonstration!

Food Preservation: Oakley found that the problem in the county was the lack of understanding of the importance of quality products and good storage procedures.

Child Development and Family Life: Oakley considered this a minor phase of the program. However, the Union Home Demonstration Club chose this emphasis because there were numerous children in members' families. The result was a thorough study and an educational exhibit visited by 2,000 families at the county fair.

Clothing: This was another minor program for the year. Demonstrations included the following topics: newer methods of tailoring, lengthening dresses, selection of colors for different types of women, blind hemming, narrow hems, washing and blocking a woolen sweater.

Housing and Agricultural Engineering: Rural electrification, kitchen improvement, remodeling and planning, as a part of housing and agricultural engineering, were major phases of the county's program for the year. Oakley noted the following problem to be addressed in the county:

> One of the greatest problems in rural electrification is getting people to understand that there are a few things they need to understand before hiring an electrician to wire their house. Instead, they choose the cheapest man to do the job, and of course, get a "cheap job," which they realize when it's too late. Too few outlets and too few circuits, or too heavily loaded circuits, along with poor lighting are the greatest weaknesses. Families, in general, have not learned the importance of making a study and then a plan for their housing problems.[38]

She also reported on the following successful educational endeavor:

> Three educational meetings on "points to consider in wiring the farm and home" were held in the county through cooperation of W. J. R. Browder, Extension Specialist in Electrical Engineering, and officials of

Southwestern Gas and Electric Company. . .
A three day wiring school was held a few
weeks following, where eleven men studied
and developed the wiring of the Owen
Williamson farm and home. When this
job was completed "open house" was held
with Miss Elizabeth Williams, Extension Home
Management Specialist, W. J. R. Browder,
Extension Specialist in Electrical Engineering,
the county and home agents, and Southwestern
Gas and Electric Company officials giving
explanations to the visitors as to the whys and
wherefores of the lighting and wiring system.
One hundred fifty adults attended the open
house meeting.[39]

Home Management: Oakley noted that home
management was of minor importance in the year's
work—although rural electrification, improvement of
rural housing, and work simplification techniques were
vitally important but were included under another
heading. However, two demonstrations were mentioned
and provided the following delightful vignettes:

A discussion and demonstration has been given
to twelve home demonstration clubs on buffet
style service for community meals; the agent
planned with the Beacon Hill Club women on
how to arrange their food on the table for serving
at a rural acquaintance meeting of the DeQueen
Chamber of Commerce in their community. . . .
approximately three hundred women observed
the demonstrations and the majority of club

women have put this into practice when the club meets in their homes for pot luck lunch.

Advantages of washing dishes from right to left have been discussed in the majority of clubs and possibly one hundred women have been shown how they could cut down the number of steps taken by rearranging their kitchens and through using the right system of dishwashing.[40]

Home Industries: Although the topic was of minor emphasis, several demonstrations were put on in order to arouse interest. The goal was to make use of native materials where possible and to make them of value in the home or for marketing. Oakley included the following list of demonstrations:

Demonstrations include eighteen on pine needle work; nineteen on making hot dish mats from corn shucks and cardboard; two on stenciling of fabrics; three on reseating chairs with fiber rush; a finished stool was shown to nineteen clubs; twelve demonstrations were given on decorating stationery with ink spattering; two on Italian hemstitching; one on etching.[41]

Health: This was one of the major emphases in the county during 1948. Oakley noted that problems included late diagnosis of diseases, lack of good sanitation practices, and low finances with which many improvements could be made around the home. County goals were to develop health facilities and service for rural families through a group insurance plan and to decrease health hazards in the home. The following activities were reported:

> Health leaders from the different clubs have been active in the cancer drive, and in informing people about the county-wide cancer clinic – Union Club leader reported 22 dollars collected from their community for the drive.

> Leaders informed their neighbors of the county-wide tuberculosis clinic which was held for a week in the county during October. 2,884 people were x-rayed, compared to 1,200 last year. A flyer distributed within the county included the following statement: "Since there are quite a number of active TB cases in the town and county, and the fact that TB rates first in deaths between the ages of 15 – 44 of all diseases, it is very important that we, as citizens, do something about it."[42]

Special Activities: Oakley provided examples of community projects throughout the county and state, as follows:

> Several clubs did special community projects this year. Some of these are: cleaning community cemetery, wired community church and gave donation toward purchase of piano; two showers to families who were burned out – by the Williamson Club. Union Club sponsored a contest in mail box improvement in their community; Wright's Chapel Club gave a box of fruit and candy, and a box of clothing to a

boy in the State Hospital for Nervous Diseases. They also gave clothing to a needy boy in the community.

Fifteen clubs have given donations of from five to twenty dollars each toward a 4-H furnishing fund.

Sevier County has participated in a collection of canned products each year for the Arkansas Children's Home and Hospital. An average of approximately 150 quarts [is] collected for this purpose each year through home demonstration clubs.[43]

Fairs and Exhibits: The Sevier County Fair Association sponsored a fair in DeQueen on September 23, 24, and 25, 1948. Home demonstration clubs' educational booths provide insight into the women's interests during the year, as follows:

- Chapel Hill – We not only need Enough Light, but it must be the Right Kind of Light
- Wright's Chapel – Better Wiring should bring (1) Enough Outlets and (2) Enough Circuits to the home
- Beacon Hill – Thrifty Thrills with cotton bags
- Harmony – How Safe is Your Home?
- Union – Child Development Through Proper Play Equipment
- Wofford's Chapel – Use of Burlap in the Home
- Norwoodville – Furniture Made at Home for Little Cost

- Walnut Springs – We Live at Home
- Williamson – Seven Steps to Balanced Nutrition[44]

Community Activities and Recreation: We are indebted to Oakley for the following description of Sevier County women's fund raising activities for the 4-H Girls' House at Fayetteville. The activities were most likely emulated throughout Arkansas. The report follows:

> The outstanding project this year in the way of 4-H Fund activities has been the Sevier County Council project of raising three hundred dollars to furnish a room in the 4–H girls' cooperative house at the University of Arkansas. Fifteen home demonstration clubs have contributed from five to twenty dollars toward this fund. Two hundred twenty five dollars has been paid into the state chairman already. Clubs raised this money through community activities such as pie or cake walks, carnivals, serving food at auction sales, sponsoring Stamps Quartet or similar type entertainment, and sale of "community made" quilts.
>
> The council, as a whole, has a plan now in action to complete the project, which is to sell recipe booklets, giving a chance on winning fifty quarts of canned products. One county council project for this fund raising plan which netted thirty two dollars and fifty cents was the sale of various household arts, such as aprons, tea towels, curtains, hot dish holders, etc.[45]

County-Wide Activities: Oakley noted that the Sevier County Council of Home Demonstration Clubs was made up of twenty home demonstration clubs. Two of the clubs had become inactive during the year. However, members of each continued to take part in council work.

In the development of the yearbook, each month's program centered on one particular phase of the work; however, clubs were allowed from one to three choices for demonstration. Exceptions could be permitted when a club had a topic about which it felt strongly.

Outlook and Recommendations: Oakley completed her annual report—and most likely gave a deep sigh of relief—by expressing a need within the county organization for "better understanding and cooperation with the United States Department of Agriculture groups where possible."[46] She then listed other major concerns that should be emphasized in 1949. Her list has been placed in bulleted form, which would be a term with which she was not familiar:

- Rural electrification
- Rural housing
- Landscaping
- Health education
- Live-at-home program
- Development of the 4-H program

Ovita Oakley's report has given us a place to close our study of the very difficult 1940s. This one report, out of at least seventy-five, has provided a sampling of the work going on in the counties. In some ways, it reflected changes in philosophy—such as the cooperation with male agents and inclusion of big projects such as home electrification. In other ways, however, it was a reflection of the earliest reports on food preservation and clothing.[47]

Endnotes

[1] 1945 Annual Narrative Report, State HDA, RG 33, NARA/Fort Worth, Texas.
[2] Ibid.
[3] Ibid.
[4] Ibid.
[5] Ibid.
[6] Ibid.
[7] Ibid.
[8] Ibid.
[9] Ibid.
[10] Ibid.
[11] Ibid.
[12] Ibid.
[13] Ibid.
[14] Ibid.
[15] Ibid.
[16] Ibid.
[17] Ibid.
[18] 1947 Annual Narrative Report, State HDA, RG 33, NARA/Fort Worth, Texas.
[19] Ibid.

[20]Ibid.

[21]Ibid.

[22]Ibid.

[23]Ibid.

[24]Ibid.

[25]Ibid.

[26]Ibid.

[27]Ibid.

[28]Ibid.

[29]Ibid.

[30]Ibid.

[31]Ibid.

[32]1948 Annual Narrative Report, Sevier County HDA, RG 33, NARA/Fort Worth, Texas.

[33]Ibid.

[34]Ibid.

[35]Ibid.

[36]Ibid.

[37]Ibid.

[38]Ibid.

[39]Ibid.

[40]Ibid.

[41]Ibid.

[42]Ibid.

[43]Ibid.

[44]Ibid.

[45]Ibid.

[46]Ibid.

[47]Ibid.

The Picture Gallery

(All pictures in the gallery were found in Record Group 33, National Archives Southwestern Branch, Fort Worth, Texas.)

Working Hard

Demonstrating and Teaching

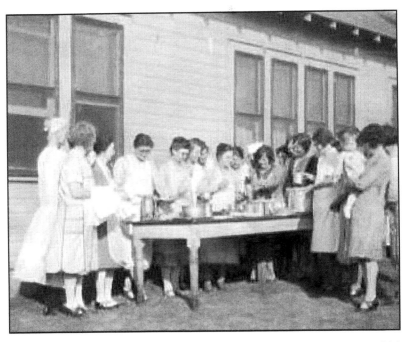

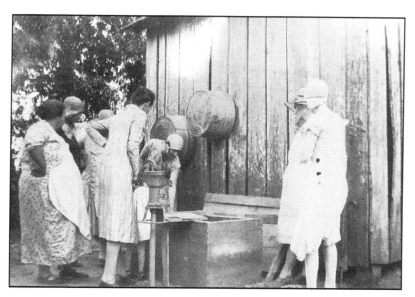

Working Together and Making Things

Taking Pride

Looking Pretty

OUR 4-H SCHOLARSHIP GIRL

MISS NELLIE BARNETTE

Having Fun

Displaying at Fairs and Camps

13

The 1950s: Time of Change for Women

Tragedy for Arkansas's Home Demonstration Work

In May 1950, Connie J. Bonslagel, strong leader of Arkansas's home demonstration work since before 1920, died as the result of an automobile accident. Her written words provided the basis for much of this history. Early on, it seemed she was most concerned about filling positions. She certainly had strong opinions and was not afraid to share them. She was particularly vocal about the devastating effect the anti-marriage policy had on her ability to retain agents. But as the 1930s and 1940s progressed, her words became more reflective; she obviously provided vital leadership that kept the home demonstration work going. In the *Good Housekeeping* article, Claudia Cranston made the following comment:

> Two factors have made the progress of the Arkansas Home Demonstration Clubs stand out above that of other states. These two factors are, first, their personal leader, Connie Bonslagel, State Home Demonstration Agent—and, second, their annual Arkansas Army Camp "Showcase."[1]

During one week's observation, Cranston recognized the strength of Arkansas's leader. Perhaps this book will keep Bonslagel's legacy alive for a little longer.

Mrs. Hazel C. Jordan was appointed state home demonstration agent on July 1, 1951. She had previously been the Northeast District agent. Jordan provided strong leadership for several decades also. She included the following minutes of the September 1951 meeting of the Arkansas Council of Home Demonstration Clubs in her first state report. The minutes provide an enlightening view of the organization—and of the early 1950s in Arkansas, as follows:

Program of Work for 1952 – Arkansas Council of Home Demonstration Clubs

Adopted at regular annual meeting of the Arkansas Council of Home Demonstration Clubs in September 1951:

It was decided: to increase state council dues from 25 cents to 50 cents per club.

Rural Arts:
The council passed a resolution suggesting:

1. That poetry and playwriting and other cultural arts have a place in our home demonstration programs and in community programs.

2. That we study the elementary fundamentals of the construction of poetry and playwriting, and make a sincere effort to better understand the beauty of these cultures.

3. That we make the rural arts something to live with, enjoy and share in our daily lives

in order that we may further develop our appreciation of the higher arts of living.

Citizenship – International Relations:
All clubs are being asked:

1. To observe United Nations Day.

2. To observe one minute of prayer for peace each day at 11:00 a.m. (national).

3. To strive to interest all women in assuming their responsibilities as informed and active citizens by:

a. Studying qualifications of candidates for government offices.

b. Keeping informed on legislation affecting the home.

c. Voting in all elections.

4. To study inflation, its causes, effects, and how to deal with it.

5. To reaffirm our concern for conservation of the natural resources of our state.

Education and Family Life

Education:
It was voted that we:

1. Ask home demonstration club members to discuss the importance of a college education with all groups of senior girls.

2. Study and discuss at home demonstration club meetings the wise use of tax money.

3. Supply more printed material on universal topics for discussion.

4. Do something to arouse our people as to what Democracy means.

5. Urge all members to cooperate with local and state organizations in solving school problems, placing emphasis on the need for developing local responsibility.

Family Life:
It was decided that the home demonstration clubs should:

1. Promote a forceful family life program.

2. Stress the importance of books as a source of information, inspiration, and recreation in a Democracy, and give recognition to club members who participate in a reading program.

3. Investigate the library resources in their communities, use the services now available, and further promote improvement in the services.

Health and Community Improvement
They agreed to:

1. Encourage health committees to further develop an educational program, including physical and mental health as affected by (1) nutrition, (2) housing, (3) early detection of disease, (4) facilities for health and medical care, (5) health insurance, and (6) immunization program.

2. Interest well-qualified women to train for nursing.

Legislation
They voted to:

1. Promote a legislative program to acquaint the members with both sides of any legislation (established or pending and whether it be local, state or federal) remaining clear of any pressure groups.

2. Name county chairmen for a legislative study.

Safety
It was decided:

1. To sponsor Pedestrian Safety in cooperation with the State Safety Council until October 30, 1952. This was to start with special emphasis during the month of November, 1951.

2. To promote safety in home demonstration clubs and to cooperate with existing state safety agencies.

4-H Club Work
It was agreed:

1. That each county council would appoint a 4-H chairman.

2. That all home demonstration club members would give emphasis to community 4-H clubs by:

(1) Furnishing adult leaders.

(2) Furnishing meeting places.

(3) Furnishing transportation.

(4) Providing recreation programs (games, refreshments).

(5) Giving demonstrations.

(6) Showing educational movies.

(7) Assisting with county camps, county banquets, and other activities.

Girls' 4-H Cooperative House
It was voted:

1. To pay on or before July 31 one dollar per club for the Girls' 4-H House bond retirement fund. This will go to the business manager, Mrs. K. M. Park, Route 2, Clarksville, Arkansas.

2. To use the same method as that for obtaining silverware for the Girls' 4-H Cooperative House to get plastic Lifetime dishes for the House. The same coupons are good for dishes.

3. To set aside $150 from the council fund to be used in landscaping of the Girls' 4-H Cooperative House and to buy hose.

4. To suggest that interested counties buy or make mattress pads for the 4-H House.[2]

Emphases in 1951

Hazel Jordan reported that the work emphasized the family as a unit. In addition, the Rural Community Improvement (R.C.I.) program had recently been launched in Arkansas to promote the working together of all organizations in a community for the betterment of each family—hence, the betterment of the community.[3]

The long-term planning program at the time indicated cooperation among the men's and women's programs. Under the program, farm people contributed materially in writing up objectives, voicing their opinions, and formulating long-term goals. Each neighborhood club or small community group elected a man and woman to represent them. Using the small groups' input, the representatives passed recommendations—through subcommittees—to the county agricultural planning committee. Both the community committees and the county agricultural planning committee were composed of men, women, boys, and girls—who found that much could be accomplished through working in small subcommittees.[4]

Jordan also indicated that interest on the part of urban women was continuing to grow. Little Rock, Pine Bluff, Helena, El Dorado, Hot Springs, Texarkana, Fort Smith, Conway, Russellville, West Memphis, and Jonesboro had organized urban women into special interest groups and had trained leaders to carry out the work.[5]

Membership Increase a Priority

In 1951, the membership goal was set at 52,000 for 1952. The following graphic provides a quick snapshot of membership trends from 1941 through 1951:

Home Demonstration Enrollment and Clubs from 1941 through 1951

Year	Enrollment	Number of Clubs
1941	64,863	2,224
1942	63,690	2,230
1943	57,532	2,074
1944	48,332	1,878
1945	40,608	1,702
1946	38,447	1,626
1947	37,421	1,643
1948	38,323	1,646
1949	39,050	1,624
1950	43,066	1,774
1951	45,947	1,781

Membership fell from its high of 64,863 in 1941 to a low of 37,421 in 1947. The discussion of the world war's effects on rural Arkansas provided numerous insights into the losses. By 1951, however, membership had gradually increased to 45,947.

Plans for membership increases included (1) a membership campaign throughout the state with training for membership leaders, (2) organization of additional special interest groups with more result demonstrations, (3) radio programs and publicity, and (4) emphasis on better training of officers and subject-matter leaders.[7] Although two of the planned activities included publicity, the remaining ones involved changing or improving the work itself to make it more appealing to women.

1956 Update of the Work

By 1956, the Extension Service had consolidated its various annual reports into the comprehensive Arkansas Agricultural Extension Service 1956 Combined Annual Report for Administrative, Supervisory, and Specialist Staff. The report had well over 150 pages and included agricultural as well as home demonstration work. Each subject-matter specialist provided insight into his or her work.

The Rural Economy

The agricultural economist, T. (second initial unclear) Atkinson, included a background for the overall work, as follows:

Many farmers feel that they are not fully sharing in the general prosperity prevailing in the United

States. Therefore, they want programs and ways of increasing the profitableness of farming. Often they do not know the causes of economic [unclear] and lack facts needed to evaluate existing programs and proposed new [ones].[8]

Atkinson noted that specific problems included rapid technological and social changes as well as supply-demand relationships.[9]

Home Furnishing

For her part, Sue Marshall, home furnishing specialist, noted that although farm incomes were lower, more families were planning carefully in order to build new homes or remodel old ones. Her work included such topics as trends in soft floor coverings, the well-furnished home, chair caning, furniture arrangement, and color selection for walls.[10]

Clothing

The clothing specialist, whose name was not readable, commented that the program's objective was to "train leaders to plan, select, make, or purchase harmonious and attractive wardrobes for each member"[11] and to help members get the most out of their sewing machines.[12]

Foods and Nutrition

The foods and nutrition specialist included the following trends, which for the most part had much more to do with women than with foods:

- Food expenditures were up considerably (although the percentages were not readable).

- Families were eating more meals away from home as well as more ready-processed foods.
- Twenty-eight percent of married women were employed outside the home. (The numerals were difficult to read and may not be reliable.)
- These homemakers had less time to prepare meals and needed information on how to "select, prepare, and serve food attractively with a minimum amount of time and effort."[13]
- Homemakers needed more knowledge of nutrition to make wise choices in buying, conserving, and planning well-balanced meals.
- Interest had shifted from preparation of individual food to planning and preparing meals.
- Homemakers were asking for more help for entertaining and for special occasions.

As a result of the above trends, the nutrition and foods work focused on "jiffy meals,"[14] meals for busy days, and simple, nutritious, and attractive holiday meals. The specialist summarized her concerns and how to meet the program's goals, as follows:

> Much of the work in building better food habits is related to the actual preparation of the food. The food value of the particular food, how to save the food value, how the food fits into the meal, and what to serve with it are [parts] of the leader training meetings in food preparation.[15]

Health Education

The health education specialist listed the numerous health concerns for rural people throughout the state, as follows:

- Lack of knowledge concerning the causal relationship of unsanitary conditions to disease. Specific problems included lack of garbage disposal, rats and insects, weeds and stagnant water, and inadequate window and door screening.
- Poor eating habits and other personal habits.
- Failure to recognize early signs of disease.
- Poor immunization practices, lack of exercise, and insufficient recreation.
- Self-prescribed diagnostic remedies.
- Lack of family physicians and inadequate health insurance plans.
- Inability of lower income families to pay for medical care.
- Lack of knowledge about existing health facilities and services.
- Lack of know-how to organize together to solve a community health problem even if it is recognized.[16]

The specialist seemed surprisingly optimistic as she noted the following successes:

Communities are getting together to solve community health problems. Parents are learning the importance of having a family physician and dentist and consulting them yearly. Mental health, heart disease, [unreadable], and health insurance are becoming recognized as important factors in a happy home life.[17]

She ended her report with the following example of "[a] typical rural county of about 6,000 population":

Seven hundred seventy-four [numerals difficult to read] people went for chest x-rays in two days. Over 100 club women had a physical examination after discussing the importance of this medical procedure in their clubs. In this same county six communities worked on an [animal] disease control program. The county agent, working with the local veterinarian, set up a schedule for vaccinating dogs against this disease. A total of 900 dogs were immunized.[18]

Family Life

The family life specialist listed objectives to assist families, as follows: (1) to gain an appreciation of the social influences of the family and community; (2) to accept responsibility for building a better world; (3) to weigh values in family living in order to emphasize the factors which point to happiness, self-confidence, and desirable adjustment for family members; and (4) to recognize adjustment problems and learn effective ways of meeting them.[19]

To meet the above objectives, the specialist provided the following topics for study and discussion:

- Affection, the Balance Wheel of Family Living
- Arkansas Family Reading Program
- Build Your Personality
- Discussion Techniques
- Family Fun
- Is Your Child Ready for School?
- Ladder of Love
- Parent-Teen Relations
- Play in the Lives of Young Children
- Stepping Stones to Happy Family Living
- Your Manners are Showing[20]

Many of the above topics may be traced to the emphases put in place in the 1930s. Each had been added as the work changed its focus from physical matters to emphasis on the emotional and social needs of rural families.

Overall, the study of home demonstration programs has provided a perhaps unprecedented look at rural Arkansas women and families over a forty-five year period. Some of the programs had been in place for the entire time, although for the most part the emphases had changed. Others were put in place during the 1930s as the focus shifted to the farm family as a unit. It may be necessary to re-read each chapter in order to comprehend the nuanced changes to the face of home demonstration work and the ways in which they reflected the changing lives of Arkansas's rural women.

Endnotes

[1]Claudia Cranston, "Learn and Live" in *Good Housekeeping* magazine, Volume No. 108, No. 4, April 1939. Retrieved from the Cornell University online Home Economics Archive: Research, Tradition, History, on February 23, 2012. (http://hearth.library.cornell.edu/cgi/t/text/pageviewer-idx?c=hearth;cc=hearth;q1=Claudia%20Cranston;rgn=full%20text;didno=6417403_1409_004;view=image;seq=203;node=6417403_1409_004%3A5.57;page=root;size=s;frm=frameset)

[2]1951 Annual Narrative Report, State HDA, RG 33, NARA/Fort Worth, Texas.

[3]Ibid.

[4]Ibid.

[5]Ibid.

[6]1941 and 1951 Annual Narrative Reports, State HDA, RG 33, NARA/Fort Worth, Texas.

[7]1951 Annual Narrative Report, State HDA, RG 33, NARA/Fort Worth, Texas.

[8]1956 Combined Annual Report, State Extension Service, RG 33, NARA/Fort Worth, Texas.

[9]Ibid.

[10]Ibid.

[11]Ibid.

[12]Ibid.

[13]Ibid.

[14]Ibid.

[15]Ibid.

[16]Ibid.

[17]Ibid.

[18]Ibid.

[19]Ibid.

[20]Ibid.

14

The 1960s: Time of Social Change

The Economic and Social Backdrop

The following section from the 1964 combined annual report for the Arkansas Agricultural Extension Service provides a telling backdrop for the work:

Arkansas is changing rapidly in its economic and social situation. The technological revolution has brought about many changes in modern agriculture. People in agricultural research, education, and industry have joined with farmers to bring their total capacity to bear on problems of food and fiber production, processing, and distribution. The result is ever-increasing amounts of food and [unreadable] for a growing population at decreasing costs per unit of output.

Considering income progress of the southern states from 1940-59, with the U. S. average income index being 100, it is noted that Arkansas is 61 [difficult to read] with the highest southern state being 91.4 and the lowest 53.6. This is a real challenge to the leadership in furthering economic development and social improvement in order to more favorably compare with other sections of the nation.

With the decreasing number of farms and the consolidation of land into larger units – many of which went under management type operations – rural people began leaving the farms. Many remained in rural areas but worked in the towns and cities nearby. Rural life became more complex, it became interwoven in the total society of the area, county and state. In fact, in a rural state like Arkansas the problems of one segment of the society, rural or other, cannot be met without their having some effect on both groups. These very changes make it necessary that Extension redesign its program and direct its efforts to meeting the challenges brought about by this different concept and approach to rural and urban progress.

Family living is a very important aspect of area and county development. Social improvement includes such things as health, housing, clothing, foods, recreation, fine arts, welfare, and education. Within Extension are well trained home economists who are in a position to give leadership to all phases of social improvement. Therefore, Extension is broadening its program in home economics to meet the needs of all the people in the county, not just home demonstration club and 4-H club members. The many problems of the consumers are being recognized in this educational program.[1]

Membership Figures

Membership numbers, which fell dramatically during and after World War II, simply never recovered. By 1965, the membership was less than half the total at the organization's height in 1941: 64,863 members in 2,224 clubs.

Year	Enrollment	Number of Clubs
1952	43,881	1,730
1953	41,866	1,660
1954	39,315	1,622
1955	39,464	1,663
1956	35,249	1,523
1957	34,527	1,490
1958	32,726	1,433
1959	31,130	1,398
1960	30,849	1,397
1961	30,801	1,404
1962	30,983	1,425
1963	30,331	1,382
1964	29,457	1,370
1965	29,161	1,362[2]

This study has shown several intertwining reasons for the losses. Some of the likely factors were women's working outside the home, decreasing numbers of farms, and rural people's commuting to jobs in the towns.

Home Economics Work

Under the subheading "Human Relations," the objective was to provide education for effective human relationships and to help families know and understand the principles of human development and personal adjustment. Accomplishments included the following:

- In Phillips County 216 families with newborn babies received the "Newborn Baby Speaks" series.
- Nine mothers of twenty-four children participated in the Child Development Short Course.
- Scott County clubs studied the causes and effects of the school drop-out situation.
- Yell County women studied "What Every Child Requires."[3]

Home management and family economics work were important. Under "Family Economics," the objective was for families to achieve higher levels of living in accordance with their needs, wants, and goals. The means to attaining these achievements would include the ability to make wise decisions in arranging their time, energy, and financial resources.[4]

Do you recall the dilemma for families when the sewing machine was invented in the mid-1800s? The discussion from a previous chapter is revisited below:

Elias Howe's patent for a sewing machine in 1846 became the prototype for many later models. However, sewing machines simply cost too much for individual families or seamstresses to purchase alone. Even the cast-iron stove cost very little compared to a sewing machine, with its precise moving parts. *Godey's Lady's Book* suggested that ten families should go together to purchase one machine. Isaac Singer's partner, Edward Clark, however, came up with a solution that would sell ten machines to ten families instead: the installment plan, with its five dollars down and high interest rates.[5]

By the 1960s, Clark's "solution" had taken hold. Research studies of the time indicated that more than 50 percent of families used credit in some form or other. Five counties had lessons on "Wise Use of Credit." The discussions included "Why Use Credit," "Cost of Credit," "How to Figure Interest Rates," and "How to Shop for Credit."

Although work in foods and nutrition, home furnishings, arts and crafts, health, and clothing continued, the emphasis in each subject obviously was tailored to the overall goals of the time. Some examples follow:

> Foods and Nutrition work in 29 counties [included] lessons on "More for the Food Dollar" as a part of the year's program in family economics.[6]

> Two new circulars on Yeast Breads and Food for Tots were written and the circular on Canning Fruits and Vegetables was revised. Leaflets on Time Saving Meals and Homemade Mixes were also revised.[7]

> The main goal [of the Arts and Crafts program] was to develop individual, family and community relationships by the creation of leisure time work.[8]

> Arts and crafts played a part in family economics during the year. Four quilting short courses were held with 47 attending.[9]

"Family Well-Being through Home Improvement" [emphasized] the importance of furniture and decorating the home in relation to the needs and interests of the individual family.[10]

Forty-five counties received special assistance in house planning or remodeling.[11]

Work with low-income urban as well as rural families was a trend in the 1960s in accordance with the earlier statement that "Extension is broadening its program in home economics to meet the needs of all the people in the county, not just home demonstration club and 4-H club members. The many problems of the consumers are being recognized in this educational program."[12] Examples of this work include the following:

In Pulaski County, the home demonstration agent held a nutrition short course in a low rent housing project. [Topics included] food for the family, meal planning, food plans, and buying food.[13]

After having received Extension training a clothing leader in Ashley County made the following contribution in working with low income families: She worked in cooperation with one of the local fabric shops and conducted a short course with 22 homemakers; they did pattern selection and fitting patterns [among other activities].[14]

The foods work seemed to mirror most accurately the 1960s woman's situation. With women working outside the home, the emphasis on time-saving meals and homemade mixes obviously reflected this trend. The lesson on getting the most for the food dollar was certainly appropriate for the time. Leaflets on yeast breads and canning were somewhat surprising but encouraging as proof that the heritage skills were still considered important.

With the overall backdrop set out at the beginning of the chapter, surely there was distress on the part of those who worked with Arkansas's people. Instead of getting better, Arkansans' plight seemed to be to stay near the economic bottom among Southern states. The work continued, however, in the quest to provide better lives for rural and urban families in spite of the overwhelming realities.

The Work with African American Women— Looking Back

As we come in our study to 1966—the year that the black and white work merged and the name was changed from home demonstration to Extension Homemakers work—it is appropriate to reflect on the separate but equally important program by and with black women from the very beginning of the organization. For example, the amazing work of early African American agents Lugenia B. Christmas, Carrie W. Moore, Cora Lee Coleman, and Annie L. Smith was spotlighted during the Great Flood of 1927.

However, the agents' normal, everyday work with black tenant wives in the Arkansas Delta and in other counties during those early years provided much more than enhancements and uplift for the women—although it accomplished those things also. Do you recall Negro District agent Mary L. Ray's wonderfully detailed account of the difficulties of just setting up a bread-making lesson? And there is no doubt their work in gardening and canning saved lives—just as the white agents' work did—as people in the Delta and other areas of Arkansas were starving in the aftermath of the floods and during the debilitating droughts of the early 1930s.

During 1936, Miss Cassa Hamilton, Negro District home demonstration agent, and Connie Bonslagel, state agent, presented the idea of a "State Home Demonstration Council" for Negro club members. At a Farmers' Conference at Arkansas Agricultural, Mechanical and Normal College, the organization was formed. A dynamic group of officers was elected. Each of the women had experience with the county council form of program planning and projecting. Under the leadership of Mrs. Cassa (Hamilton) Lawlah, Mrs. Fannie Mae Boone, Mrs. Ella P. Neely, and Mrs. Marguerite P. Williams, and the dedicated officers, the organization "helped homemakers develop a better understanding of the wise use of their resources – time, money, and energy."[15]

In a county-by-county history prepared by the Arkansas Extension Homemakers Council during the late 1970s, work by and with black women was highlighted in twenty-two counties. Although other counties had Negro work over the years, the twenty-two counties may have been ones that had a functioning county council in 1965 when the separate work ended.

Two Unique Perspectives

Throughout their history, black women flourished as they accepted leadership roles in their clubs and county organizations. Although we salute the early agents, members, and lay leaders, our focus turns now to two of our own women who have willingly shared their stories for this history.

Mrs. Jettie Williams, Little River County Member

Mrs. Jettie Williams of Little River County provided a wonderful perspective on the news that the black and white clubs would be combined. Williams recalled that in 1963, her local club was encouraged to come to the district meeting at Hot Springs. There the members were told the black and white clubs would merge and the organization's name would be changed to Arkansas Extension Homemakers. She noted that it was especially good for the black members since it had become difficult to retain a black agent in the county.[16]

Williams and fellow members were excited with the change since both groups of women could come together to share their skills. She noted that the local black and white homemakers' clubs had always been friends and would share news of their clubs as well as recipes and craft ideas. When she and the other members returned home from the meeting, "we called all our members and told them of the great things that we had witnessed at the meeting. We told them that we needed to add and bring our children as 4-H club members."[17]

Mrs. Azzie McGehee, Desha County Member

Mrs. Azzie McGehee is another long-time member who personally experienced the changes that occurred in 1966.

Records indicate that in 1951, there were twenty-nine Negro home demonstration agents working with some 13,700 members. Each of the twenty-nine counties had a Negro home demonstration council organized to further the work of the community clubs.

In 1950, the young and single Azzie O'Neal began working as the secretary in McGehee (Desha County) for Mrs. Lois B. Perkins, Negro home demonstration agent, and Mr. Charlie Reed, Negro agricultural agent. After uniting in marriage in 1950 to Alonzo McGehee, Jr., and relocating to the Almstead community, Azzie O'Neal McGehee joined the Almstead Home Demonstration Club in 1951. In 1952, she resigned from her secretarial position with the Extension Service because she had small children at home but continued to be a member of the club.

In 1955, she moved from the country to McGehee, where there were no black clubs for her to join. So, instead, she organized a 4-H club and led the young people for many years. In 1955, she also returned to work for the Extension Service as secretary to Mrs. Perkins, Negro home demonstration agent, and Mr. R. T. Webb, Negro agricultural agent. She worked there until December of 1965. In January of 1966, she began working for the U. S. Agricultural Stabilization and Conservation Service and worked for that federal agency for twenty years.

Mrs. Azzie McGehee is a lovely woman who does not mind telling that she is eighty-one years old. She is a member of the McGehee Extension Homemakers Club and continues to lead 4-H young people.

Extension Homemakers and 4-H work seem to have been her "cup of tea." Not one to sit still, she enjoys attending meetings, learning new skills, entering exhibits in the county fair, and meeting new people. She was secretary of her club for eighteen years. Now, she is treasurer and photographer. Through her Extension Homemakers Club, she has chaired fundraisers for scholarships for graduating 4-H seniors and has participated in adopting three residents of the local nursing home who have no families. She remains the 4-H club leader, where she and the young people provided New Year's parties at the local nursing home. They brought bags of bananas, grapes, and candy, and sang for the residents.

Thinking back to her brief home demonstration days in the early 1950s, she joined the Almstead Club to make yeast breads, can vegetables, do arts and crafts, sew and refurbish, and make home furnishings. Her first remembrance was of learning how to can fruits and vegetables in a pressure cooker, using the right size jars and jar tops. Her least favorite activity—can we blame her?—was building a chicken house. She had to dig the holes with a post-hole digger and then finish the job using saw, hammer, and axe.[18]

Endnotes

[1] 1964 Annual Narrative Report, State HDA, RG 33, NARA/Fort Worth, Texas.

[2] Arkansas Extension Homemakers Council, *History of Home Demonstration Work, 1914 –1965; Extension Homemakers Work 1966 – 1977 in Arkansas* (no city/no date), yearly figures scattered throughout the report.

[3] 1964 Annual Narrative Report, State HDA, RG 33, NARA/Fort Worth, Texas.

[4] Ibid.

[5] Strasser, 138–139.

[6] 1964 Annual Narrative Report, State HDA, RG 33, NARA/Fort Worth, Texas.

[7] Ibid.

[8] Ibid.

[9] Ibid.

[10] Ibid.

[11] Ibid.

[12] Ibid.

[13] Ibid.

[14] Ibid.

[15] Arkansas Extension Homemakers Council, *History of Home Demonstration Work, 1914 –1965; Extension Homemakers Work 1966 – 1977 in Arkansas* (no city/no date), 311.

[16] Jettie Williams, "The African American Experience of Arkansas Extension Homemakers Club Southwest, Yesterday Today and Tomorrow, Centennial Celebration, 1912 – 2012," a paper forwarded to Betty Oliver of the Cooperative Extension Service and then to Elizabeth Hill in March 2012. Copy of utilized pages retained by author.

[17] Ibid.

[18] Telephone interviews with Mrs. Azzie McGehee by Elizabeth Hill during mid-April 2012, based on oral history of Mrs. McGehee prepared as a part of the state-wide oral history project through the Pryor Center for Oral History at the University of Arkansas. Although there was no record retained of the conversation, the written essay was shared by email.

15

Long-Term Commitments to Children and Youth

Although the one hundred-year history of home demonstration/Extension Homemakers work has been told chronologically, sometimes decade by decade, that style was not appropriate for two important long-term commitments. Each of the following stories is told from its beginning. The first one has an ending date; the second is continuing.

Girls' 4-H Cooperative House at the University of Arkansas

Most Extension Homemaker members seem to know about the Girls' 4-H House on the University of Arkansas campus that was built in about 1951. In 1938, the Arkansas Council of Home Demonstration Clubs Board of Directors recommended to the Council that they undertake to build a house for forty or more 4-H girls at the University comparable to the sorority houses. The Council voted to adopt this as a state-wide activity. Apparently, the fundraising started immediately—with a campaign to raise $1.00 per club member, as is shown below:[1]

> [From Miller County, 1938:] The home demonstration club members have joined in a state-wide campaign of selling product maps of

Arkansas to obtain funds for the establishment of a home for 4-H Club Girls who wish to attend the College of Agriculture in Fayetteville. The new home for 4-H girls will be in Fayetteville located near the University campus. A free trip was offered to Camp Joe T. Robinson, women's state camp, to the one who sold the most maps. . . . Ninety-nine product maps have been sold to date at 58 cents each being $57.42 and $10.00 was donated by the Fouke Home Demonstration Club.[2]

[From Nevada County, 1938:] The council expects to raise $100 for the scholarship [to help a boy or girl with expenses at the University] and $100 for the native stone house at Fayetteville for former 4-H girls by getting out a cook book to sell at 35 cents a copy.[3]

During World War II, home demonstration clubs worked to encourage their members, neighborhood clubs, and county councils to buy bonds. They sponsored pie suppers, white elephant sales, and auctions. Since the purpose of buying the bonds was "to help the boys get home," the women were comfortable inviting entire communities to participate. The bond purchases had two purposes: to help to win the war, and to save cash to be applied to help finance the 4-H Girls' House at Fayetteville. In 1945, 571 clubs in sixty-eight counties participated. County councils in all seventy-five counties had invested over $43,000 in bonds for this purpose since the war began on December 7, 1941.[4]

By 1947, $53,659.49 had been paid into the 4-H House fund. A double lot had been purchased. Eight counties had contributed $300 each above the building fund to furnish one of the rooms, and several other counties had made smaller contributions toward furnishings.[5]

In 1950, the cornerstone was laid, and the house was dedicated to the following four ideals: service, loyalty, cooperation, and understanding. Tribute was paid to the late Connie Bonslagel, who took a leading part in the drive to obtain funds. (A portrait of Bonslagel that hung in the house is now on display at the Arkansas 4-H Center in Ferndale. The portrait was painted by Adrian Brewer of Little Rock and presented by Miss Annie Golightly of Memphis.)[6]

Architect E. Chester Nelson designed the building, which included living space, a game room, twenty bedrooms, a glassed-in porch, and a music room. The massive stone house, built on a corner lot one block from campus, was completed and dedicated in April and May, 1951, respectively. It provided housing for forty women students, who paid $35 per month in cash or commodities from their families' farms.[7]

In its history of the work through 1977—which was something of an outline in two-year increments—the AEHC provided only cryptic comments about the house throughout ensuing years. In 1956/1957, the history noted that the last mortgage on the house was burned. Expenditures amounted to $162,261: $3,105 for lots, $147,766 for construction, $11,300 for furnishings, and $500 for landscaping. Extensive repairs began in 1956.

In 1976/1977, the annotation was simple and straightforward: "Board of Directors of Arkansas Extension Homemakers Council voted to sell the 4-H House."[8]

The house was sold to a fraternity in 1977 and was later used as a residence for other groups. It was torn down in 2003 to make way for the Garland Center. According to an article in the *Arkansas Democrat-Gazette* in 2003, the demolition of the building was a traumatic experience for preservationists and others who valued the property for its history and beauty. Workers salvaged the cornerstone, several mahogany doors, and light fixtures. Eric Hand, the writer, continued:

> Gary Scarborough owned the property from 1996 to 2001 before selling it to Chi Alpha, who sold it to the university last year.
>
> He said he loved it for its rock façade and its unique strength, derived from concrete floors and fire walls on each floor, including the attic. He said he has been told the building was the strongest in Fayetteville and was once used as a bomb shelter.
>
> "In the short period of time I owned it, I had so many women come up to me and say, "I wouldn't have come to college if it wasn't for that building," he said.[9]

Shirley Mathey provided a poignant look at her experiences as a student and resident of the house. She had been a 4-H'er and attended camps at Fayetteville.

She grew up knowing that she could attend the University of Arkansas. When she arrived as a freshman in 1952, she spent the first day cleaning her room just to get over her homesick feeling. Her first roommate was a girl from Monette, and the second one was Barbara Keil, with whom she had lots of fun. Keil was tall, and Mathey was short, but they were good together. She remembered the shared responsibilities, which she called heavy duty but not unreasonable. She particularly remembered serving breakfast. [This was a cooperative house in which the residents shared the housekeeping duties.]

Having lived in a farm home, Mathey felt like she was now living in a palace! She recalled having afternoon coffee in the living room, using tiny cups and saucers, and having the music room, where she and Keil played and sang. Even the washer and dryer in the basement were things she did not have at home. Oh yes, they had a special place to store their luggage!

The meals were wonderful, and everyone ate together at the same time each evening. The head person would fill the plates and pass them to each one. The girls learned new ways to arrange and present food.

The years passed quickly, and she graduated in 1956. She was a home economics teacher for many years. She enjoyed the University of Arkansas, but her most important contacts were in the 4-H House. A house-mate, Virginia Tucker Rowland, started a newsletter to former residents and kept it going until about 2003. Although Rowland died from a fall on April 4, 2012, her legacy will continue this summer as former 4-H House girls meet for their annual reunion. This year they will all go to the Crystal Bridges Museum together.

Mathey closed by saying they are all getting older and cherish their togetherness. They were not aware of the house's destruction until after the fact. Of course, they were saddened by the loss.[10]

In just a few paragraphs, Mathey was able to convey her feelings for the house and to confirm home demonstration women's committed efforts to provide the lovely residence for 4-H girls as they studied at the University.

A Commitment to Children's Hospital

According to a wonderful, vignette-filled history of Arkansas Children's Hospital by Steven G. Hanley, the hospital's early years were characterized by a hand-to-mouth existence. Ruth Beall, who became superintendent in 1934 of what was then the Arkansas Children's Home and Hospital, had been the administrator for the Benton County Tuberculosis Association before coming to Little Rock. Through this organization, she had worked with the home demonstration clubs in Benton County and knew that the clubs, under direction of the county agent, taught health, diet, and homemaking skills to rural Arkansas women. Here, she reasoned, was "a vast reservoir of rural women who had little cash but abundant goodwill."[11] She appealed to the statewide organization; soon "jars of home-canned fruits, vegetables, jams and jellies were pouring in from across the state."[12] The women also sent homemade pajamas, layettes, and other items for the children. Thus began a precious relationship that has lasted for seventy-eight years.[13]

By 1940, the State Council of Home Demonstration Clubs had sponsored for several years the program of contributions to Arkansas Children's Home and Hospital. Thousands of jars of canned goods, clothing, bedding, towels, and toys were presented to the institution each year by the rural women, sometimes as Thanksgiving and Christmas boxes. County councils were responsible for the program in the various counties. Excerpts from the 1940 state report follow:[14]

> When this program was first adopted, contributions were mostly in the form of canned foods but it has now grown or been extended to include other types of food and articles for household use. Included in the gift from 35 clubs in Benton County, one of the heaviest contributors, this year were the following items: 3 quilts, 5 sheets, 13 pair pillow cases, 32 towels, 4 bushels sweet potatoes, 1,045 quarts canned fruit and vegetables, tea towels, bandage material, reading matter, pictures, garments.[15]

When asked just what, if anything, the gifts from the home demonstration clubs meant to the maintenance of the hospital, Beall answered, with tears in her eyes, "Had we not had this help back in 1934, I honestly think we would have had to close."[16] Although 1934 will be remembered as one of the devastating drought years, the women shared what they had.[17]

In 1945, the Office of Home Food Supply of the U. S. Department of Agriculture, through its Food Pool Plan, sent out a call for organizations—including Arkansas's home demonstration clubs—to can additional produce. Organizations were given two choices: can for shipment overseas or can and contribute an additional 10 percent to a favorite charity. Over the years, Beall had told the council how much the gifts had meant to the institution. She added that the hospital's high nutrition standards would be difficult to maintain without these gifts. Therefore, the committee voted to ask all home demonstration clubs to increase by 10 percent their regular gifts for 1945. The remainder of the report follows:[18]

As a result, the Children's Home and Hospital has the largest supply of canned food ever stored there. The executive committee, working with the supervisor of the hospital, found that the most needed foods were tomatoes, green beans, and beef or chicken soup stock, since many meals were served to sick children. This gave the women a better idea as to the varieties of products to contribute to the collection. The supervisor of the hospital reported that nothing but the very highest quality products were sent in and that they had received large quantities of soup stock and tomatoes. This year 1,072 clubs in 71 counties contributed to this piece of work. A few counties that had not contributed before cooperated in the donations this year.[19]

In 1947, 1,033 clubs in seventy counties presented the institution with 13,902 quarts of canned foods, 1,544 cotton goods articles, and 911 home-made toys and other articles.[20]

In a 1968 ceremony, Arkansas Children's Hospital dedicated the hospital's Clothing Room with a permanent plaque that read, "Dedicated to Arkansas Extension Homemakers Council."[21] In responding to the dedication, Mrs. H. E. Jameson, president of the state council, made the following comment:

> There were many difficult days in our organization, and we know some problems must have faced you here in the hospital, but some of the youngsters who came to the back entrance to help us unload our cars of the food, bedding, toys and clothes could not have helped us had you and your staff here not been able to help them.[22]

For her response to the dedicatory remarks, Hazel Jordan, whose title at the time was State Leader, Extension Home Economics, noted that Ruth Beall knew practically every home demonstration agent in the state because food was so important at the time. She reminded the audience that in most counties, the home economists and their councils asked each homemaker to can one extra jar for the hospital.[23]

An Update from Children's Hospital

Arkansas Children's Hospital is celebrating its centennial anniversary this year just as Extension Homemakers are doing! What a lovely thing it is to know that these two wonderful organizations were begun in the same year.

In March 2012, the following article was included in *Vital Signs*, the hospital's employee newsletter. It is printed below by permission:

Vital Signs – Volunteer Corner
March 2012

"Our most precious commodity at Children's Hospital has always been the good will of the people of our state." – ACH Hospital Administrator Leland McGinnis
(from Steve Hanley's book,
A Place of Care, Love and Hope: A History of Arkansas Children's Hospital)

As Arkansas Children's Hospital reflects on our last 100 years, we all know that volunteers and community supporters have played an integral role here at Arkansas Children's Hospital. In reading through Steve Hanley's book about the history of the hospital, it becomes clear that volunteers, community supporters and employees have willingly aided the Arkansas Children's Home and Hospital throughout our 100 years.

From the all-volunteer medical staff that was named in 1925 to the groups that donated canned food, household items, and free laundry service in 1928, the people of Arkansas have always believed in Arkansas Children's Hospital. The ACH history book reminisces days when volunteers were organized to investigate the homes of people who wanted to adopt children and the hard times when all employees were dismissed (except the cook and laundress) and a group of volunteers cared for the children so the hospital could remain open.

In the 1930s, Ruth Olive Beall appealed to the Home Demonstration Clubs (now known as Extension Homemakers Clubs) to provide jars of home-canned fruits, vegetables, jams and jellies. By the early 1940s, these groups had asked the hospital for a list of needs and decided to make clothing, bedding and stuffed toys for the children as well. These groups still support the hospital today by making pillows, blankets, hats and other items for our patients.

It is overwhelming to see the dedication and support given to us by our ACH volunteers. To give selflessly of their time to help in any way – whether it be rocking a baby, playing a game with a child or even helping in an office or the gift shop – ACH volunteers have and will continue to make a difference here at Arkansas Children's Hospital. Thank you, ACH volunteers, for all you have done and will continue to do![24]

Congratulations to Arkansas Children's Hospital for its one hundred years of providing loving care for Arkansas's children.

Endnotes

[1]1947 Annual Narrative Report, State HDA, RG 33, NARA/Fort Worth, Texas.

[2]1938 Annual Narrative Report, State HDA, RG 33, NARA/Fort Worth, Texas.

[3]Ibid.

[4]1945 Annual Narrative Report, State HDA, RG 33, NARA/Fort Worth, Texas.

[5]1947 Annual Narrative Report, State HDA, RG 33, NARA/Fort Worth, Texas.

[6]Arkansas Extension Homemakers Council, *History of Home Demonstration Work, 1914 –1965; Extension Homemaker Work 1966 – 1977 in Arkansas* (no city/no date), 15-16.

[7]Ibid.

Arkansas Alumni Association postal-size card, "4-H House," dated 2011.

[8]AEHC History, 22.

[9]Eric Hand, "4-H House's Time Runs Out," in *Arkansas Democrat-Gazette,* May 18, 2003. (Typed, attributed copy of article received from Shirley Mathey via email forwarded by Betty Oliver, Cooperative Extension Service, to Elizabeth Hill on February 29, 2012.)

Arkansas Alumni Association postal-size card, "4-H House," dated 2011.

[10] Email from Shirley Mathey to Elizabeth Hill, received April 18, 2012.

[11]Steven G. Hanley, *A Place of Care, Love, and Hope: A History of Arkansas Children's Hospital,* Second Edition. (No city: no publisher, 2007), 39.

[12]Ibid.

[13]Ibid.

[14]1940 Annual Narrative Report, State HDA, RG 33, NARA/Fort Worth, Texas.

[15]Ibid.

[16]Ibid. 1940 state.

[17]Ibid. 1940 state

[18]1945 Annual Narrative Report, State HDA, RG 33, NARA/Fort Worth, Texas.

[19]Ibid.

[20]1947 Annual Narrative Report, State HDA, RG 33, NARA/Fort Worth, Texas.

[21]Undated program from Arkansas Children's Hospital dedication ceremony with scripts for Jameson and Jordan attached. Received from Betty Oliver, Cooperative Extension Service, April 2012.

[22]Ibid.

[23]Ibid.

[24]Melissa B. Wolfe, "Volunteer Corner" in *Vital Signs*, Arkansas Children's Hospital's employee newsletter, March 2012. Forwarded by email from Melissa Wolfe to Elizabeth Hill on April 2, 2012. Permission to print in full granted on April 4, 2012.

16

The Rest of the Story

June 2011 Interviews

Before the June 2011 state AEHC meeting in Hot Springs, every county was invited to provide names of individuals—members or agents—to be interviewed about their experiences in home demonstration/Extension Homemakers work. Interviewees were not prepared in advance; they were surprised when their names were called during a luncheon meeting. A schedule of interviews was set up, and individuals reported to be interviewed—in groups of three or four.

Despite the lack of preparation time, each person who was interviewed added to the overall understanding of the work. Participants were asked about how and why they joined the organization, what they found when they got there, how the work has changed over the years, and their opinions about those changes.

The following thirty-six individuals provided an unexpectedly candid and concise analysis of Extension Homemakers work during the past forty or so years:

Peggy Barnett, Garland
Krista Brimer, White
Judy Brink, Garland
Anna Mae Brown, Pulaski
Jo Ann Carr, Jefferson
Betty David, Yell
Bonita Gandy, Logan
Andrea Hartley, Jefferson
Jean Harvell, Izard
Anne Jackson, Pulaski
Yvonne James, Benton
Johnette Johnson, Montgomery
Peggy Leger, Perry
Ellen McCloskey, Pulaski
Ivaline Moody, Craighead
Pauline Myrick, Lincoln
Ann Nix, Little River
Juanita Nutt, Perry
Sue Palsa, Prairie
Colene Parker, Madison
Patsy Parsons, Logan
Lillian Pittman, Greene
Bonnie Ray, Sebastian
Kay Sanders-Chick, Baxter
Marilyn Scroggins, Boone
Marilyn Shearin, Mississippi
Kaye Shrout, Montgomery
Judy Simmons, Bradley
John Stoll, Lawrence
Faye Suitt, Pulaski
Kim Tate, Izard
Jeri Vangilder, Pope
Fredonia Waldron, Pulaski
Juanita Webb, Drew

Candes Wilson, Washington
Maureen Zoerner, Ouachita

How and Why Members Got Into the Work—and What They Found When They Got There

Peggy Barnett of Garland County did not grow up in rural Arkansas. When her husband retired from military service, she took her four-year-old and joined a club, where she learned cooking, sewing, and crafts. She found home demonstration work to be educational—certainly more than crafts—and she enjoyed the lessons. Later, she became chairman of the arts and crafts fair. This is a juried fair with 385 exhibitors! The club bought its own building, and she learned to work in the kitchen where she and others made chili and doughnuts to sell at the fair.

Krista Brimer of White County has been an EHC member since 2006. When Krista joined her club, she felt unworthy because she did not possess the level of homemaking skills she thought appropriate for EHC members. However, her club has progressed into a multi-faceted organization through its community and educational functions. She has found that members can contribute to the community while they continue to learn.

Judy Brink moved to Garland County from Illinois in 1999. She had joined an Illinois club in 1979. She was in 4-H and became a junior leader. She found her Arkansas club to be more active than the one in Illinois.

Anna Mae Brown of Pulaski County (77-year member) was a 4-H'er and joined the Brady Club during the Great

Depression. Anna Mae provided a view of the distant past as well as more recent history but will be featured later as attention is turned toward the future.

Jo Ann Carr of Jefferson County (22-year member) joined the Whitehall Club at its organizational meeting and was elected as its first president. She liked the meetings, lessons, and crafts.

Betty David of Yell County joined an EHC club when she moved back from California in 1981. Her mother already had a job waiting for her as the clothing leader. David had lovely memories of childhood experiences as a 4-H'er. She remembered going to Fayetteville and modeling a dress she had made. When they made the mattresses, she sat underneath and poked the needle back through! When she married, she joined the home demonstration club, which met in homes and had demonstrations in cooking, canning, and clothing.

Bonita Gandy of Logan County (25-year member) recalled attending 4-H meetings at school. She especially remembered a biscuit-baking contest for which she and her mother worked really hard. As she recalls, the biscuits turned out just fine. She is drawn to the educational aspects of EHC, and she supports the organization's role in preserving our homemaking heritage.

Andrea Hartley of Jefferson County remembered growing up in a small town as part of a farming community. Her mother was not a part of EHC work, but her aunt took her to meetings with her. Hartley was interested in the crafts the women worked on.

Jean Harvell of Izard County, who was in 4-H, joined a home demonstration club in 1959 when she returned to Melbourne from Illinois where she had moved for work. Her sister and some friends had organized the Maple Club. It was the only social activity besides church. Later, she joined the Red Bud Club, which just last week finished making dresses for a church's mission trip to Peru. Members made thirty little girls' dresses and nineteen pairs of pants.

Anne Jackson of Pulaski County joined in 1966—the year her fifth daughter started to school. She commented that she wanted to do something for herself—not realizing it was for the whole family.

Yvonne James of Benton County said her mother and mother-in-law wanted her to join when she returned to Arkansas in 1980. Her early passion—which has continued—was her club's extended project to preserve a wonderful old school building. The club meets in a little club house beside the school.

Johnette Johnson of Montgomery County (11-year member) worked outside the home her entire life. She always wanted to quilt; when she moved to Mount Ida on Lake Ouachita, she joined a quilting club that met every Monday. Fellow members assured her their EHC club went hand-in-hand with the quilting club: they were all members of both. So she joined EHC and served as county council president for six years. She especially likes the work for underprivileged children in the county. She is honored to be a part of the organization.

Peggy Leger of Perry County joined EHC in 1995 when she moved to Bigelow after leaving the Air Force. Having been raised in rural areas, she knew how to cook and can. Juanita Nutt—a fellow Californian—invited her to join. She found an organization that did not emphasize home skills as Juanita found in 1964.

Ellen McCloskey of Pulaski County joined EHC in 2005, but throughout her childhood she was a member of 4-H in the community off West Markham in Little Rock. After college, Ellen went to Brazil as a 4-H leader through the Peace Corps during 1963 through 1965! In 1982, she joined an international development office of the U. S. Department of Agriculture. Her work led her into third world countries—where she realized that home demonstration practices from the very early days would have helped. Ellen is a member with Anna Mae Brown.

Ivaline Moody of Craighead County joined in about 1970 when her boys were a pretty good size. She had never learned to preserve food. Canning and freezing were a part of her learning process. She learned to sew in school, and in 1976 she had a best-of-show at the fair in a three-piece cotton outfit. In EHC, she honed her sewing skills and learned more professional techniques.

Pauline Myrick of Lincoln County started with 4-H as a volunteer leader. She grew up in the community but moved away and then returned. She remembers being "elected" as 4-H leader and then learning the news! The ones who elected her must have known what they were doing: She kept the job for thirty-three years! As an EHC member, she was state president from 1994 to 1996.

Ann Nix of Little River County knew she wanted to join EHC when she retired. Someone invited her to a Mother's Day tea, so she asked a friend to come. They joined that day. She went to a meeting in Arkadelphia and learned to make pretty cancer caps on looms. She has made over 200 of the caps.

Juanita Nutt of Perry County joined a home demonstration club in 1964. She was newly married, and her friend Mabel Ritter invited her to attend. She learned how to sew, can, and garden. She had never done any of these things before. She thought that the deeper you planted a bulb, the better it would grow! She knew how to cook a little, but having come from California, she had never heard of poke salet and okra. She learned how to cook both of these Southern delicacies.

Sue Palsa is a retired agent from Prairie County. After college, Sue became a school teacher until she left the workplace to raise her family. She began her work with the Extension in 1989, although there was no vacancy in Prairie County at the time. She eventually was able to return to her home county, and she reminisced about the wonderful opportunities and people in Prairie County. Of the ten clubs in her county, one was a very early one. She retired in 2007.

Colene Parker of Madison County joined EHC in 1972. She recalled that in the 1970s, club members were busy trying to retain the "heritage skills," i.e., food preservation, quilting, crocheting, and household arts.

Patsy Parsons of Logan County joined a home demonstration club and honed her skills in sewing. Her son grew up behind her sewing machine. She entered sewing contests and recalled winning a contest with a double-knit pantsuit.

Lillian Pittman of Greene County (15-year member) likes to try new things. A friend asked her to join, and everything her club is involved in encourages her to do creative things at home. She likes to sew with cotton, and she likes competition. Does her club work make her a better homemaker? She is sure it gives her the confidence to try.

Bonnie Ray of Sebastian County (35-year member) remembered going to 4-H club meetings during school hours. She had lots of good memories of 4-H experiences during the late 1940s and early 1950s. She made a dress when she was nine years old. She joined EHC as a young married woman but dropped out and worked in PTA for twenty-one years while her children were in school. Then she and her husband moved to the country, where she joined a club.

Kay Sanders-Chick of Baxter County retired from the U. S. Department of State and moved to Arkansas in 1992. Neighbors—mostly newcomers to the state also—invited her to visit an EHC club as she built her home. Kay had retired from a high-energy, stressful job, so she was drawn to the leadership element of the organization. Right now thirty to thirty-five women attend the meetings. In her isolated community—where the roads were not paved until the 1970s—two club women organized and supported children through 4-H work in the 1950s and 1960s. The women had come from other states just as Kay had done.

Marilyn Scroggins of Boone County joined a home demonstration club in 1955 because a friend invited her. She grew up in 4-H work in Ohio and later in Arkansas. As a young mother, she enjoyed the demonstration work in cooking, clothing, canning, and gardening. Since August 2010, Marilyn's club has met in her basement every Friday and made quilts for wounded military men and women for flights from Germany. The request came from a commander to one of the members as she visited her military daughter in Germany. In a telephone update in April 2012, Marilyn reported that EHC members had recently sent their one hundredth quilt in honor of the centennial.

Marilyn Shearin of Mississippi County (25-year member) had remembrances that started with her mother—a sixty-year member. She recalled helping her mom in the kitchen at the fair. She also remembered the judging, a club house, family gatherings, and lots of crafts.

Kay Shrout of Montgomery County, an agent for thirty-seven years, recalled her early fifteen years as an agent in Madison County, which had an active EHC program. When she left, members assured her that they had trained her! Kay agreed.

Judy Simmons of Bradley County (20+ year member) has had a passion for the work since she joined. She recommended just applying the goals and principles of the EHC creed in order to help make a better world.

John Stoll of Lawrence County (5-year member) helped his wife in all kinds of EHC projects after he retired. He said he began following her around just as a volunteer. However, two years ago she became state president, and he became a member so that he could participate with her in state-level projects. Childhood memories included sleeping on a homemade mattress in the community called Opposition. In Ravenden, the canning kitchen became the school kitchen for a little two-room schoolhouse.

Faye Suitt of Pulaski County joined EHC during 1978 but worked as a secretary in the state office for twenty years before that. As an employee, she found the up-to-date information for homemakers to be phenomenal. When she changed jobs, she joined an EHC club and still appreciates the research-based information she receives.

Kim Tate of Izard County (25-year member) reminisced that her mother joined in 1971. At that time, women did not have babysitters, so Kim went with her mom. She enjoyed crafts and what the members learned. She was a 4-H'er and a 4-H leader. She expressed a hope that EHC work would continue and that later generations would be drawn to the work.

Jeri Vangilder is an agent in Pope County. She recalled her grandmother cleaning the house and making her special banana cake for home demonstration club meetings during the late 1950s and early 1960s. Most of the members were her grandmother's age— probably about age forty-five—which, of course, seemed very old to Jeri. Vangilder majored in home economics because of her home ec teacher's encouragement. She started work in July 1977 as a junior field assistant in Cleburne County during the summer after her junior year of college—at $1,000 for the ten weeks.

Fredonia Waldron of Pulaski County grew up in one-half of a country grocery store. Her mother told of canning with tin cans rather than glass jars. Waldron joined EHC in the 1960s and served during the 1970s. Then she went into the military service for thirty years and returned to Pulaski County, which was a new county for her.

Juanita Webb of Drew County was a 4-H'er as a child. She became a 4-H leader and then joined EHC, where she has been a member for more than thirty years. She joined a club because of her interest in homemaking skills and community service opportunities.

Candes Wilson of Washington County joined EHC in 1982. Her early memories were of her grandmother and mother quilting for needy families. When she joined in the early 1980s, her first big project was getting Arkansas-produced and Arkansas-packaged foods for a tasting party for the national EHC convention. The party was on the lawn at the University of Arkansas at Fayetteville. Unfortunately, a sudden thunderstorm turned the lovely lawn party into a disaster that still haunts Candes!

Maureen Zoerner of Ouachita County got involved in Calhoun County—in Locust Bayou. She joined the newly organized club although she had no idea what it was all about. They met in homes, and their agent would work with club members on making things. Zoerner learned what the organization was all about and served as AEHC state president from 2000 to 2002.

The remaining topics of the interviews, "How the Work Changed Over the Years" and "Interviewees' Opinions about Those Changes," are included later as a reflective piece. In the meantime, members and agents were able to shed light on some of the well-known activities of the past.

Noteworthy One-Time Activities

Some projects during the past forty-or-so years have become legendary—almost to the level of the mattress-making of years gone by. Just about everyone knows a little about them, but the number of individuals who actually participated is growing smaller. A few of the interviewees were able to provide eye-witness accounts, which we all should cherish! Each one of the following accomplishments is important to retain in our collective memory.

Surveys of Arkansas's Cemeteries

During a spring 2011 conversation with the writer about historical resources in Arkansas, Dr. Wendy Richter, State Historian and Director of the Arkansas History Commission, mentioned the cemetery surveys conducted in the late 1960s by Extension Homemakers. Richter commented on how important the surveys were in supplementing Arkansas's vital statistics records because births and deaths were not officially recorded until 1914.

During the June 2011 interviews, several club members vividly remembered their late 1960s experiences trudging through thick brush to find long-forgotten cemeteries. They cringed as they recalled chiggers, wasps' nests, snakes' holes, barbed wire fences, tall grasses, and a hot Arkansas sun. Everyone chuckled as one member recalled a headstone that suddenly moved and fell over. She seemed to remember that a rabbit jumped from behind. The mood was more reflective as someone else recalled that sometimes they found a fruit jar with a piece of paper inside. On the piece of paper they found the name of a deceased newborn baby. They tried to secure the fruit jar a little more deeply into the ground.

Others remembered cemeteries far off the beaten path, found only through tracking devices, map searching, and sometimes, the guidance of a local citizen. When possible, each surveyor placed a piece of plain white paper over the marker's etched name and dates. Then she rubbed over the uneven area with a pencil just as we all used to do as children in elementary school. Many of the stones were plain and offered no means of identification of the decedent.

Each county compiled its cemetery book, some with directions to cemeteries' locations. Members sold the hard-bound books for several years. Individuals from all over the country continue to call for information in locating a loved one's grave. Sometimes club members are able to supply the requested information. A member of the Madison County Historical Society kindly emailed information about the county's surveys. Copies of several survey books are housed at the Arkansas History

Commission archives directly behind the State Capitol in Little Rock.

The "Every Child by '74" Project

Betty Flanagan Bumpers, former First Lady of Arkansas, is a member of the National Women's Hall of Fame. In reading about Bumpers, we realize that she should have been an Extension Homemaker. She has a passion for her community and the world and the wherewithal to do something about it. The Hall of Fame website states: "[S]he has dedicated her life to issues affecting children's health, empowering women, and the cause of world peace."[1]

When Bumpers became First Lady of Arkansas, we had one of the lowest immunization rates in the nation. Bumpers spearheaded a state-wide program for childhood vaccinations. As a result, Arkansas achieved one on the highest immunization rates in the country. The "Every Child By '74" project brought together the Arkansas League for Nursing, State Health Department, Arkansas National Guard, State Nurses Association, State Medical Society, Cooperative Extension Service, faith-based organizations, and other volunteers. The campaign was so successful that the Centers for Disease Control and Prevention used it as a model for other states.[2]

Long-time Extension Homemakers recall that in at least one national publication Bumpers gave a great deal of credit to our organization for making the program successful. In an interview, Anne Jackson of Pulaski County called her own work in the campaign her favorite Extension Homemakers memory. She recalled that

Bumpers was right there in the trenches—working with the people who were going out and volunteering in the schools and with the parents. Jackson said she did clerical work as the children and parents came in for the inoculations. Juanita Webb of Drew County recalled working as a volunteer also—seeing that the children were in place. She added that nowadays her club helps with influenza inoculations—just providing a drink of water. "Sometimes they have to wait in line quite a while."[3]

A Priceless Contribution

Dr. Jeffrey R. Kaiser, a neonatologist and researcher at the University of Arkansas for Medical Sciences and Arkansas Children's Hospital, had a difficult challenge performing his brain blood flow research study of very premature infants, sponsored by the National Institutes of Health (NIH) and the National Institute of Neurological Disorders and Stroke (NINDS). He was measuring brain blood flow with a pencil-sized ultrasound transducer that was taped on the temples of babies as small as one to two pounds. Sometimes it took up to twenty pieces of tape to secure the transducer. This was problematic because premature infants' skin is very fragile, and tape could pull off their skin. This just would not do.

Then, one of Dr. Kaiser's research assistants scoured the UAMS Neonatal Intensive Care Unit (NICU) and found a crocheted hat in a baggy, with a label saying that the hat was donated by the Arkansas Extension Homemakers. The research assistant placed the hat on one of the larger study infants, and realized that this cap could hold the transducer in perfect position, without the need for tape! The caps could hold the transducer in place for hours, allowing Dr. Kaiser to gather important information about why some premature infants have bleeding in their brains.

Dr. Kaiser realized that the Arkansas Extension Homemakers caps would be perfect to make his $2.5 million dollar research work. He knew nothing about the Arkansas Extension Homemakers at that time. He contacted them and met with several ladies to discuss the research study. Within a month, he was given over 100 crocheted caps small enough to snugly fit on the heads of the premature infants! He was also presented hundreds more at yearly AEHC conferences. The caps were colorful, and the study infants' parents loved them. The parents were given the caps after the research study was over—a beautiful memento of their stay in the UAMS NICU.

When describing his research study in medical journals, Dr. Kaiser always acknowledges the Arkansas Extension Homemakers' contribution. Dr. Kaiser has since secured more NIH funding and has learned a lot more about brain blood flow in premature infants, and ways to prevent preemies from bleeding in their brains. According to Dr. Kaiser, it was because of the beautiful crocheted hats made by ladies of the Arkansas Extension Homemakers Council that his research has been successful.[4]

Dr. Kaiser's work should be a source of great pride to every Extension Homemaker.

Continuing Commitments of Note

Participants shared about some important continuing commitments, as follows:

The County Fair Work

Fairs were an important part of home demonstration work from almost the very beginning. Extension homemakers nowadays have become an integral—and vital—part of their individual counties' fairs.

Marilyn Shearin of Mississippi County has fond memories of her mother's sixty-year home demonstration/Extension Homemakers work. She remembered helping her mom in the kitchen at the fair. She also recalled using the home demonstration clubhouse for gatherings, including a barbecue chicken dinner for all members and their families.

And fairs are still important to the work. Interviewees talked of judging 4-H entries as well as going to other counties as judges. They admitted that sometimes they are appreciated and sometimes not. The entrant who does not receive a blue ribbon may not appreciate their work so much. They stressed, however, that when they judge, they praise as much as they can, but they also teach entrants how they can improve their work.

Judy Brink, who moved her membership from Illinois to Garland County in 1999, commented that her Arkansas club is more active than the one in Illinois—especially regarding fair activities. Down here, Extension Homemakers own their own building and kitchen on the fairgrounds. When her county's fairgrounds were sold, club members worked with the fair board to ensure that a new building was provided. We are pleased to report that it was.

Interviewees commented that in addition to judging, Extension Homemakers are often responsible for the cultural arts building. Cultural arts include baking, sewing, knitting, needlework, adult and children's craft projects, horticulture, art, and quilting—all in one building. But the women do not work with chickens and cows. They leave that responsibility to the fair board.

John Stoll of Lawrence County, who started out helping his wife with her Extension Homemakers Club work, "came in the back door—but I get a great deal of joy out of the work that EHC does in seeing that the county fair operates."[5] Stoll serves as co-chair of the woodworking program at his county fair.

Pennies for Friendship

During her interview, Pauline Myrick spoke of the ACWW and Pennies for Friendship. She reminded her group that ACWW stands for Associated Country Women of the World—and Pennies for Friendship is a fund-raising method used to support the association's endeavors. At the March 2012 officers' training session at Ferndale, a large glass jar labeled "Pennies for Friendship" was passed from member to member. A little research provided additional insight into the program, as follows:

> ACWW, Associated Country Women of the World, who live in rural and urban areas, representatives of many races, nationalities and creeds, believe that peace and progress can best be advanced by friendship and understanding

through communication and working together to improve the quality of life for all people through:

- relief of poverty
- relief of sickness and the protection and preservation of health
- advancement of education[6]

It is gratifying to know that Arkansas homemakers have contributed for many, many years to a program to help women and their families throughout the world. Let's continue to fill that big glass jar at every opportunity!

A Changing Organization

As might be expected, the thirty-six individuals who were interviewed had quite a lot to say about the changes they have seen in the organization over the years. Their answers were thoughtful and reflective. In the 1970s, the organization was focused on retaining the heritage skills of previous years. Clubs did more hands-on, life-skills activities. For example, a member might have taught floral arranging after collecting flowers from a garden or field. At one point—in the 1980s—there were thirteen separate programs of work, including food preservation, meal planning, clothing, policy, etc. Clubs were teaching all the subjects that families needed to support themselves. More recently, the thirteen programs of work were replaced by four: nutrition, health, resource management, and family life.

Some remembered when crafting was the main focus. Then the pendulum swung, and clubs were not allowed to mention crafting in their reports. Of course, it must be remembered that the organization is an educational entity—as we learned in chapter one—and that fact remains today. As the organization seemed to struggle to find its place in a rapidly changing world, its name became Arkansas Association for Family and Community Education, in accordance with the national organization's name change. After a few years, members voted to return to Extension Homemakers and later dropped out of the national organization because they felt it did not reflect who they were as an organization.

Although the programming may have evolved because of outside influences or policy changes, the fact that the membership is getting older cannot be overlooked. Programs nowadays focus on helping members grow older gracefully, in better health, and more prepared all-around. Or—as one interviewee commented—members are growing older, but they're fighting it all the way. Programs are tailored to the members' needs and interests. Recent topics have included nutrition, health, money management, the parenting journey, and the personal journey.

Another member noted that even during the past ten or twelve years, there have been major changes. Clubs no longer have the little crafty, little food thing. Programs are now geared to bring members into the modern world: how to talk to your doctor, how to purchase an airline ticket and plan your vacation, how to use a computer, and how to manipulate a digital camera, for example.

Programs come from members' wants and needs. The Strong Women program—a national program that originated at Tufts University—provides strength training that improves balance and flexibility. It is often offered to the public in such venues as senior centers and churches. For participants over seventy years of age, a doctor's permission is required. Men and women attend, and some physicians regularly prescribe the program for patients who need strength training.

Leader training has changed also. In the 1970s, leader training was conducted by the home economist, who taught the lesson; leaders took the information back to their communities. One agent commented that the women today are so talented and have such leadership skills that the agents provide the information for them but the women do not necessarily need training in the subject matter. They are self-starters and are able to facilitate the discussion or invite an appropriate subject-matter expert to lead the meeting.

It is obvious by reading interviewees' brief biographies earlier in this chapter that members often wait until they retire from the workforce to join an Extension Homemakers club. Members nowadays are better educated than their grandmothers and mothers were. It is also apparent that Arkansas attracts well-educated, capable retirees from out of state, some of whom are drawn to Extension Homemakers work because it offers leadership opportunities as well as educational and community service activities.

And, of course, we now have men joining our clubs! Wouldn't our foremothers have gotten a chuckle out of that? The men are fitting right in, however, enjoying the work, accepting responsibilities, and contributing to the organization. And they are obviously being accepted by the women members.

No doubt, each of these groups adds a layer of richness and texture to the overall organization.

Would My Daughters Join?

Interviewees were concerned that for the most part younger people do not join Extension Homemakers clubs. One member placed the situation in perspective by asking a rhetorical question: If her club started an evening club, would any of her five daughters come? Her answer was an emphatic "No." Younger women who work outside the home have neither the time, energy, nor desire to attend meetings. Of course, as a homemakers' organization, we want our young people to spend non-working time with their families. And, besides, we know that if the children are involved in sports, the whole family is involved in sports. And there are other factors to consider, as follows:

- **Retaining 4-H girls:** It is even difficult to retain 4-H girls after they become adults because they often move to other counties or areas.

- **Accommodating young moms:** Today's organizations of all kinds may not be as accommodating to young families as our clubs were in previous years. Several interviewees mentioned going to meetings with their mothers; some took their own children and felt comfortable in doing so. More recently, however, that often is not an accepted practice. We have become accustomed to leaving children at home with babysitters.

- **Competing with other organizations:** In the past, the home demonstration club was often the only social outlet in the community other than the local church. Today, however, women have their own transportation and are willing to drive several miles to organizations that meet their needs.

A Revival of the "Heritage Skills"

An important development within EHC work is the realization that people in the community—particularly younger individuals—need and want to learn the so-called "heritage skills." Do you recall Ellen McCloskey's biographical sketch? As a U. S. Department of Agriculture international development employee in third world countries, Ellen realized that home demonstration practices from the very early days would have been helpful in the work. Here in Arkansas, agents and members alike have discovered those same needs among our young people today—and in some cases they are working to meet those needs.

Sharing With the Community

For example, in Garland County, members started an SOS ("Sharing our Skills") program. It started with a Saturday cooking lesson in which club members provided the ingredients and taught attendees how to prepare the meal. Then participants actually prepared the food in what members called a strictly hands-on demonstration. Men and women attended, and Job Corps young people especially responded. The boys loved to cook. Then the group divided into two parts: one group actually became an Extension Homemakers club with leaders provided by the mentoring club.

During 2010–2011, the club offered cooking classes to its members and to the public on weekdays. Advertising was by word-of-mouth and the agent's weekly newspaper column. Topics included cooking in the crockpot, using healthier recipes, preserving strawberry jam, and pickling carrots. As many as forty people attended—50 percent from the public; it was necessary to have two separate classes. Participants represented various age groups—from young adults to middle-aged individuals. The last class was for pressure cooking and canning—but no one signed up for that one. Club members planned to offer similar classes next year, including bread making—although not necessarily from scratch.

As was noted, there is a need once again for these fundamental homemaking skills. Participants may not choose to join the Extension Homemakers club; however, members are able to share needed information and skills within the community.

Special Interest Clubs

Another recent trend is the organization of special interest clubs. Interviewees were excited about the possibility of attracting new members with such emphases as basic sewing and cooking skills. Many young wives and mothers simply do not have the basic homemaking skills, and there is no one else to teach them. One member said she teaches cooking classes at her church. People have asked her why she does not teach them through her Extension Homemakers club. Another individual commented that there is a need to share canning and food preservation skills with lower income women who cannot afford a freezer.

In one county, fifteen small clubs have been replaced by two or three large special interest clubs. Women and lots of men attend an upholstery club. The classes are open to the public, and participants may upholster a couch. The Strong Women program attracts younger women who will come out at night for exercise. They do not like crafts, but they will help with community-wide projects by helping set up, etc.

Special interest clubs incorporate three regular lessons into their meetings during the year. In the remaining months, the lessons include new techniques and procedures in the special interest subject, i.e., cooking, quilting, scrapbooking, or needlework. Otherwise, the clubs meet standard requirements for affiliation.

Mentoring 4-H Boys and Girls

Many of the interviewees had fond memories of their experiences as 4-H members. Over and over again, they talked about how their clubs are choosing to mentor 4-H boys and girls. For example, one club has a workshop for 4-H members every Tuesday. Extension Homemakers teach the kids how to make jelly, can pickles, bake cookies and breads, and practice basic sewing steps. The club had to divide the 4-H'ers into two separate groups because there were so many who wanted to learn.

Another club member also talked about being involved with 4-H youths. Club members made a quilt last summer with the 4-H'ers. They also taught them canning, sewing, and cooking. She commented that the boys really liked the projects. During the last sewing class, she taught two boys how to use roto-cutters.

Although many Extension Homemakers choose to mentor 4-H youths, there is an exciting new opportunity for all clubs. At the March 2012 annual officer training at the 4-H Center at Ferndale, Dr. Ann Sortor, Associate Director, FCS & 4-H Youth Development, announced a new initiative entitled "The 4-H Program for Healthy Living." The program will target growing obesity among our children throughout the state. The State AEHC Council and the seventy-five county councils will share the cost of the program. Dr. Sortor asked members to assist the county agents in administering the program, which will be an inter-generational effort.

Community Service

Although some community service projects have been accomplished on a state-wide basis, as we have seen, most clubs find a need in their own community and work together to try to meet that need. As examples of the varied activities, the award-winning project books for 2011, which will be featured at the 2012 state meeting in Hot Springs in June 2012, are listed below by district, as follows:

2011 Ouachita District Awards for Project Books – Summaries

Karen Bell Fox, Ouachita District Director
Sally Patterson, Ouachita Associate District Director
Bettie Huntley, Ouachita Associate District Director

Calhoun County – Calhoun County Homemakers – Emergency EXIT Totes for Children

The Calhoun County Homemakers provided children's clothing in a variety of sizes. Toiletries and handmade totes to hold the items were also provided for children who may be taken from their homes in emergency situations. The community and the DMA Apparel business were instrumental in helping.

Cleveland County – Cleveland County EHC – Wilma the Dairy Cow

"Wilma the Dairy Cow," an educational program, was given to Head Start students to teach them how and where we get our dairy products. They saw a live cow being milked. They were also served ice cream. The students had many questions about the cow, milk, and dairy products.

Cleveland County – "Y" EHC – Ornament Workshop

The "Y" Extension Homemakers Club organized a Christmas ornament workshop for community children. Each child made two or more ornaments to take home. The club provided ornaments and snacks for the children.

Cleveland County – Rison EH Club – Hope Women's Resource Center

Hope Women's Resource Center was the Rison Extension Homemakers community service project. The program enabled the club to help by providing baby clothes and personal items needed for the expectant mothers. Educational materials were purchased by the club.

Cleveland County – New Home EHC – Financial Frauds, Scams, and Your Money

"Financial Frauds, Scams, and Your Money" is a program to increase awareness of various phone, internet and personal frauds. Guests from the community and surrounding areas were given contact information, and plans are to update the fraud alerts periodically.

Garland County – Loyal Ladies EH Club – HS Boys and Girls Club Spa Baton Corps

Members of the club contributed their treasures and time to a garage and bake sale in June. They made craft items throughout the year, making a profit of $83.40. Each member had something to contribute, whether it was time or talent. The EHC Arts and Crafts Fair items sold were our secret seasoning, shawls, and crocheted necklaces, totaling $213.51. Our club contributed $50 to Garland County Humane Society, $50 to the Guardian Angel Cat Club, $100 to the Area Council on Aging, $45 to the Angel Tree for the Salvation Army, and also contributed many clothing items, toys, personal hygiene items, canned goods, and $200 to the Jackson House Special Project.

Garland County – Designing Women EH Club – Pines Nursing and Rehab Center/Crafts

Our club certainly believes this project was a success. The residents of the Pines Nursing and Rehabilitation Center look forward to our monthly visits. The craft projects have been engaging and stimulating to the residents, and we look forward to future craft projects with them.

Garland County – Garland County EH Club – Sharing Our Skills (SOS)

In 2008, Phyllis Pipkin invited the Job Corps to attend the Sharing Our Skills (SOS) program. As a result, a brand new Extension Homemakers Club was formed and was called the Cooking Corps. The young people took instantly to cooking, with skills sharpened to measure, chop, dice, and slice to prepare economical meals. Other skills taught were kitchen safety, cleanliness, and food shopping. The club currently meets on a Saturday and helps in the kitchen at the EHC Arts and Crafts Fair. They also help with traffic control at these two events, thus earning the club money to pay dues and attend council meetings.

Garland County – Park/Heights EH Club – Relay for Life Luncheon

Park/Heights Club has been participating in the Relay for Life luncheon since it began several years ago. Our goal is to raise funds to aid in cancer research.

Garland County – La Casa EH Club – Walker Bags

The new and improved walker bags are brighter and trimmer. This year patients were very pleased with them. Our coverage has been limited to the HSV and surrounding area. We have established a reputation as the "Walker Bag Club" as we have made and distributed more than 400 bags . . . and we're still going strong!

Little River County – Arden EH Club – Got You Covered

Eighty-six knitted caps for newborns and 58 polar fleece caps for cancer patients were made by the Arden Extension Club. The items were delivered to Arkansas Children's Hospital, Little River Memorial Hospital, Little River Hospice, Wadley Hospital, St. Michael's Hospital, and the American Cancer Society.

Montgomery County – Montgomery EH Council – Experimental Summer Feeding Program for Children

The Summer Feeding Program for Children helps families in Montgomery County. Many children in our county do not have adequate food when school is not in session. Businesses and individuals donated $1,740 to purchase food for seven families with sixteen children. The local grocery donated milk and fresh fruit. EHC and local church members donated 3,850 volunteer hours.

Montgomery County – Joplin EH Club – Back to School Backpack Program

Backpacks and school supplies for two schools were donated by EHC members, county residents, and local businesses. An estimated $1,000 in school supplies was collected, and the backpacks were donated by EHC members. This effort supplied approximately 100 children.

Nevada County – Nevada County EHC – 4-H Arts and Crafts Fair Workshop

Our county helped conduct two 4-H Arts and Crafts Fair Workshops this year. EHC members planned, coordinated, and then conducted a pillowcase project. Each workshop had 15 participants who learned basic sewing skills. Finished products were entered in the county fair and the Southwest Arkansas District Livestock Show and Fair.

Nevada County – Fairhills EH Club – Community Sewing Workshop

A sewing workshop in basic and advanced sewing skills was hosted by our club for participants from the local community. This free workshop also showcased many great examples of other crafts such as quilts, needlework, crotchet items, knitted items, and cross-stitch.

Nevada County – Women of Purpose EHC – Arise, Restore the Woman in You Women's Conference

The conference theme – "Arise, Restore the Woman in You" – invited women to enjoy a day of restoration and renewal, while listening to guest speakers, music in ministry, break-out sessions, and shopping. One hundred seventy-five participated in the event held in Prescott.

Pike County – Pike County EH Club – Helping Hands Touching Little Lives

A project born from the love of sewing and the missionary efforts of several people in the county who traveled to Zambia to work in orphanages allowed club members to extend community service to the world. Dresses, diaper shirts, bibs from pillowcases, and diapers from T-shirts were sewn using donated fabric, yard sale bed sheets, and other fabric. The group planned, published information about, and conducted workshops. Twenty-three members and community people, plus workshops conducted with 4-H'ers, produced 128 dresses to be sent to Zambia at Christmas for little girls' Christmas joy.

Polk County – Homestead EH Club – Teddy Bears of Love

A project to bring together Extension Homemakers and nursing home residents in a fundraising project also assured the nursing facility of having lots of candy for their Halloween "Trick or Treat" goblin visitors.

Polk County – Polk County EHC – Hearts and Hammers

After a tornado hit Mena, we participated in a community-wide project to say "Thank You NY" in your effort to help rebuild Mena. The local committees of Hearts and Hammers truly helped our community move forward and toward healing. Extension Homemakers are proud to have had a role to play in giving freely of our time, talents, and monies. The job is not yet finished.

Pulaski County – Pulaski EH Club – Supporting Our Troops

This project involved active personnel, as well as the families left at home, and included articles for troops, school supplies, and toys for children of military families. We also sent cards to recovering soldiers at military hospitals.

Pulaski County – Sharon EH Club – ACH Items

Our club has been helping Arkansas Children's Hospital for the past three years. This year we made dolls, 173 hats, 197 pillows, 58 blankets and 188 Christmas stockings, donating about 1,377 hours, and enjoying all of them. We were given fabric, stuffing, and threads from people who are not in the club. We spent only $29.32. Everything else was donated.

Sevier County – DeQueen EH Club – Eating Smart, Being Active

This project involved leading and teaching youth in food preparation, purchasing and safe handling, with emphasis on nutrition. The art of developing good habits in a variety of settings was also taught. Twenty-two children and eight adults attended in June, and thirty-seven children and eleven adults attended in August.

Sevier County – Sevier EH Council – Recorded History of WWII Veterans of Sevier

The Sevier County Extension Homemakers Council has great respect for the veterans of our armed forces, and we wanted to preserve the history of their experiences as told in their own words.

Sevier County – Union Extension Homemakers – Pillows and Pads

Nine members of our club made pillows and pads for patients at Brookwood Nursing Home. The pads were made for wheelchairs to help protect patients' bodies and make the chairs more comfortable. This was a very rewarding project to help others be more comfortable.

2011 Delta District Awards for Project Books – Summaries

Charlotte Wright, Delta District Director
Marnette Reed, Delta Associate District Director
Barbara Jones, Delta Associate District Director

Craighead County – Black Oak EH Club – Red Cross Disaster Comfort Kits

This project stems from the need for disaster comfort kits for the Red Cross. After a brief description, the eight club members created and delivered kits containing various personal items. The cost of the kits was $100 plus $65 for donated items.

Craighead County – Greensboro EH Club – Scam Awareness

Members of the Greensboro EH Club hosted a planned educational seminar for the Greensboro community. Stephen Svetz of the Attorney General's office presented the seminar on scams. Eighteen members of the community attended. EHC members assisted in distributing information and serving refreshments. The community received valuable information on old and new scams.

Craighead County – Oak Grove EH Club – Angel Wraps

Members of the Oak Grove EHC have participated in many projects over the years; however, none has touched them as deeply as Angel Wraps for the NEA Clinic's Charitable Foundation's ShareHope. The "Angel Wraps" are infant demise kits used by both Jonesboro hospitals. More than 60 tiny garments were made by the club during the year.

Craighead County – Opportunity EH Club – Helping Neighbors Food Pantry

Opportunity EH members were instrumental in helping feed the needy in the community by donating approximately 450 pounds of nonperishable food items, $50 in cash, and birthday supplies (all items valued at approximately $400) to the Helping Neighbors Food Pantry.

Craighead County – Pleasant Grove EHC – Blankets, Lap Pads and Neck Pieces for Autistic Children

Pleasant Grove EHC made blankets, lap pads and neck pieces to be used by occupational therapists in area schools and day cares to soothe children with autism or ADHD. Using donated rice, the club spent $130 for materials. If purchased, these items would have cost in excess of $400.

Craighead County – West Mart EHC – Walker and Chair Bags

The community service project chosen by the West Mart EHC of Jonesboro was to provide walker and chair bags to St. Elizabeth's Place. We later donated 14 additional bags to individual friends and relatives for their use. The bags were handmade with all fabric and notions donated by EHC members. Cost of fabric, notions, and travel to St. Elizabeth's Place was $75.

Cross County – Hickory Ridge EH Club – Hand Rolls for Nursing Homes

Our community nursing homes are very thankful for the hand rolls made by the Hickory Ridge EHC. They feel we have made a tremendous improvement to the nursing home residents' lives. We enjoyed working together as a club and volunteering our service to make someone else's daily life a little easier. We feel that as an EHC, we will continue to improve the lives of our local residents by striving to meet the community's needs.

Jackson County – South Tuckerman EHC Club – Walker Bags/Purses

Walker bags and purses for the Lindley Health Care and Rehab Center was an enjoyable, educational, and worthwhile community project. It was an honor to be asked and to be able to supply this need. We strive to make a difference in the lives of our community.

Jefferson County – Jefferson County EHC – UAMS Cot Sheets

The UAMS Kids First Daycare recently had a need for cot sheets. The Jefferson County Extension Homemakers made and presented over 100 of these needed sheets. The special children enjoy anything with new colors and textures. It makes their naps more enjoyable.

Jefferson County – Grace Willing Workers EH Club – Workshops for Trinity Village Medical Care

Grace Willing Workers EHC chose to enrich Trinity Village Medical Care. Seventeen club members participated in three club workshops to make items for the center. In addition, visits were made during the holidays to distribute items and interact with the residents. The 50 residents benefited greatly from the extra attention our club provided.

Jefferson County – Camden Road EHC – Help for New Mothers

Help for New Mothers was a project that was a benefit to our community. You may never know when a person is in need, especially a new mother. This project appeals to all segments of our society, and if we help one needy mother become a better mother or have a better start as a new mother, then the project is successful.

Jefferson County – White Hall Willing Workers – Hand Rolls for White Hall Rehab

The White Hall Willing Workers EHC was asked by the White Hall Nursing and Rehab Center for hand rolls for their patients. The Rehab unit requested them in different colors and textures. The club made 60 sets of hand rolls, which were very much appreciated. The colors made them feel better about using them.

Lincoln County – Lincoln County EH Club – AARP Driver Safety

The Lincoln County EHC sponsored an AARP Driver Safety Program for drivers 50 and older. Cars, traffic rules, driving conditions and even the roads traveled everyday have changed since many received their first licenses. This was an opportunity to promote safer driving skills, help older drivers maintain their mobility, and promote independence among older adults.

Lonoke County – Lonoke County EH Club – Breads 'N' Threads 4-H Camp

Lonoke County EHC presented a Breads 'N' Threads 4-H Day Camp to teach basic sewing and cooking skills to 26 students aged 9 through 16. Twelve Homemakers and one 4-H leader volunteered over 100 hours.

Poinsett County – Whitehall EH Club – Pillows for Head Start

A need for pillows at the Head Start program in Harrisburg triggered this project. Working with Head Start, the club made and presented each child in the program with a pillow for nap time. The children will be able to take their pillows home at the end of the school year. This project raises the awareness of how important it is to help others in the community.

Poinsett County – Poinsett County EHC – Bread of Life Food Pantry

The need for food in Poinsett County sparked this project. Due to the economy, many families are in need of services the Bread and Life Food Pantry provides. Working together as a group, the Poinsett County EHC Council provided some food for the families in the county. The project helped the members of EH Clubs see how important it is to help other families in the community who are struggling to provide for their families.

Poinsett County – Lucky 13 EH Club – Turbans for Breast Cancer Patients

Lucky 13 EH Club had two workshops to make chemo turbans in honor of National Breast Cancer Month. The turbans were presented to June Morse, manager of Hope Circle in Jonesboro. Our members feel very blessed to be able to make the community aware of Breast Cancer Month.

Prairie County – Idlewild EH Club – Hope Chest

The Idlewild EHC adopted Prairie County Hope Chest in DeValls Bluff. Ten members donated items worth approximately $250 to the Hope Chest. The project was very rewarding and made a huge difference to the organization.

Prairie County – Oak Prairie EH Club – Food for the Hungry

The Oak Prairie EHC donated nonperishable items to the Prairie County Food Bank in Des Arc. Ten members donated 95 pounds of nonperishable food items.

Prairie County – Biscoe EH Club – Boppy Pillows for New Moms

Thirty-five Boppy pillows for new mothers to lay their baby on as he/she nurses is an attempt to increase the number of breastfeeding mothers in our county. This project was requested by the Prairie County Health Department.

Prairie County – Busy Hands EH Club – 4-H Clubs Project

The Busy Hands EHC partnered with the local 4-H clubs for this project. We supplied items needed for their club and also volunteered time on many occasions to help in whatever way possible.

Prairie County – Prairie Piecemakers Quilt Club – Quilts for Valor

The Piecemakers Quilt Club made 20 quilts to be sent to a hospital in Germany for distribution to wounded soldiers in Iraq and Afghanistan. Fabric was cut, kits assembled, and quilts were constructed, quilted, and hemmed. The EHC name was attached to each quilt.

Prairie County – Riceland EH Club – Helping the Protectors of Our Country

The Riceland Extension Homemakers Club chose to help our soldiers by sending care packages overseas. So many times people fail to show respect and appreciation for these men and women who put their lives in danger to protect our homeland.

White County – El Paso EH Club – For the Least of These

Five club workshops and 19 members made 140 teaching dolls, 21 holiday lap robes/blankets, 16 hand-knitted or crocheted hats, and 20 pillows for the Arkansas Children's Hospital. We also purchased $100 worth of toys, games, books, underwear, and socks for the patients. The members spent $815 and donated 340 hours.

White County – Bald Knob EHC – Pillowcases for Patients/Residents

The Bald Knob Extension Homemakers Club sewed 200 pillowcases for the community. They were donated to Searcy Children's Home, White County Domestic Violence Center, the local hospice agency, and CARTI of Searcy.

2011 Ozark District Awards for Project Books – Summaries

Linda Chapman, Ozark District Director
Carolyn Morris, Ozark Associate District Director
Barbara May, Ozark Associate District Director

Baxter County – Oakland/Promise Land Extension – Knitting for Noggins Homemakers Club

We chose Arkansas Children's Hospital's request for knitted hats as a community service project. Members spent fall and winter evenings turning out adorable warm hats, resulting in over 200 hats being delivered.

Baxter County – Baxter County EHC – Baxter House Adult Day Services

The Center's budget was cut. The Baxter County EHC members picked up the slack by buying supplies needed on a daily basis by the House, as well as providing special parties for the clients.

Baxter County – Patchwork Extension Homemakers Club – The Christmas Stocking Project

Members read letters published in the *Baxter Bulletin*'s

Christmas Wish List. The letters were very heart-rending, requesting food, clothes, and toys. Our participation with leadership and caring made the stockings and ditty bags very important to the children and elderly at Christmas time.

Benton County – Benton County EHC – "Med List for Your Wallet"

As a way of emphasizing "Medwise" practices, our county printed 1,200 Medicine List Cards for wallets and purses. The cards can be used to list any medications used, allergies, doctors' names, and the name of your pharmacist. People in the healthcare field appreciate patients having this information with them at all times. This project is ongoing.

Boone County – Harrison EHC – Quilts for Military

Club members mailed quilts to Ramstein/Lansthul, Germany. The quilts are given to our wounded military prior to and during their travel aboard transport planes from Germany to U.S. military hospitals. Nine members and friends spent five hours a week and much time at home making these gifts of warmth, comfort and appreciation for their service.

Boone County – EHC Quilters – Quilts for Kids

Our "Quilts for Kids" project is a new category at the county and district fairs. We met with the newspaper to get the word out. It proved to be a popular part of the fair, and at least ten less fortunate children in this area will reap the benefits in the coming year.

Cleburne County – Good Springs Extension Homemakers Club – Margie's Haven House

This is a "safe house" where women and children can go to escape domestic violence. Many of the residents arrive with only the clothes they are wearing. Twelve members brought items, such as toothpaste and toothbrushes, to monthly club meetings, valued at $1,324.50.

Cleburne County – Cleburne County EHC – The Craft Fair

We conducted fund raisers to make improvements and provide maintenance to the EHC educational building at the fairgrounds. The Craft Fair offers participants an opportunity to sell their goods in a friendly setting to local citizens who buy gifts for themselves and others.

Conway County – Oppelo Twilite EHC – Bingo and More

Members enjoyed visiting residents of the Morrilton Health Care Center, providing bingo prizes, assisting with bingo games, making lap robes, walker totes, and greeting cards, and taking treats to residents. The ladies' favorite bingo prizes were the long necklaces that would fit over their heads.

Conway County – Conway County EHC – Community Immunity

We helped make Morrilton a "Community Immunity" city by assisting the Arkansas Department of Health with a mass flu clinic. We provided food to the nurses and those assisting in registration and other areas. The club also took the leadership in getting the word out.

Conway County – Petit Jean EHC – Bell Ringer

Our club brought excitement and personal achievement to the residents of River Chase Care Center by participating in the Handbell Music Makers Club. The project was very rewarding and satisfying.

Conway County – New Horizon EHC – Kiwanis Hospital Dolls

This was a gratifying project. We partnered with Morrilton Kiwanis Club members to supply hospital dolls to frightened children awaiting medical treatment.

Conway County – Birdtown EHC – Our Boys in Uniform

For over 60 years, our club has helped many people. Each month we send "care boxes" to our men and women in uniform. We try to send articles they cannot get, such as local newspapers, goodies, jerky, candies, cards, and pictures.

Conway County – Hilltoppers EHC – Backpack Food for Kids

We chose to help the Morrilton primary schools with "Backpack Food for Kids." During the year, we brought kid-friendly food to our club meetings. Items included Vienna sausages, moon pies, canned beans, applesauce, peanut butter, snack crackers, etc. Many children would not have anything to eat in the evenings or over the weekend if it wasn't for the food sent home in their backpacks.

Crawford County – Rena EHC – Reaching Out to Others

We have deep feelings of compassion for those less fortunate. By making donations to "Reaching Out to Others," we hope to make a difference in the lives of all those who pass through the doors of the Gospel Rescue Mission. Members donated 75 hours and $900.

Crawford County – River Belles EHC – Feeding the Hungry

We joined with the Alma Community Outreach organization again this year with the "Feeding the Hungry" program. We collected canned goods each quarter and presented them to the director of the program. Twelve-member teams collected $600 in food during 48 volunteer hours.

Crawford County – Bond Special EHC – Blankets for Kids

We joined forces with First Church of Nazarene's outreach "Blankets for Kids" sponsored by World Vision. We completed 100 blankets. Fifty blankets were shipped to World Vision Denver destination Africa to children orphaned by AIDS, and the remaining 50 will be distributed to disadvantaged children in the Fort Smith-Van Buren area.

Faulkner County – Roadrunner EHC – Homeless Sleep Mats

We helped the homeless in the county by making plastic sleep mats. Over 2,500 plastic bags, 240 volunteer hours, and $20 were donated for this project. Some cut and looped plastic strips and others crocheted the mats. The mats were given away as they were completed.

Izard County – Izard EHC – Manna House

We donated time, money, and items to the Manna House Thrift Store. Each volunteer spends ten or more hours a week working in the store pricing, sorting, and displaying items – clothing, kitchen supplies, furniture, etc. We also shop there in addition to donating.

Izard County – Gid EHC – Gift Bags

Members packed and delivered 30 bags to the parents of patients in Arkansas Children's Hospital. Bags held personal care items to clean and refresh guests until they secured their own needs.

Izard County – Zion EHC – Personal Care Bags

After the February 5, 2008, tornado, we decided to make Personal Care Bags for anyone involved in a local emergency. We presented five bags each, for men and women, plus additional supplies to the volunteer fire department, who will make them available as needed.

Johnson County – Oark EHC – Snuggles for Seniors

Our project "Snuggles for Seniors" took eight months to complete. Fifteen club members spent 155 hours on the project. The results were 14 lap robes, 10 shawls, and 125 pairs of fleece booties delivered to three assisted-living facilities in our area.

Johnson County – Johnson County EHC – Local Food Banks

We raised $1,000 at the annual spaghetti luncheon. Food drives throughout the year at county and club functions brought in an additional 800 pounds of canned foods. The money and canned goods were donated to local food banks.

Johnson County – ReRuns EHC – Christmas Bags

We purchased items and packed holiday decorated bags. These were presented at Christmas to the Birch Tree Community, a local mental health recovery halfway house. Gifts were given to residents and staff.

Madison County – Aurora Ladybugs – EHC Community Christmas Party

To see the community coming together for new and renewed fellowship was very gratifying for the Annual Aurora Community Christmas Party. This was spiritually uplifting, and all were ready to celebrate the birth of Jesus and for Santa to arrive at our homes with our families.

Marion County – Bull Shoals Brown Church and Monarch EHC – Salvation Army Project

Members of three Marion County EHC Clubs dressed one or two bears provided by the Salvation Army in one of three categories – knit or crochet, sew with fabric, or use a purchased outfit. Thirty-seven members volunteered 111 hours for the project. Our bears, with love added, helped the Salvation Army provide gifts for children at Christmas time.

Pope County – Crow Mountain EHC – Knit for Noggins

For the fifth year, our club used Knit for Noggins as its project. We feel we have made a difference in the lives of 1,068 children at Arkansas Children's Hospital, as well as enrich the lives of our volunteers and the program. Many people in the community donated supplies to help with our 2,790 volunteered hours this past year.

Pope County – Sunnyfield EHC – Decorating Nursing Home Doors

Decorating the doors for residents of the nursing home, who do not have family members, is our community project. Members meet at the nursing home and decorate the doors assigned by the activity director. This is a very rewarding project for our club and the community.

Sebastian County – Sebastian County EHC – Be MedWise Arkansas

Members volunteered 145 hours sharing information about "Be MedWise Arkansas." The volunteers prepared and taught lessons to their fellow club members and helped organize and host a community-wide workshop in Sebastian County. These efforts allowed 100 people to gain skills on how to interact with doctors and pharmacists and learn more about the safety of OTC medicines, prescription meds, and supplements.

Sebastian County – Excelsior EHC – Pink Bud Nursing Home Project

Twenty-nine members worked 220 hours making, sewing, stuffing, delivering items, and visiting residents at Pink Bud Nursing Home. Value of time and contributions was approximately $5,284.

Sharp County – Hardy Country Ladies – Shawls for Nursing Home

Forty-two shawls were completed and delivered to Eaglecrest Nursing and Rehabilitation Center and Ash Flat Healthcare and Rehabilitation Center. The shawls provided warmth in a cheerful and comforting way. Each shawl took approximately 10 hours or a total 420 volunteer hours. The estimated value of each shawl was $15, which valued the shawls at $630.

Yell County – Spring Creek EHC – Ronald McDonald House

In helping the Ronald McDonald House, Spring Creek EHC helped local parents who stayed at the house while their child was being treated at Arkansas Children's Hospital. Each year we donate shower items and money. This is a project we will continue for years to come.

Yell County – Yell County EH Council – Huggy Bears

Over 400 handmade Huggy Bears are giving comfort to children at Yell County hospitals and clinics. The facilities are thankful to us for supplying these huggable handmade bears that comfort their little patients during stressful situations. Club members enjoy making the Huggy Bears and are proud to serve our county through this project.[7]

These 2011 project-book award winners have provided immeasurable support to their communities and beyond.

Anna Mae Brown, Seventy-Eight-Year Member, Pulaski County

In looking toward the future, we have chosen to focus on someone whose history in Extension work goes all the way back to the Great Depression. Anna Mae Brown of the Brady Club in Pulaski County received her seventy-seven year pin at the 2011 state meeting. That means she joined an adult home demonstration club in 1934! Just before being honored at the luncheon, she participated in one of the oral interview sessions. The wonderful thing about Anna Mae's interview is that she didn't stop at either the past or the present. Instead, she looked toward the future as she recognized a need that she hopes Extenion Homemakers will fill. Her interview has been loosely transcribed and is presented in part below (minus her sweet chuckle):

I was a 4-H'er. We learned how to have projects, and we raised chickens, and mostly I learned to sew. In sewing, it helped me to provide my living. I worked at a dress factory. I had music. I've taught music to 4-H'ers. We even helped with the school music because we were in the Depression. And we learned to improvise a lot of our materials, and when we didn't have sugar we learned how to use syrup and dried fruit for our sweetness.

And we also built a club house and—we built two club houses. We gave our other one away and we bought property with playgrounds for our club and community. It was the centerpiece of our community because all denominations and cultures came together through our club. My mother was president for a while. I've been president.

We had a gathering of our preschool—we started that in our club. My little boy was about five years old and so he was getting ready for school. We had the doctor and county nurse out, and I was over the children. [This was a health clinic at the beginning of school.] The doctor came out with his stethoscope and the nurse, and

he asked the little girl to open her mouth.
Well, he had examined a couple before then.
And they did fine—and my little boy was down
below that—and then they asked her to open her
mouth and she let out a scream and my little
boy went under the club house and stayed there
'til it was over. So he never got examined. And
I was the leader of it!

It was quite an adventure. We helped with
the school – it needed our club. They used it.
I think Ellen [Ellen McCloskey, who was also
interviewed] went to school down there in our
club house. We had school for first grade in our
club house.

And it was a gathering—it was an atmosphere
that couldn't be described—it was just all a big
family. There was a lady that lived up on the
hill—she'd get up at night and if she saw a light
in someone's house during the night, she'd send
someone down to check on them. The men built
the first club house at night. We hired someone
to have the second one built.

We just had such a broad adventure there. It's
hard for me to remember it all. I was on the
board of stewards during the time of transition
and all when we sold part of our property—to the
school and post office.

Then we built a new club house. We have a
nice facility there now—on Rodney Parham Road
[right off I-630 at 201 South Rodney Parham—

near the intersection with Markham]. We're still meeting there.

Our home had a community Christmas tree in our yard—my dad planted a Christmas tree. During the Depression we made animals for the WPA—little stuffed animals—we got up enough money to give the children some candy to go with the animal. My dad worked at the Buick Company and he always furnished a basket of oranges to go with it. One man told me one day, he said, "Ann, where did they get the oranges?" It was the first orange he'd ever seen. Well, Dad did it but he wouldn't want anyone to know it.

It's been a great experience. My son was a member of 4-H, and he won a first place in judging forestry at Fayetteville. He was a missionary after that. He did like Ellen—he ventured out—he's now a missionary on the coast of Mexico working with the Spanish people there. . . .

In our church I was elected as Granny of the Church. But I'm coming in contact with little nine-year-old and ten-year-old girls. They're hungry for something. Their mothers are busy, but [the little girls] are looking for something to achieve. And I think when I was in 4-H there was a little cookbook that started us off with simple things to cook.

When our boys—our young men—marry a girl now, she doesn't know how to boil water. And if there could be something that we could do to intervene with a cookbook or something to show them how to keep house. . . . Of course, you get everything in packages that are already fixed.

But I feel sorry for the little girls—they're hungry and wanting somebody to help them. . . . I find this a new opening that we need to do something about our children and our young people.[8]

Anna Mae Brown has provided a lovely example of a woman who recognizes needs and seeks ways to fill those needs even after seventy-eight years of leading, learning, and serving others.

As We Close

As this organization of Arkansas homemakers celebrates its past and contemplates its future, it seems appropriate to end with the Extension Homemakers Mission Statement and Creed, which follow:

Mission Statement

The mission of this organization shall be to empower individuals and families to improve their quality of living through continuing education, leadership development, and community service.

Extension Homemakers Creed

I believe in the Extension Homemakers Club program and accept the responsibilities it offers to be helpful to others and to provide for continuous improvement in all levels of living.

I believe that through working together in a group we can enlarge the opportunities, enrich the life of our people, and create a more contented family and community life.

I believe in my own work as a homemaker. I believe that the greatest force that molds character comes from the home, and I pledge myself to create a home which is morally wholesome, spiritually satisfying, and physically healthful and convenient.

Endnotes

[1] National Women's Hall of Fame website. http://www.greatwomen.org/ women-of-the-hall/search-the-hall-results/details/2/210-Bumpers, accessed April 5, 2012.

[2] Ibid.

[3] Oral interview by Elizabeth Hill with Juanita Webb, June 2011, Hot Springs, Arkansas.

[4] Email to Elizabeth Hill, received April 19, 2012, from Jeffrey R. Kaiser, MD, MA, Associate Professor of Pediatrics and Obstetrics and Gynecology, Section of Neonatology, UAMS College of Medicine, UAMS Graduate School, University of Arkansas for Medical Sciences, Arkansas Children's Hospital, 1 Children's Way, Slot 512-5, Little Rock, AR 72202.

[5] Oral interview by Elizabeth Hill with John Stoll, June 2011, Hot Springs, Arkansas.

[6] Associated Country Women of the World website. http://www.acww.org.uk/, accessed April 24, 2012.

[7] List of project winners for 2011 received by Elizabeth Hill from the office of Betty Oliver, Cooperative Extension Service, Little Rock, Arkansas, via email dated March 2012.

[8] Oral interview by Elizabeth Hill with Anna Mae Brown, June 2011, Hot Springs, Arkansas.

Bibliography

American Red Cross, *The Mississippi Valley Flood Disaster of 1927: Official Report of the Relief Operations*, 1927.

Arkansas Alumni Association postal-size card, "4-H House," dated 2011.

Arkansas Council of Home Demonstration Clubs. *History of Home Demonstration Work in Arkansas 1914-1965*. S.I.: s.n., 1970.

Arkansas Extension Homemakers Council. *History of Home Demonstration Work in Arkansas 1914-1965: Extension Homemaker Work 1966-1977*. S.I.: s.n., 1978.

Arnold, Eleanor. *Voices of American Homemakers*. Bloomington: Indiana University Press, 1985.

Associated Country Women of the World website. http://www.acww.org.uk/, accessed April 24, 2012.

Barnett, Peggy (Garland County). Interview by author, June 7, 2011, Hot Springs, Arkansas. Audio recording in possession of author.

Bernhard, Virginia. *Hidden Histories of Women in the New South*. Columbia: University of Missouri Press, 1994.

Blackman, Ruby L. *A Study of Twenty-nine Home Demonstration Clubs in Lee County, Arkansas*. Thesis (M.S.)—Prairie View A & M College, 1962.

Bliss, R. K., T. B. Symons, and M. L. Wilson. *The Spirit and Philosophy of Extension Work As Recorded in Significant Extension Papers*. Washington (D.C.): Graduate School, United States Department of Agriculture and Epsilon Sigma Phi/National Honorary Extension Fraternity, 1952.

Bolin, Winifred D. Wandersee. "American Woman and the Twentieth-Century Work Force: The Depression Experience," in *Woman's Being, Woman's Place: Female Identity and Vocation in American History*, 296-312, edited by Mary Kelley. Boston: G. K. Hall & Co., 1979.

Brimer, Krista (White County). Interview by author, June 8, 2011, Hot Springs, Arkansas. Audio recording in possession of author.

Brink, Judy (Garland County). Interview by author, June 8, 2011, Hot Springs, Arkansas. Audio recording in possession of author.

Brown, Anna Mae (Pulaski County). Interview by author, June 8, 2011, Hot Springs, Arkansas. Audio recording in possession of author.

Brown, D. Clayton. "Prosperous Farms and Happier Homes: Arkansas Agricultural Extension Service, 1911-1966." *Prologue*. Vol. 30, No. 2, Summer 1996, n.p. http://www.archives.gov/publications/

prologue/1998/summer/Arkansas-extension.html, accessed April 1, 2011.

Brunner, Edmund de S. and E. Hsin Pao Yang. *Rural America and the Extension Service: A History and Critique of the Cooperative Agricultural and Home Economics Extension Service.* New York: Teachers College/Columbia University, 1949.

Carr, Jo Ann (Jefferson County). Interview by author, June 8, 2011, Hot Springs, Arkansas. Audio recording in possession of author.

Copeland, Thomas Wayne. *Good Neighbors: Agents of Change in the New Rural South, 1900 to 1940.* Dissertation (Ph.D.)—The University of Mississippi, 2011.

Cranston, Claudia. "Learn and Live" in *Good Housekeeping* magazine, Volume No. 108, No. 4, April 1939. Retrieved from the Cornell University online Home Economics Archive: Research, Tradition, History, on February 23, 2012. (http://hearth.library.cornell.edu.)

Creswell, Mary E. "The Home Demonstration Work," in *Annals of the American Academy of Political and Social Science*, Vol. 67, New Possibilities in Education, Sep., 1916.

David, Betty (Yell County). Interview by author, June 7, 2011, Hot Springs, Arkansas. Audio recording in possession of author.

Davis, Siobhan. "Not Readily Visualized by Industrial Workers and Urban Dwellers: Published Images of Rural Women from the FSA Collection." In *Reading Southern Poverty between the Wars, 1918-1939*, 48-74, edited by Richard Godden and Martin Crawford. Athens: The University of Georgia Press, 2006.

Delegard, Kirsten. "Women's Movements, 1880s–1920s." In *A Companion to American Women's History*, 328-347, edited by Nancy A. Hewitt. UK: Blackwell Publishers, 2002.

"Flu Epidemic of 1918," The Encyclopedia of Arkansas History & Culture website. http://encyclopediaofArkansas.net/encyclopedia/entry-detail.aspx?entryID=2229. Accessed March 3, 2012.

Frysinger, Grace E. *Home Demonstration Work*. Washington, D.C.: U. S. Dept. of Agriculture, 1933.

Gandy, Bonita (Logan County). Interview by author, June 8, 2011, Hot Springs, Arkansas. Audio recording in possession of author.

Gordon, Lisa D. "Education and the Professions." In *A Companion to American Women's History*, 227-249, edited by Nancy A. Hewitt. UK: Blackwell Publishers, 2002.

Graves, John William. *Town and Country: Race Relations in an Urban-Rural Context, Arkansas, 1865-1905*. Fayetteville: The University of Arkansas Press, 1990.

Gunderson, Gordon W. "The National School Lunch Program Background and Development," National School Lunch Program website, accessed November 28, 2011. http://www.fns.usda.gov/cnd/lunch/AboutLunch/ProgramHistory_2.htm#EARLY, np.

Hand, Eric. "4-H House's Time Runs Out," in *Arkansas Democrat-Gazette,* May 18, 2003. (Typed, attributed copy of article received from Shirley Mathey via email forwarded by Betty Oliver, Cooperative Extension Service, on February 29, 2012.)

Hanley, Steven G. *A Place of Care, Love, and Hope: A History of Arkansas Children's Hospital,* Second Edition. No city: no publisher given, 2007.

Harris, Barbara. *Beyond Her Sphere: Women and the Professions in American History.* Westport, Conn.: Greenwood Press. 1978.

Hartley, Andrea (Jefferson County). Interview by author, June 7, 2011, Hot Springs, Arkansas. Audio recording in possession of author.

Harvell, Jean (Izard County). Interview by author, June 8, 2011, Hot Springs, Arkansas. Audio recording in possession of author.

Helena World, 1927. Microfiche housed in the archives of the Arkansas History Commission, Little Rock, Arkansas.

Heywood, Eunice. *Education for Action: A Thirty Year History of the National Extension Homemakers Council, 1936-1966.*

Hill, Kate Adele. *Home Demonstration Work in Texas.* San Antonio: The Naylor Company, 1958.

Hoffschwelle, Mary S. "'Better Homes on Better Farms': Domestic Reform in Rural Tennessee." In *Frontiers: A Journal of Women Studies,* Vol. 22, No. 1 (2001), 51-73. http://0-muse.jhu.edu.iii-server.ualr.edu/journals/frontiers/v022/22.1hoffschwelle.pdf, accessed December 9, 2011.

Hogan, Mena. *A History of the Agricultural Extension Service in Arkansas.* Thesis (M.S.)—University of Wisconsin, c.1942.

Jackson, Anne (Pulaski County). Interview by author, June 7, 2011, Hot Springs, Arkansas. Audio recording in possession of author.

James, Yvonne (Benton County). Interview by author, June 8, 2011, Hot Springs, Arkansas. Audio recording in possession of author.

Jensen, Joan E. *With These Hands: Women Working on the Land.* Old Westbury, New York: The Feminist Press, 1981.

Johnson, Johnette (Montgomery County). Interview by author, June 8, 2011, Hot Springs, Arkansas. Audio recording in possession of author.

Jones, Jacqueline. "Tore Up and a-Movin': Perspectives on the Work of Black and Poor White Women in the Rural South, 1865-1949," in *Women and Farming: Changing Roles, Changing Structures*, 15-34, edited by Wava G. Haney and Jane B. Knowles. Boulder: Westview Press, 1988.

Jones, Lu Ann. *Mama Learned Us to Work: Farm Women in the New South.* Chapel Hill: The University of North Carolina Press, 2002.

Kidd, Stuart. "Dissonant Encounters: FSA Photographers and the Southern Underclass, 1935-1943." In *Reading Southern Poverty between the Wars, 1918-1939*, 25-47, edited by Richard Godden and Martin Crawford. Athens: The University of Georgia Press, 2006.

Kilmer, Joyce. "Trees."

Leger, Peggy (Perry County). Interview by author, June 7, 2011, Hot Springs, Arkansas. Audio recording in possession of author.

Mathey, Shirley (former 4-H House resident). Email correspondence received by the author on April 18, 2012.

Matthews, Joseph L. "The Cooperative Extension Service of the United States." In *Rural Social Systems and Adult Education; a Committee Report Resulting from a Study Sponsored by the Association of Land Grant Colleges and Universities and The Fund for Adult Education by the Ford Foundation*, edited by J. Allan

Beegle, 51-79. Baltimore: The Michigan State College Press/Waverly Press, Inc., 1953.

McCloskey, Ellen (Pulaski County). Interview by author, June 8, 2011, Hot Springs, Arkansas. Audio recording in possession of author.

McGehee, Azzie (Desha County). Telephone interviews by author during mid-April 2012, based on oral history of Mrs. McGehee prepared as a part of the state-wide oral history project through the Pryor Center for Oral History at the University of Arkansas. The conversation was not recorded but was verified by email.

McKimmon, Jane S. "Home Demonstration Work—Its Beginning" (part of a talk at the Association of Southern Agricultural Workers Thirtieth Annual Convention, Houston, February 1928) in *The Spirit and Philosophy of Extension Work As Recorded in Significant Extension Papers*, edited by R. K. Bliss, T. B. Symons, and M. L. Wilson. Washington D.C.: Graduate School, United States Department of Agriculture and Epsilon Sigma Phi/National Honorary Extension Fraternity, 1952.

Miller, Paul A. *Cooperative Extension: An Historical Perspective*. Rochester: Rochester Institute of Technology, 1976.

Moneyhon, Carl H. *Arkansas and the New South*. Fayetteville: The University of Arkansas Press, 1997.

Moody, Ivaline (Craighead County). Interview by author, June 8, 2011, Hot Springs, Arkansas. Audio recording in possession of author.

Moore, Danny Blair. *"Window to the World": Educating Rural Women in Mississippi, 1911-1965.* Thesis (Ph.D.)—Mississippi State University, 1991.

Myrick, Pauline (Lincoln County). Interview by author, June 8, 2011, Hot Springs, Arkansas. Audio recording in possession of author.

National Archives Wiki for Researchers. http://www.ourarchives.wikispaces.net/World+War++1+{posters (ARC identifier 512582/Local Identifier 4-P-143). Accessed June 30, 2011.

National Extension Homemakers Council. *An Official History of National Extension Homemakers Council, Inc.,* 1930-1990. Burlington, KY: The Council, 1991.

National Extension Homemakers Study: Program Benefits, Leadership Development, and Volunteer Outreach. Edited by Ava D. Rodgers and Bonnie Tanner. Washington, D.C. [?]: U.S. Dept. of Agriculture, Extension Service, Family Education, 1981.

National Symposium on Home Demonstration Work (1958: Michigan State University). *Report of Proceedings of the National Symposium on Home Demonstration Work at Kellogg Center for Continuing Education, Michigan State University, March 23-28,*

1958. Madison, WI: National Agricultural Extension Center for Advance, 1958.

National Task Force for the Study of Community Organization and Leadership Development in Extension CRD Work. *An Evaluation of Community Organization and Leadership Development in Cooperative Extension's Community Development Program.* [State College]: Cooperative Extension Service, Mississippi State University, 1977.

Nix, Ann (Little River County). Interview by author, June 8, 2011, Hot Springs, Arkansas. Audio recording in possession of author.

Nutt, Juanita (Perry County). Interview by author, June 7, 2011, Hot Springs, Arkansas. Audio recording in possession of author.

Palsa, Sue (Prairie County). Interview by author, June 8, 2011, Hot Springs, Arkansas. Audio recording in possession of author.

Parker, Colene (Madison County). Interview by author, June 7, 2011, Hot Springs, Arkansas. Audio recording in possession of author.

Parsons, Patsy (Logan County). Interview by author, June 8, 2011, Hot Springs, Arkansas. Audio recording in possession of author.

"Past County Officials of Cleveland County, Arkansas," Cleveland County Arkansas USGenWeb Genealogy Site, accessed December 9, 2011.

www.argenweb.net/cleveland/county-officials-
1874---1941.htm.

Pittman, Lillian (Greene County). Interview by author,
June 8, 2011, Hot Springs, Arkansas. Audio recording
in possession of author.

Rasmussen, Wayne D. *Taking the University to the
People: Seventy-five Years of Cooperative Extension.*
Ames: Iowa State University Press, 1989.

Ray, Bonnie (Sebastian County). Interview by author,
June 8, 2011, Hot Springs, Arkansas. Audio recording
in possession of author.

Reiff, Lynne Anderson. "Revitalizing Southern Homes:
Rural Women, the Professionalization of Home
Demonstration Work, and the Limits of Reform,
1917-1945." In *Work, Family, and Faith: Rural
Southern Women in the Twentieth Century,* 135-165.
Edited by Melissa Walker and Rebecca Sharpless.
Columbia: University of Missouri Press, 2006.

Reiff, Lynne Anderson. *"Rousing the People of the
Land": Home Demonstration Work in the Deep South,
1914-1950.* Thesis (Ph.D.)—Auburn University, 1995.

Sanders-Chick, Kay (Baxter County). Interview by
author, June 8, 2011, Hot Springs, Arkansas. Audio
recording in possession of author.

Schlereth, Thomas J. *Victorian America: Transformations
in Everyday Life, 1876-1915.* New York:
HarperPerennial, 1992.

Schneider, Dorothy, and Carl J. Schneider. *American Women in the Progressive Era, 1900-1920*. New York: Facts on File, 1993.

Schwieder, Dorothy. *75 Years of Service: Cooperative Extension in Iowa*. Ames: Iowa St. Univ. Press, 1993.

Scott, Roy V. *The Reluctant Farmer: The Rise of Agricultural Extension to 1914*. Urbana: University of Illinois Press, 1970.

Scroggins, Marilyn (Boone County). Interview by author, June 7, 2011, Hot Springs, Arkansas. Audio recording in possession of author.

Shearin, Marilyn (Mississippi County). Interview by author, June 7, 2011, Hot Springs, Arkansas. Audio recording in possession of author.

Shrout, Kaye (Montgomery County). Interview by author, June 8, 2011, Hot Springs, Arkansas. Audio recording in possession of author.

Simmons, Judy (Bradley County). Interview by author, June 8, 2011, Hot Springs, Arkansas. Audio recording in possession of author.

Simons, L. R. *Early Development of Cooperative Extension Work in Agriculture and Home Economics in the United Sates*. [Ithaca, N.Y.]: New York State College of Agriculture, 1962.

Smith-Lever Act of 1914.

Stockley, Grif. *Race Relations in the Natural State.* Little Rock: The Butler Center for Arkansas Studies, 2007.

Stoll, John (Lawrence County). Interview by author, June 7, 2011, Hot Springs, Arkansas. Audio recording in possession of author.

Strasser, Susan. *Never Done: A History of American Housework.* New York: Pantheon Books, 1982.

Suitt, Faye (Pulaski County). Interview by author, June 7, 2011, Hot Springs, Arkansas. Audio recording in possession of author.

Swain, Martha A. "A New Deal for Southern Women: Gender and Race in Women's Work Relief." In *Women of the American South: A Multicultural Reader*, edited by Christie Anne Farnham, 241-257. New York: New York University Press, 1997.

Tate, Kim (Izard County). Interview by author, June 7, 2011, Hot Springs, Arkansas. Audio recording in possession of author.

University of California Department of Home Economics. Volunteer Student Service. "Save Meat." War Emergency Series No. 8. November 1918. Found in: The American Association of Family and Consumer Sciences Records, #6578, Division of Rare and Manuscript Collections, Cornell University Library. http://exhibits.mannlib.cornell.edu/meatlesswheatless/meatless-wheatless.php?content=ten. Accessed June 30, 2011.

U. S. Department of Agriculture Cooperative Extension Service. *Record Group 33.* National Archives and Records Administration Southwestern Branch, Fort Worth, Texas. Digital photocopies made by Richard Hill and Elizabeth Hill in May and August 2011. Paper photocopies made by Rose Ellis in May 2011. Digital and paper photocopies in possession of the author.

U. S. Federal Extension Service. *Changing Styles in Home Demonstration Work.* [Washington, D.C.]: Federal Extension Service, U. S. Dept. of Agriculture, 1965.

Vangilder, Jeri (Pope County). Interview by author, June 7, 2011, Hot Springs, Arkansas. Audio recording in possession of author.

Waldron, Fredonia (Pulaski County). Interview by author, June 7, 2011, Hot Springs, Arkansas. Audio recording in possession of author.

Ward, Florence E. *Home Demonstration Work Under the Smith-Lever Act, 1914-1924.* Washington: U. S. Department of Agriculture, 1929.

Warner, Paul D., and James A. Christenson. *The Cooperative Extension Service: a National Assessment.* Boulder: Westview Press, 1984.

Webb, Juanita (Drew County). Interview by author, June 7, 2011, Hot Springs, Arkansas. Audio recording in possession of author.

Williams, Jettie (Little River County). "The African American Experience of Arkansas Extension Homemakers Club Southwest, Yesterday Today and Tomorrow, Centennial Celebration, 1912 – 2012," a paper forwarded to Elizabeth Hill in March 2012 by Betty Oliver of the Coopertive Extension Service. Copy of utilized information retained by author.

Wilson, Candes (Washington County). Interview by author, June 7, 2011, Hot Springs, Arkansas. Audio recording in possession of author.

Wolfe, Melissa B. "Volunteer Corner" in *Vital Signs*, Arkansas Children's Hospital's employee newsletter, March 2012.

Zellar, Gary. "H. C. Ray and Racial Politics in the African American Extension Service Program in Arkansas, 1915-1929." *Agricultural History*, Vol. 72, No. 2, African Americans in Southern Agriculture: 1877-1945 (Spring, 1998): 429-445. Published by: Agricultural History Society. Stable URL: http://www.jstor.org/stable/3744391, accessed October 12, 2011.

Zoerner, Maureen (Ouachita County). Interview by author, June 8, 2011, Hot Springs, Arkansas.

Contributors to the History

Despite my fear of leaving out the name of someone who contributed to the history, I must express my appreciation to the following individuals who provided information and insight into the work or who assisted me in some other way:

Peggy Barnett, Krista Brimer, Judy Brink, Anna Mae Brown, Carolyn Brown, Jo Ann Carr, Pauline Collins, Melody Curtis, Betty David, Rose Ellis, Bonita Gandy, Andrea Hartley, Jean Harvell, Ana Hollis, Anne Jackson, Yvonne James, Johnette Johnson, Jeffrey R. Kaiser, M.D., Peggy Leger, Shirley Mathey, Azzie McGehee, Ellen McCloskey, Elizabeth McGinley, Ivaline Moody, Pauline Myrick, Ann Nix, Juanita Nutt, Betty Oliver, Sue Palsa, Colene Parker, Patsy Parsons, Eva Marie Pearson, Lillian Pittman, Bonnie Ray, Wendy Richter, Joy Russell, Kay Sanders-Chick, Marilyn Scroggins, Marilyn Shearin, Kaye Shrout, Judy Simmons, John Stoll, Faye Suitt, Kim Tate, Jeri Vangilder, Patricia Vaughan, Fredonia Waldron, Juanita Webb, Jettie Williams, Candes Wilson, Melissa Wolfe, and Maureen Zoerner.

Thank you also to each one who provided club scrapbooks for my review.

Made in the USA
Charleston, SC
02 March 2013